CONTENTS

FLOOR COVERINGS

FOR HISTORIC BUILDINGS
A Guide to Selecting Reproductions

HELENE VON ROSENSTIEL

GAIL CASKEY WINKLER

The Preservation Press

The Preservation Press
National Trust for Historic Preservation
1785 Massachusetts Avenue, N.W.
Washington, D.C. 20036

The National Trust for Historic Preservation is the only private, nonprofit national organization chartered by Congress to encourage public participation in the preservation of sites, buildings and objects significant in American history and culture. Support is provided by membership dues, endowment funds, contributions and grants from federal agencies, including the U.S. Department of the Interior, under provisions of the National Historic Preservation Act of 1966. The opinions expressed herein do not necessarily reflect the views or policies of the Interior Department. For information about membership in the National Trust, write to the above address.

Printed in the United States of America
96 95 94   5

Library of Congress Cataloging in Publication Data

Von Rosenstiel, Helene.
    Floor coverings for historic buildings: a guide to selecting
  reproductions / Helene Von Rosenstiel and Gail Caskey Winkler.
        p.   cm.

    Bibliography: p.
    Includes index.
    ISBN 0-89133-130-1
    1. Floor coverings—Catalogs.   I. Winkler, Gail Caskey.
  II. Title.
  NK2115.5.F55V66 1988
  747'.4—dc19   87-22310

The Preservation Press gratefully acknowledges the assistance of F. Schumacher and Company and The Wool Bureau in the production of this book.

Cover and title page: IMPERIAL TRIANGLE. Pile carpet. Schumacher. (See page 246.)

Endleaves: Upright loom used in handknotting a carpet. From Diderot's *Encyclopedia*. (The Athenaeum of Philadelphia)

Pages 8–9: MAPLE LEAF. Ingrain carpet. Family Heir-Loom Weavers. (See page 141.)

Pages 38–39: TROPICAL LEAVES AND FLOWERS. Brussels or Wilton carpet. J. R. Burrows and Company. (See page 194.)

FLOOR COVERINGS FOR HISTORIC BUILDINGS
A Guide to Selecting Reproductions

INTRODUCTION

FLOOR COVERINGS FOR HISTORIC BUILDINGS

Floor coverings predate houses. Clean sand, sweet grasses and the skins of animals probably softened the primitive caves of our earliest ancestors. Such materials provided aesthetic and tactile pleasure, just as floor coverings do today. For most of recorded history, floors and floor coverings were synonymous; the packed earth, brick, tile, stone or wood was both structural and visible. One of the earliest known woven floor coverings, a rug little more than six feet square and dating to the fifth century B.C., was found in the Altai Mountains of Central Asia and now is in the collection of the Hermitage Museum in Leningrad. Its wool pile was woven with a Ghiordes knot, the same used in Turkish carpets. From Central Asia, apparently, the art of weaving rugs spread through Asia, North Africa and Europe.

Some carpets are still handknotted, the most obvious being Oriental rugs from Asia and the Near East. But beginning in the early 18th century, European weavers began to produce certain types of pile carpets on handlooms that, during the 19th century, were adapted to water or steam power. These technological advances permitted households other than the wealthiest to have carpeted floors for the first time in history.

Here we need to define terms that will be used throughout this book. A "floor covering" is any material used to finish a floor, including wood, brick, stone, tile, linoleum, vinyl, matting and carpeting. "Carpets," "carpeting" and "rugs," however, are soft floor coverings, and the names tell us a little about the history of their use. The term "carpet" is derived from a Latin word for carding wool

Ingrain carpet shown in an anonymous portrait of a child, c. 1830 (detail). (Frank S. Schwarz and Son Gallery, Philadelphia)

11

that gradually came to mean any thick wool cloth used to cover tables or beds. The word acquired its modern definition during the 18th century when Europeans began to emulate the Eastern practice of placing carpets on floors. "Rug" comes from a Scandinavian term for coarse wool cloth used as a cloak or coverlet and, by the early 19th century, meant a small mat for the floor, particularly one used in front of a hearth. Today, "carpet" and "carpeting" signify large floor coverings that are often installed wall to wall and fastened in place, while "rug" retains the meaning of a smaller floor covering that is not tacked down.

LEVELS OF AUTHENTICITY

Sometimes one is fortunate to find historic floor coverings surviving in place. This is more common with hard finishes such as brick, stone, tile and wood. These materials may need only gentle cleaning or replacement of a few damaged sections to restore them to their original appearance. However, carpets and floorcloths (painted canvas) are far less durable. If we are lucky enough to find these floor coverings still intact, care must be taken to preserve them. They should not be subjected to normal wear. As carpets age, their fibers become brittle. Walking on or vacuuming these fragile fibers causes abrasion and the ultimate loss of surface pile. Nineteenth-century hooked rugs present another problem because they were often worked on burlap, which self-destructs over time, powders and leaves the hooked face unsupported. The burlap backing of early linoleum makes those floor coverings equally fragile. And the oil in the paints used on 18th- and 19th-century floorcloths eventually dries out, leaving only dried pigments on their surfaces. While it is possible to use these historic materials in museum rooms that the public will not enter, ideally they should be saved to serve as documents on which reproductions can be based.

When no historic floor covering exists or when the original cannot be used, a modern product must be substituted. Whether the decision is made to choose a pattern offered by a manufacturer or to reproduce an original from a particular building, the first question to be tackled is authenticity. Here it is important to under-

stand two terms, "reproduction" and "adaptation." A reproduction is a modern product that copies a known, historic example. An adaptation, however, is either a modern treatment of a historic document or a completely new design perhaps loosely based on historical precedent. The choice between a reproduction and an adaptation rests on two considerations: a sensible assessment of the needs of the purchaser and an understanding of the differences between past and present methods of production.

Let us consider first the needs of the purchaser. While curators of museums and historic houses have a public obligation to interpret period interiors as accurately as possible, the owner of a much-beloved old house may not. And even if both homeowner and curator wish to reproduce a historic floor covering, they will encounter factors that will alter the decision.

CUSTOM WORK. According to the most rigorous definition of museum restoration, if research proves that a

Period reproduction carpet in the parlor of the Ebenezer Maxwell Mansion (1859), a house museum in Philadelphia. (Ebenezer Maxwell Mansion)

13

Second floor of Congress Hall (1787–89, 1793–95), Philadelphia. An ingrain reproduction was used for rooms seen only from the doorway, while more durable level-loop Wilton carpeting woven in the same pattern was made for heavy-traffic areas. (Thomas L. Davies, National Park Service)

particular type of carpeting was once used, it should be replaced, regardless of the preferences of curator, board members or donors. And if a sample of the original carpet survives, the committee may be obliged to reproduce its exact pattern and colors. Custom work requires locating a mill that will reproduce the pattern, scale, pile and color of the original. However, custom work is both expensive and time consuming because it usually requires creating an entirely new design. The design must be drawn to full scale with colors duplicating the originals. If a Jacquard attachment is needed to weave the design, then point papers must be made and cards cut and stitched together for each repeat of the pattern. A loom must be specially prepared and a small sample woven for approval. Each step involves additional expense and time, and it is not unusual for custom work to require 18 months to complete. Some mills will accept small orders for custom work, others will undertake only large runs of carpeting, and a great many simply find the undertaking unprofitable. In short, time and cost may preclude documentary reproduction.

SPECIAL ORDERS. There is a second choice: a special order from a manufacturer's existing line where pattern and scale are appropriate to the target date of the restoration. This solution is also necessary when no actual sample or visual documentation survives but when written records, such as an inventory, prove that a specific type of floor covering was in the building during the targeted period. Some carpet mills have archives containing historic documents on which they base their modern lines. Many of these mills will do special orders of available designs, including custom coloring, adding borders from their collection and producing the carpet in either cut or looped pile. Such orders usually require 4 to 10 weeks.

STOCK ITEMS. When custom designs and special orders fall outside the budget for re-creating the floor covering of a historic building, the only alternative is to select a stock item, a ready-made product with pattern and colors acceptable for the target date of the project. The best of these designs have been adapted from historic sources with perhaps slight alterations in scale or color to accommodate modern tastes or manufacturing techniques. However, too many adaptations of historic designs wander so far from the source that the finished product is only vaguely similar to the original. Unfortunately, most manufacturers of ready-made floor coverings rarely distinguish between reproductions and adaptations, and they often do not identify the documents from which their designs were taken.

Durability is another consideration. Ingrain carpeting is fragile and quickly wears out under hard use. These defects were less serious during the 19th century when heavy walking shoes were rarely worn in the house and ingrain carpeting was relatively inexpensive. Also, many wools used today are softer, and consequently less durable, than those used in the past. A steady stream of visitors through the rooms of a house museum or public building will quickly soil and damage ingrain carpeting that is now expensive to replace. One solution adopted in most large museums is to restrict admission to restored rooms. However, the flow of visitors in historic houses often leads through rooms or hallways containing reproduction floor coverings. If the budget does not permit regular replacement of carpeting, only three alternatives are available: no carpeting, obtrusive runners over fragile carpeting or a more durable carpet reproducing the appropriate pattern and colors. Independence National Historical Park experienced just this problem in Congress Hall. When the National Park Service restored the chamber of the House of Representatives and the offices and hallway leading to the Senate chamber, an ingrain carpet was reproduced for the floor. With tens of thousands of visitors, the carpet quickly deteriorated. Constant replacement was out of the question, and the traffic pattern could not be altered. The solution adopted by the Park Service curators was to reproduce the ingrain pattern in a more durable Wilton-weave carpet with a looped pile. This carpeting was laid in the hallway and the House of Representatives while ingrain remained in the rooms viewed from the doorways. The result is not absolutely authentic but by reproducing the color and scale of the original pattern, the original appearance of these spaces was captured.

Upright loom and tools used in handknotting a carpet. A cartoon of the design was placed above the weaver's head. From Diderot's *Encyclopedia*. (The Athenaeum of Philadelphia)

CHANGING TECHNOLOGIES

The previous examples show that considerations in restoration exist beyond the aim of absolute authenticity. In addition to these problems, there is another: some historic floor coverings simply cannot be reproduced. For example, the machines used in the 19th century to print tapestry carpets and linoleum are no longer in production. In these cases, the only choice is to seek an adequate alternative to the original floor covering.

Modern manufacturing techniques present yet another set of difficulties. As indicated, historians of the decorative arts generally agree that a reproduction should match the original document in pattern, scale and color. However, should a reproduction be the same fiber as the original? During the 18th and 19th centuries carpets were made only from natural fibers such as wool, cotton and jute. Today, many reproductions of historic patterns contain synthetic fibers—the most common being nylon—that are often blended with wool to improve the abrasion resistance of cut-pile carpets such as Wilton. Furthermore, the dyes used during the 18th and 19th centuries came from animal, vegetable and mineral sources while modern carpets use artificial dyes—first discovered in the 1850s and little used before the last quarter of the 19th century.

Chenille cloth, the first step in making machine-woven chenille Axminster carpets.

Chenille fur (pile) after cutting.

Cut-and-folded chenille fur.

Transverse section of chenille, showing the fur inserted.

Section of a chenille Axminster carpet. (All, The Athenaeum of Philadelphia)

AXMINSTER CARPETS. Weaving methods also have changed since the 18th and 19th centuries so that the modern names applied to carpets do not always match the historic names. A short history of carpet manufacturing yields several examples. One type is Axminster, which denotes a luxurious, cut-pile carpet. Its origins date to the second half of the 18th century when seamless, handknotted carpets—imitating Orientals—were first made in Axminster and elsewhere in England. Similar handknotted carpets were manufactured in America by the 1790s.

While handknotted Axminsters continued to be woven in England, several types of machine-woven carpets, also called Axminsters, were developed in the 19th century. The first was a "chenille Axminster" patented in 1839 by James Templeton of Glasgow, Scotland. This carpet, also known as a "chenille" or "patent chenille Axminster," was woven in two stages. The first step was to weave the chenille "fur" (pile) of the carpet and the second was to weave the fur into a fabric foundation that served as the carpet backing. Templeton's patent chenille Axminsters were seamless and up to 33 feet wide, making them the first woven broadloom carpets. New England carpet manufacturers began to weave chenille rugs and carpeting by the mid-19th century, and they continued to be woven in England as late as the mid-20th century.

In 1867, approximately 30 years after Templeton's patent, Halcyon Skinner perfected another type of Axminster loom for Alexander Smith and Sons Carpet Company of Yonkers, N.Y. Skinner's loom used endless chains of wool—rather than the two-step chenille method—to weave a carpet known as "Royal Axminster." Today, Skinner's invention is called a "spool Axminster" and is the most complex loom used in carpet manufacturing. The name comes from the spools on which the yarns are wound before the carpet is woven. Each spool holds as many ends of variously colored yarns as there are tufts across the width of the design, and the number of spools needed corresponds to the number of rows of tufts that make up one full repeat of the pattern along the length of the carpet. Once wound with yarn, the individual spools

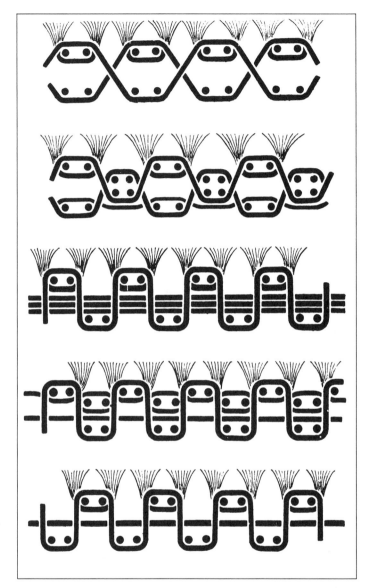

Cross section of Axminster carpet weaves. (The Athenaeum of Philadelphia)

are placed on a continuous chain, with each colored thread pulled through a funnel to form a tuft of pile. Spool Axminster looms can weave carpets with virtually limitless numbers of colors.

In 1892 Brintons of Kidderminster, England, perfected yet another type of Axminster loom still used today and known as a "gripper Axminster." This loom uses a Jacquard attachment to control individual grippers that

plant tufts of colors and thus form the pattern. Gripper looms are easier to prepare for weaving than spool looms and are used instead of spool looms when small runs of custom carpeting are needed. Unfortunately, gripper looms generally limit patterns to 16 colors including those added by careful "planting" (replacing a standard color in the pattern with a special one).

These changes in Axminster production mean that

Patterned spool Axminster loom. Each spool travels a complete circuit to produce one pattern repeat. (The Wool Bureau and Brintons Limited)

Gripper Axminster loom, which can use only a limited number of colors. (The Wool Bureau and Brintons Limited)

reproducing a document Axminster carpet is not always possible. For instance, handknotted Axminsters are no longer made in America. And while spool Axminster looms are still producing carpets, a custom order would be out of the question unless a large yardage is needed such as for hotel or commercial use. Smaller runs are woven on gripper Axminsters but, because they are limited in their use of color, they cannot accurately reproduce a historic spool Axminster carpet.

BRUSSELS, WILTON AND TAPESTRY CARPETS. Another problem presented by changing technologies involves Brussels, Wilton and tapestry carpets. English weavers used handlooms to produce Brussels (looped-pile) and Wilton (cut-pile) carpeting beginning in the mid-18th century. Both types were woven in strips typically 27 inches wide and stitched together by hand to make wall-to-wall carpeting. In England and America, the handlooms required highly skilled weavers to operate them; consequently, Brussels and Wilton carpeting, although less expensive than handknotted Axminsters, were beyond the reach of most 18th- and early 19th-

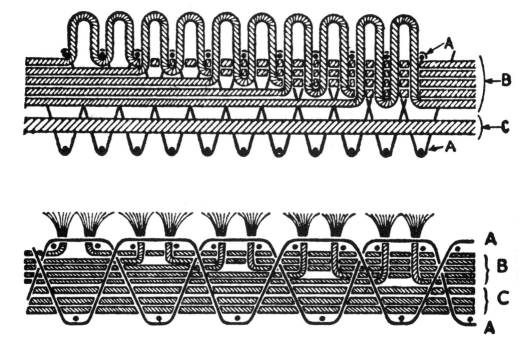

century households. In fact, Brussels and Wilton carpets were affordable to middle-class Americans only after Erastus Bigelow invented the first power loom for weaving them in 1846 and opened a factory in Clinton, Mass., in 1849. English mills switched to power looms still later in the 19th century.

By then, Brussels and Wilton carpeting had competition from another source, the so-called tapestry carpets. In 1832 Richard Whytock of Edinburgh, Scotland, invented a weaving process using preprinted woolen warp threads wound on large drums that formed the face of looped or cut-pile carpets. Whytock's invention permitted an almost limitless number of colors and greatly reduced the amount of expensive wool needed to weave a pile carpet. These two factors made tapestry carpets the popular choice for middle-class consumers during the second half of the 19th century. To distinguish Whytock's carpets from the traditional weaves, they were called "tapestry Brussels" (as opposed to "body Brussels") and "velvet" (as opposed to Wilton). Beginning in 1847 the Higgins Company of New York City was the

top

Section of a five-frame Brussels carpet, showing the chain (A), pile warp (B) and stuffer warp (C). (The Athenaeum of Philadelphia)

bottom

Section of a five-frame Wilton carpet, indicating the chain (A), pile warp (B) and stuffer warp (C). (The Athenaeum of Philadelphia)

first American manufacturer to weave both tapestry Brussels and velvet carpeting. By the 1880s James Dunlap of Philadelphia had invented a second method for printing tapestry carpets, one that did not use drums wound with yarn. It consisted of weaving an entire carpet in undyed wool and then printing the pattern on the surface by rolling the carpet through a steel drum that pressed the dyes into the wool pile.

Of these three types of carpets, only one—the Wilton—is still produced today. Brussels carpeting woven on actual Brussels looms ceased production during the 1920s as tastes changed in favor of cut-pile and seamless carpets. Today, carpeting with the appearance of Brussels is actually woven on Wilton looms and is identified as "level-loop Wilton" by the carpet industry. Drum-printed tapestry carpets are no longer manufactured, although carpets continue to be printed in a manner similar to Dunlap's invention. However, modern printed carpets are tufted, not woven, and then shot with dyes using neoprene (synthetic rubber) molds. The steps needed to take a printed carpet into production make it virtually impossible today for a factory to produce a small, custom order duplicating the complex, realistic designs found on a 19th-century tapestry carpet. And finally, the term "velvet" no longer designates a drum-printed carpet; to the modern industry it means a cut-pile carpet woven on a Wilton loom without a Jacquard attachment. Thus, velvet carpeting now has a luxurious surface of a single color or simple striped design. It should not be confused, however, with modern tufted carpets occasionally identified as velvets. These are available in any local carpet store, but, while some densely tufted varieties are suitable for private homes, they are not correct for historic houses or museums.

FLOORCLOTHS AND LINOLEUM. In addition to carpeting, floorcloth and linoleum manufacturing also were subject to changing technologies. While the earliest floorcloths were handpainted or stencilled, these techniques were generally replaced by block printing in factories during the 19th century. However, linoleum, invented in 1863 in England, proved far more durable than painted floorcloths, and by the early 20th century

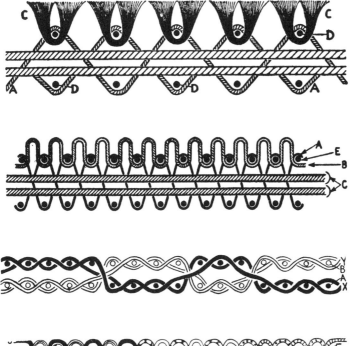

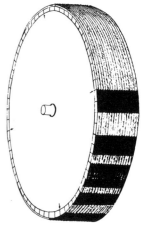

above
Tapestry printing drum, covered with partly printed yarn. Each warp row would have a drum.

left, top to bottom
Sections of tapestry velvet, tapestry Brussels, two-ply ingrain and three-ply ingrain carpets. (All, The Athenaeum of Philadelphia)

floorcloths had lost their market to this competitor and factory production ceased.

The few small firms that have revived floorcloth manufacturing today use either handpainting or stencilling, but not wooden blocks, to replicate 18th- and 19th-century patterns. Linoleum has suffered a similar decline. It continues to be manufactured in Europe but only in styles that became popular around World War I, including granite, jaspé (random striations) and solid colors. Patterns popular during the 19th century, such a those resembling encaustic and transfer-printed tiles, can be found only in vinyl flooring today, and few are acceptable authentic substitutes.

DOCUMENTING FLOOR COVERINGS

Before beginning to re-create a historic interior or refurnish a building, it is important first to determine the purpose of the project. Is historical accuracy of paramount concern, or will a period flavor be acceptable? Is the building to reflect a general interpretation of a particular period in the past or the specific taste of a previous owner or family? The answers to these questions should be sought by owners, curators or committees in charge of historic structures, public or private. At the same time, a target date for restoration or refurnishing should be determined.

INITIAL ANALYSIS. The greater the attempt to recreate a specific period in the past or to illustrate how a specific individual may have lived in a house, the more detailed the initial analysis must be. Answers to pertinent questions will dramatically influence the nature and cost of the restoration and most certainly will help determine the nature of the floor coverings selected. For example, when developing the furnishing plan, the age and the use of the structure over time must be determined. For a residential structure, one should know the family's social standing in the community and how much they might have spent in decorating the house. Were they people of sophisticated taste who followed the latest styles? Were current fashions available to them, or did they live so far from centers of trade and transportation that even the best they could obtain would have seemed old-fashioned to residents of coastal cities? Did the family leave written records, or were they sufficiently well known that the newspapers mentioned their activities? Is there any physical evidence—paint samples, bits of wallpaper, a fragment of carpeting, nail holes in window casings—to suggest how the house was decorated? Once these questions are answered and the restoration plan determined, additional information can be sought to flesh out the final scheme.

Documentary evidence—as opposed to physical evidence from the structure itself—is found in libraries, museums, public archives and private collections, and may include the U.S. census, wills, inventories, tax and church records, genealogies, auction catalogs, city directories, newspapers, shipping records, bills of sale, diaries, journals, letters, photographs, paintings and drawings. Each of these documents may provide specific clues of what to look for when examining the structure.

For a residential structure, questions to pose include: Was the owner married? Did children, other family members or servants live in the house? At what age did the owners die? The answers to these questions will help determine room use and decoration. The best bedchamber occupied by the owners, for example, was generally better furnished than the children's bedchambers; both were generally far more elaborate than rooms for servants. If the owner was elderly, the house might have had furnishings acquired over a lifetime; unless the house was recently built or the owner was wealthy, the chances are it would not be decorated in the latest fashion. The owner's occupation and the location of the house also will provide clues about the family's status in the community, but it is important to remember that what constitutes status can change over time. During the 18th and early decades of the 19th century, for instance, merchants were among the community elite and often lived in the heart of the city; but as industry became more important than commerce as a basis of wealth, bankers and factory owners, who often lived in newer areas on the periphery of the city, replaced the merchant class.

WILLS AND INVENTORIES. The local city or county courthouse is invaluable when researching a specific owner because it is a repository for wills and inventories. Wills often list specific items bequeathed to family members and friends. Estate inventories, taken at the time of death, indicate personal property, including household furnishings, and assign each item a value. Furthermore, household inventories are generally recorded on a room-by-room basis. Consequently, they contain valuable information on room use: how they were furnished and, on the basis of cost, how stylish the contents. Floor coverings often were included in these inventories and occasionally are carefully recorded as to age and type. For example, in the 1868 inventory of the Philadelphia home of Henry Deringer (inventor of the pistol that bears his name) the velvet carpet in the parlor was valued at $145, while the ingrain in the second parlor, which served as his dining room, was only $13. The dining room ingrain was computed at 60 cents a yard, while that in a bedchamber was only 50 cents. Deringer's inventory thus confirms the usual practice of better carpets in more public rooms, with the best carpet in the parlor. If no inventory of the appropriate period can be found for the house, a careful examination of inventories of individuals with similar wealth and social standing may provide guidance as to types and costs.

AUCTIONS AND SALES. Sometimes auction catalogs and newspaper accounts of sales supply information about household furnishings. Auctions were held when an estate was liquidated at the time of death and the house and its contents sold. When the Philadelphia firm of M. Thomas and Sons sold the contents of a house at 189 Spruce Street on November 10, 1856, the catalog detailed the type and amount of floor covering for each room in the house, including Venetian carpeting in the halls, 83 yards of tapestry carpet in the parlor, 32 yards of English oilcloth in the dining room and 58 yards of Canton matting in the front chamber of the second floor. Not all auction catalogs are as helpful, however, because the furnishings were often collected in a few rooms for the sale and, consequently, may not reveal where the pieces were used.

FURNISHING RECEIPTS. Rarely is one lucky enough to find an owner who saved all the bills for decorating

The Forest, c. 1845. Its floors were covered with an Axminster carpet, hearth rugs and oilcloth. (Drew University Library-Archives)

and furnishing a house, although vestry records and published reports may yield useful details for public and institutional buildings. William Gibbons, a wealthy South Carolina planter, built a summer home, The Forest, near Madison, N.J., in 1836 and ordered most of its furnishings and decorations from New York City merchants. His receipts survive in the archives of the present owner, Drew University, and provide valuable hints about the decoration of the house during the family's tenancy. For example, on March 17, 1845, Henry Andrew of New York City billed Gibbons $675 for "1 Axminster Carpet & Windowpieces to order" and "2 Hearth Rugs to Match." Where the carpeting was installed is uncertain because both the parlor and the dining room originally had two fireplaces. It is certain, however, that Gibbons laid the carpet wall to wall and ordered separate pieces sewn on to fill the window recesses. Later, on April 12, 1845, Henry Andrew charged $38.19 for "30⅝ Square Yards Oil Cloth 18'5" x 14'11"," which may have been intended as a drugget (crumbcloth) in the dining room, perhaps to protect the Axminster carpet.

Henry Andrew's bill for floor coverings used in William Gibbons's summer home, The Forest (1836), near Madison, N.J. (Judi Benvenuti, Drew University Library-Archives)

DIARIES AND LETTERS. Occasionally, one is fortunate to find diaries, journals and letters that shed light on decoration. These may have been kept by the owner's family or other persons who visited them. The diary of Sidney George Fisher is filled with interesting details of life between 1834 and 1871. Following a December 26, 1856, visit to Champlost, a country house near Philadelphia, Fisher recorded, "The hall has been refitted, the walls covered with embossed leather, the floor with a very beautiful carpet, two shades of green, & some new furniture and objets d'art brought by Miss Fox from Europe to decorate it. It is very handsome." Clues such as these provide a basis on which to plan a restoration or furnishing project.

DIRECTORIES AND NEWSPAPERS. City business directories and local newspaper advertisements also indicate the kinds of household furnishings manufactured in a community or sold there. During the 18th century wealthy residents of major seaports could acquire the most current European fashions, as could Tidewater

A decorative broadside advertising Joseph Swartz's Carpet Manufactory in Philadelphia, c. 1852. (The Athenaeum of Philadelphia)

Venetian carpet and mats shown in the painting *Grandmother's Delight* by Charles Cole Markham, c. 1860. (Frank Schwarz and Son Gallery, Philadelphia)

planters who traded directly with London agents. But primitive transportation networks often prevented such furnishings from reaching households away from major centers of trade. Until the second half of the 19th century, residents of rural communities depended generally on the products of local artisans. Advertisements indicate what types of skilled craftspeople were working in the community during the target date for the restoration project.

PAINTINGS AND PHOTOGRAPHS. Paintings, drawings, engravings and, by the second half of the 19th century, photographs, offer visual documentation of decoration used during the target period. These sources may indicate the type of floor covering (if any) used in a room, the pattern and scale of the design, how the material was installed and sometimes its color. Knowledge of the types of floor coverings available at a specific time and the sorts of patterns that were popular is essential for correctly interpreting visual documents. For example, both Venetian and list carpets were striped and woven in narrow widths. They can usually be distinguished in photographs or drawings; Venetian had a regular striped pattern along the warp (length) of the goods, while list was less highly striped and the thick, multicolored weft stuffers created an irregular appearance across the width of the carpet strips, which rarely matched where they were seamed. Both Venetian and list carpets were flatwoven, meaning they had no pile and were reversible. Ingrain was also flatwoven carpeting, but unlike Venetian or list it had geometric and floral patterns. Fortunately, ingrain sometimes can be differentiated in prints and photographs from other types of patterned carpets by subtle yet distinctive shaded bands that run across the width of each carpet strip.

Understanding the social class and wealth of a person whose decoration is being studied also helps suggest the sort of floor covering shown. When a painting, drawing or photograph lacks the details needed to determine precisely what sort of carpet was present, economic and social factors may help one make an educated guess. For instance, more ingrain carpeting was woven in America during the 19th century than any other type. However, middle-class households were the major market for this product. Families with greater income generally purchased more expensive carpets, including Brussels, Wiltons, tapestries and Axminsters. An inventory can often confirm the type of floor covering illustrated in the visual documents pertaining to the specific house.

SURVIVING SAMPLES. Occasionally, historic floor coverings survive in situ. Tile and wood floors are of course more durable than carpeting, oilcloth and paint. But sometimes these more perishable finishes remain through accident, neglect or the care of previous owners. For example, written records proved that when The Athenaeum of Philadelphia (1847, John Notman) was completed, the vestibule floor was covered with oilcloth and the reading room floor with ingrain carpeting. Neither floor covering apparently had survived. However, when a large bookcase at the west end of the reading room was removed during restoration in 1975, a surviving piece of

Surviving sample of original ingrain carpet, c. 1847, from The Athenaeum of Philadelphia, discovered during a 1975 restoration. (The Athenaeum of Philadelphia)

Piece of little-worn ingrain carpet, c. 1825–50, now in The Athenaeum's collection. (The Athenaeum of Philadelphia)

the original ingrain carpeting was discovered. A section of original painted floor similarly was found under a heavy piece of furniture in the Vail House (c. 1830), now part of Speedwell Village in Morristown, N.J.. When a family in Port Hope, Mich., acquired a late 19th-century house, they were delighted to find the original carpeting on the parlor floor, although much faded and worn. In cleaning the attic and closets, the owners then discovered an unused piece of the same carpet with colors as vivid as the day it had been woven.

These surviving examples of original materials are called documents. In contrast to wallpaper, bed and window hangings, and household furnishings, relatively few floor coverings survive for several reasons. First, 18th- and 19th-century carpeting was made primarily of wool and was subject to the ravages of moths and carpet beetles. Furthermore, being underfoot, abrasion and soil reduced the pile or wore holes in flatwoven constructions such as ingrains. Serious water damage from leaks or potted plants caused areas of rot. Before carpet padding was introduced in the late 19th century, new carpets were sometimes laid over old ones, which hastened their demise. Or, if a family purchased a new carpet for a parlor, they might recut the old one to fit a less important room such as a bedchamber. Years of continued service ensued until the carpet was thrown away or, as sometimes was the case with ingrains, cut down for horse blankets. Finally, just as today, used carpeting was discarded because it was not as easy as a set of curtains to store in an attic trunk.

PROPER PERIOD INSTALLATION

Proper installation is as important as the pattern, colors and scale of the floor coverings chosen to reproduce the appearance of a historic interior. Manufacturers' showrooms or retail outlets can recommend individuals in your area who specialize in the installation of their products. Careful measurement is the first step and usually should be done by the individual responsible for supervising the final installation. In some cases a measured drawing of the floor plan is necessary. This is particularly true when borders are part of the design of tile, hardwood or

wall-to-wall carpeting or when custom carpets are required. Whether the carpeting is produced in one piece to fit a room or woven in 27-inch widths that are stitched together in the factory or on site, a measured plan will prevent serious mistakes.

Many of the carpet patterns included in this book are woven on 27-inch looms just as they were in earlier centuries. These carpets should be sewn together by someone familiar with the peculiarities of installing woven carpeting. Too many installers today use heat-sensitive tape to seam carpeting; this product is successful with tufted carpets that became common after World War II but is unsatisfactory for most woven installations.

Heat-sensitive tape should not be used to install grass matting. Here the best methods are those used historically, which included tacking each strip in place with nonrusting nails for wall-to-wall use or stitching together the strips to form a rug. U-shaped staples also work for wall-to-wall installations and are nearly invisible but were not used until the 20th century. When Japanese tatami matting is chosen to replace a period floor covering, the fabric binding along the edges must first be removed.

Finally, it is essential to install any carpeting over firm, durable padding. The purpose of padding is to protect the backing of a carpet from grinding into the dirt that has filtered through it to the floor below. These small particles can be very abrasive and literally wear away the back of the carpeting, eventually causing pile loss. An adequate pad must never compress to a thickness less than 1/8 inch or it will fail to protect the carpeting. Consequently, the best padding is not the thickest but the densest. Hair pads, while more expensive than products of urethane or foam rubber, offer the best protection.

Unlike carpeting, floorcloths were historically placed directly on floors without padding. Most modern producers of floorcloths recommend that technique today. Early linoleum was installed by nailing in place; mastics were used by the end of the 19th century. Unless the linoleum is intended for a museum, the manufacturer's recommendations should be followed. For other types of floor coverings, the manufacturer's installation instructions also may be used.

Restored parlor of San Francisco Plantation (1850), Reserve, La., with a carpet custom made by Stark Carpet Corporation. (San Francisco Plantation)

INTRODUCTION

How to Use the Catalog

The catalog portion of this book is divided into five chronological periods that coincide with changes in floor covering styles and manufacturing technology. Each chapter begins with a brief history of the types of floor coverings available at that particular time and concludes with a list of suitable reproductions and adaptations for each type. Both hard finishes (wood, brick, tile, resilient flooring, floorcloths and matting) and carpeting are included. In many cases, a product is suitable for several time periods and thus is listed in all applicable chapters (although it may be illustrated only once, generally with its period of most prevalent use).

Individual catalog entries are listed by flooring type and supplier's name (in alphabetical order) and give the following information when it is available:

Product name

Indication of flooring type, including whether it is a reproduction or an adaptation

Description of the pattern

Country of origin

Date of the original or appropriate time period

Guidance on period appropriateness or installation

Information on the document and its location

Fiber content

Dimensions and size of the pattern repeat

Construction details

Catalog number or numbers

Available colors suitable for the period

Separate border when offered

Special collection name

Building or organization for which the item was made or examples of sites where it is installed

Availability (custom made, special order or stock item)

A glossary of common floor covering terms, a reading list and sources of additional information, all included in the appendix, provide helpful explanations to supplement the text.

Also presented in the appendix is a list of floor covering suppliers, given alphabetically as well as by specialty category. The distribution of floor coverings is somewhat complex, particularly for carpeting. Carpet manufacturers, for example, may or may not design and sell directly or solely the items they manufacture. Carpeting is distributed in the following varied ways:

1. Wholesale to a customer, such as a hotel chain, requiring a large quantity of carpeting. Many manufacturers will not custom weave for or sell directly to an interior designer, private institution or individual because of the time and high costs involved. This is becoming increasingly true as more clients seek reproductions.

2. Retail to carpet stores generally offering a wide variety of products from a number of manufacturers.

3. Through a design showroom, such as those operated by Scalamandre and Schumacher, which are accessible only to the trade. Design showrooms may sell either floor coverings made exclusively for them or products from a variety of manufacturers.

4. Through an agent representing a single company. In particular, British manufacturers work through American representatives who can furnish American consumers with information and product samples.

Furthermore, because it is nearly impossible to copyright a design, a manufacturer may produce a pattern similar to one already made by another company, perhaps changing colors and details. Small design changes may also permit a manufacturer to sell to other purchasers a previously exclusive pattern, one perhaps done for a historic house museum.

Thus, in the following catalog sections, readers will find some pattern names, numbers and descriptions repeated under different suppliers' names; others have the same name but different order numbers. Patterns appear under the names of manufacturers, manufacturers' representatives and design showrooms, indicating the availability of many carpet designs from a variety of sources. Information also is provided on manufacturers and suppliers who perform custom work. Readers who wish to order an item or who require additional information should contact the company indicated, using the address in the list of suppliers. Or, contact an interior designer, who will provide access to a design showroom or assist in making arrangements with the manufacturer or supplier.

CATALOG
OF REPRODUCTION
FLOOR COVERINGS

1750 TO 1800:
THE COLONIAL AND EARLY
FEDERAL INTERIOR

Most American homes of the last half of the 18th century would be considered sparsely furnished by today's standards. Low levels of artificial lighting, few curtained windows, furniture arranged along the walls instead of in intimate conversation groupings and a general absence of carpeting characterized most houses of the period. These interiors do not fit with nostalgic images that, until recently, were promoted by most museums. Yet we must remember that for most of the period America was a European frontier outpost inhabited predominantly by provincial British men and women. The beginnings of the industrialization that would so transform the 19th-century home were felt in England by 1780. Only the wealthiest few could afford the luxury of carpets, upholstered furniture and lavishly curtained windows that today are accepted as standard in the majority of middle-class homes. As an English colony, America was expected to export raw materials and import finished ones. These trade arrangements resulted in high costs for finished goods, which prohibited most Americans from richly embellishing their houses.

As mentioned in the introduction's section "Documenting Floor Coverings," inventories can yield fairly accurate pictures of the contents of houses. In 1775, for example, when Philadelphia was the largest city in America—and one of the largest in the English-speaking world—floor coverings of any type appeared in less than three percent of the inventories. Even among the wealthiest of these city dwellers, floor coverings were mentioned in less than 20 percent of the inventories. These findings were not pecu-

CHURCH MEDALLION RUG. Oriental rug. Karastan Bigelow, Colonial Williamsburg Reproductions. Cream, dark blue, tobacco and red.

41

liar to Philadelphia but common throughout the colonies and the early Republic.

WOOD FLOORS. Most Americans lived on floors of bare wood; brick and marble floors were as rare as carpets in most colonial houses. In New England, which had virgin stands of enormous white pine, colonists sawed the wood into planks commonly 12 to 26 inches wide. The edges were sometimes cut to form shiplapped joints, and the planks were surface-nailed directly onto the joists. As these giant trees were consumed toward the end of the 18th century, yellow pine planks (typically cut in five- or six-inch widths) were substituted. Throughout the 18th century the best floors were made of long boards that spanned the length of the room and required no piecing.

In the middle and southern colonies somewhat harder yellow pine was used during the period. A 1769 insurance survey of the Philadelphia home of Samuel Powel, the last mayor before and first mayor after the Revolution, described a "doweled floor" of yellow pine. The planks varied from 4½ to 6 inches wide and were joined by horizontal dowels. This was the best flooring available because it was composed of evenly sized boards and its tight seams were less likely to warp; it was also the most expensive. In the poorest construction, boards of varying widths were pieced, abutted and face-nailed to the joists.

Modern homeowners planning to re-create an old wood floor should consider three points. First, by the second half of the 18th century, random-width boards were the mark of a floor of poor quality. Second, at no time during the 18th century were floorboards attached to joists using wooden dowels. The so-called pegged floor is a 20th-century invention, possibly based on a misunderstanding of 18th-century carpentry practices such as that used to lay Samuel Powel's floor. Finally, pine floors were never treated to the high-gloss finishes associated with hardwood floors at the end of the 19th century and so treasured by owners of old houses today. Early floors were cleaned by scrubbing with water and sand, to which wood ashes were sometimes added; this practice certainly precluded any sort of varnish coat.

PAINTED FLOORS. While not varnished, pine floors were sometimes finished with paints composed of white

Original brick floor in the front entrance hall at Stenton (1728), Philadelphia. Brick floors were rare in colonial houses, while wood floors such as the one shown here were more common. (Thomas L. Davies, National Society of the Colonial Dames of America in the Commonwealth of Pennsylvania)

lead, pigments and linseed oil. This finish was particularly popular in New England, possibly because white pine is softer than yellow pine. Colors of surviving 18th-century floors are mainly yellows, dark reds, grays and browns, while surviving patterns often have narrow borders and centers composed of swirls, pinwheels, stylized oak leaves or other designs generally painted freehand. By the end of the century bolder colors, including blues, greens and white, were added to the palette and more complex, stencilled designs were used. Geometric shapes such as squares, diamonds and cubes were favored throughout the 18th century and were sometimes marbleized, thus imitating vastly more expensive flooring. Naturally, floors fin-

above

Painted canvas floor-cloth reproduced by Grigsby/Hallman Studio from a 1739 design by John Carwitham. (Catherine Wetzell)

above right

Reproduction marble-ized floorcloth installed in the hall of the Cupola House (c. 1725, 1758), Edenton, N.C. (Woodward Memorial Funds, The Brooklyn Museum)

ished this way were not scrubbed and required occasional retouching as the paints wore.

FLOORCLOTHS. The step from painted pine floors to painted floorcloths is a small but expensive one. Early records of their use include the household inventories of such colonial dignitaries as William Burnet (1688–1729), governor of Massachusetts, and Robert "King" Carter of Virginia (1663–1732). Before the Revolution, most floor-cloths found in America probably came from England. After the war, however, Americans produced them in numbers to compete with the English trade. The work was done by house and ship painters as well as firms specializing in interior decoration. In 1793 Joseph Barrell of Charlestown, Mass., canceled a floorcloth he had ordered through his London agent, explaining that he could now obtain what he desired in America.

Good-quality floorcloths were made from four to seven coats of oil-based paint applied to both sides of a canvas and followed by a decorative pattern created freehand or with stencils. The best were made from a single piece of seamless canvas. George Washington purchased a floorcloth costing $14.28 on January 11, 1796—no small expenditure at that time. Throughout the 18th century, house painters' account books record the repainting of worn floorcloths, which suggests that owners protected their investments and wanted them to last as long as possible.

Some idea of popular patterns comes from John Carwitham's *Various Kinds of Floor Decorations Represented Both in Plano and Perspective* (London, 1739), which contained 24 illustrations of designs suitable for "Pavements of Stone or Marble or . . . Painted Floor Cloths." Floorcloths were most often placed in entry halls, parlors and rooms used for dining. Designs varied; some floorcloths were a single color, sometimes ornamented with a border design, while others had overall geometric patterns of squares, diamonds or cubes—the latter painted in three colors—and all could be marbleized. Floorcloths were also painted to imitate carpets; the account book of a Boston painter in 1771 recorded the painting of four yards of canvas in "Turkey Fatchion." Some designs were rather unusual. Another Boston entry of 1788 listed an order for "a Poosey-Cat on one Cloath and a leetel Spannil on ye. Other." The size and intended use of a floorcloth may have determined its design. Wall-to-wall floorcloths imitating marble tiles were suitable for entry halls, while "poosey-cats" and "spannils" seem more likely in sitting rooms.

MATTING. Another floor covering associated with the last half of the 18th century was matting woven of various natural materials such as grass or straw. The best products apparently came from the Far East, because the terms "Canton" and "Indian" matting appear in inventories and advertisements. George Washington ordered quantities of Canton matting for Mount Vernon beginning in 1759. His original orders were placed with a London agent; however, when America began direct trade with China in the 1780s, Washington purchased through Robert Morris of Philadelphia.

Matting could be used as a year-round floor covering or as a summer replacement. Unlike floorcloths, matting was woven in strips, usually 36 inches wide, and stitched together to form larger carpets or simply tacked directly to the floor with the edges abutting. Housekeepers were advised never to use soap but to wash their matting with saltwater to prevent yellowing. Matting was also available in checkered patterns employing colors such as red or black to contrast with uncolored grasses. Several mattings that imitate early ones are available today, although none comes in colors.

Mats are occasionally recorded in inventories or paintings, but these utilitarian objects must have been common because of the condition of most colonial streets. That eminently urban American, Benjamin Franklin, praised the regularity and breadth of Philadelphia streets, but because most were unpaved, he confessed that "in wet Weather the Wheels of heavy Carriages plough'd them into a Quagmire . . . and in dry Weather the Dust was offensive." He added that it was not uncommon to see "the Inhabitants wading in Mud . . . often over Shoes in Dirt," while shopping at the central food market. Rough mats of braided rope, imported Spanish rush or bristly corn husks undoubtedly were placed at entry doors to remove what shoe scrapers had not. Within the house, softer mats of woven rags might be used at the thresholds of rooms or near beds. One late 18th-century inventory recorded a straw mat in a room designated "the nursery."

MASONRY FLOORS. Brick or marble-tiled floors were rarely seen in 18th-century America. Bricks often were used for fireplace hearths or as flooring in rooms associated with cooking or food storage. Marble was sometimes chosen for hearths or fireplace surrounds in the best rooms of the wealthy, and occasionally fireplaces were faced with imported tiles. Delft tiles from Holland, for example, were used around the fireplace openings in two houses north of Philadelphia, Graeme Park (1722), built by Sir William Keith, the provincial governor of

Pennsylvania, and Hope Lodge (c. 1750), built by Samuel Morris, a prosperous Quaker mill owner.

EARLY CARPETS. As already mentioned, carpets were rare in 18th-century American houses. While Samuel Morris had Delft-faced fireplaces, his household inventory taken on his death in 1770 listed no floor coverings at all. This is not too surprising considering both their cost and the fact that Hope Lodge was a country, rather than a city, house. No matter how prosperous, 18th-century rural households invested less in showy furnishings than did their urban counterparts. The residents of a city house or a Tidewater plantation, however, might acquire some status from the furnishings displayed in their houses. Furthermore, because great planters, city merchants and their families formed the majority of people considered well-to-do in the 18th century, they had both the means and the access to buy luxurious materials such as carpeting.

Handknotted Oriental carpets woven in the Near East, sometimes called Turkey carpets, were found in few colonial homes. Through most of the 18th century, American paintings depict them as table covers—an Anglo-Dutch tradition—as they were far too valuable to walk on. Only by the last decades of the century do they appear on floors, and then only in the homes of the most prosperous families. Furthermore, paintings of the period show a marked preference for strong, geometric patterns such as those found in rugs from Smyrna and Ushak.

AXMINSTER CARPETS. By the 1750s English weavers located in Exeter, Axminster and Moorfields were producing "domestic Orientals." Like true Oriental carpets, the English copies were knotted by hand on vertical looms, and several weavers might be employed to create a single, wide, seamless carpet. All English products so woven eventually came to be called Axminsters, a name derived from the longest-operating weaving center. The carpets copied Oriental rugs and patterns from the French Royal carpet manufactory at Savonnerie, and two firms, in Axminster and Moorfields, worked neoclassical designs for architect Robert Adam. On July 26, 1787, Abigail Adams visited the factory at Axminster, recording in her diary, "The carpets are equally durable with the Turkey, but surpass them in colors and figure." Because English carpets copied Oriental patterns, it is difficult to determine which type is shown in paintings of the late 18th century. However, there is no mistaking which type of carpet Benjamin Franklin bought in England in April 1766, for he wrote home that he had celebrated the repeal of the Stamp Act by purchasing "a large true Turkey carpet [which] cost 10 guineas, for the dining room parlor" in his Philadelphia home.

Before the 1790s Axminster carpets were exceedingly rare in America; no documented survivals have yet been found. But by 1787 American Axminsters were advertised in Philadelphia. They were made by William Peter Sprague, who was born in either Kidderminster or Axminster, England, about 1750, and who probably worked at Thomas Whitty's carpet factory in Axminster. At the end of the Revolution, Sprague and his family emigrated to Burlington, N.J., where he established his first factory before moving to Philadelphia in 1790. In the following year, he wove an Axminster carpet for the Senate chamber and in April was paid $215.25 by George Washington for a carpet "for the large dining room" in the house the president occupied in Philadelphia. Despite this early American production, the cost of Axminsters kept them beyond the reach of most households. When Sprague died in 1808, Axminsters ceased to be woven in Philadelphia.

BRUSSELS AND WILTON CARPETS. During the last half of the 18th century, British mills wove three other types of carpeting that were exported to America: Brussels, Wilton and ingrain. Unlike Axminsters, these carpets were woven in strips that were seamed together before laying. Brussels carpets, presumably named for their city of origin, were first woven in England about 1740 in Wilton and shortly thereafter in Kidderminster. Wilton carpets developed slightly later as a variation of Brussels. Both had worsted face piles, which in the case of Brussels were looped and in Wilton were cut. Both were produced on narrow looms in strips 27 inches wide. (The origin of the 27-inch standard possibly derives from the ell, a unit of measurement calculated by the Flemish at 27 inches, or from the fact that 27 inches was the span woven by a handweaver at an Axminster loom.) The patterns included floral medallions and geometric designs such as squares or octagons with clusters of flowers or oak leaves in their centers. Colors were subtle; paintings show carpets in brown and olive green, sage with pink, blue green with red, and cream with black and mauve. Brussels and Wilton carpets remained fairly expensive until production was mechanized in the 19th century.

INGRAIN CARPETS. Ingrain carpeting—also known as Scotch, English, Kilmarnock and Kidderminster after British weaving centers—began about 1735. It was woven in 9- to 54-inch widths, with 36 inches as standard. It had a reversible, flat surface composed of wool and worsted and was far less expensive than Brussels, Wilton or Axminster and thus was more commonly used. While most ingrain carpeting sold in colonial America was from Great Britain, there was some domestic production as well. Home looms produced patterned goods for floors but most of these were not true ingrains, which are double weaves. William Peter Sprague produced ingrain carpeting in addition to Axminsters in his Philadelphia factory. Visual documents and surviving examples of carpets suggest that these 18th-century ingrain patterns were woven in bright, highly contrasting colors such as black with yellow and green with yellow and orange.

In addition to the "true Turkey carpet" he purchased in 1766, Franklin sent his wife enough carpeting from London in 1758 to make up one large and two small carpets. He directed that "it is to be sow'd together, the Edges being first fell'd down, and Care taken to make the Figures meet exactly: there is Bordering for the same." These seamed goods were either Brussels, Wilton or ingrain, although the latter would certainly have been the easiest for an amateur to sew together.

LIST CARPETS. While Franklin could afford manufactured carpets, most Americans could not. Some households undoubtedly wove their own carpets or rugs. Eighteenth-century inventories occasionally record list carpeting, which takes its name from "list," meaning narrow strips of fabric or the selvages of cloth that formed the weft. The weft created a random pattern, while the warp threads formed regularly spaced stripes. Either way, the finished product was generally 36 inches wide, and panels of list could be seamed together to form larger carpets.

NEEDLEPOINT RUGS. American women also made needlepoint rugs or carpets, of which there are no known surviving 18th-century examples. Documented 18th-century English needlepoint carpets are made from wool worked on canvas in either the cross-stitch or the tent stitch. The Metropolitan Museum of Art has one from the early 19th century that is room size and even shaped to fit into the recesses on either side of the fireplace. It reportedly took family members two years to complete. Such carpets would have been special and presumably treated with great care. The fact that no colonial example apparently survives may suggest how few were actually made.

WOOD FLOORING

AGED WOODS

▶ ANTIQUE CYPRESS. Flooring planks. ½″, ⅝″ and ¾″ thick, 2″–11″ wide, 2′–12′ random lengths. Special order.

▶ ANTIQUE DISTRESSED AMERICAN CHESTNUT. Flooring planks. ⅝″ thick, 3″–7″ wide; ¾″ thick, 3″–10″ wide; 1″ thick, 3″–10″ wide; 2′–12′ random lengths. Special order.

▶ ANTIQUE DISTRESSED OAK. Flooring planks. ⅝″ and ¾″ thick, 3″–10″ wide; 6/4″ thick, 3″–12″ wide; 2′–12′ random lengths. Special order.

▶ ANTIQUE FIR. Flooring planks. ⅝″ thick, 3″–12″ wide; ¾″ and 6/5″ thick, 3″–15″ wide; 2′–12′ random lengths. Special order.

▶ ANTIQUE MILLED AMERICAN CHESTNUT. Flooring planks. ⅝″, ¾″ and 6/5″ thick, 3″–7″ wide; 2′–12′ random lengths. Special order.

▶ ANTIQUE MILLED OAK. Flooring planks. ⅝″ and ¾″ thick, 3″–10″ wide; 6/4″ thick, 3″–12″ wide; 2′–12′ random lengths. Special order.

▶ ANTIQUE POPLAR. Flooring planks. ⅝″ thick, 3″–12″ wide; ¾″ thick, 3″–15″ wide; 6/4″ thick, 3″–15″ wide; 2′–12′ random lengths. Special order.

WIDE PINE BOARDS. Wood flooring. Carlisle Restoration Lumber Company.

▶ ANTIQUE WHITE PINE. Flooring planks. ⅝" thick, 3"–12" wide; ¾" thick, 3"–15" wide; 6/4" thick, 3"–15" wide; 2'–12' random lengths. Special order.

▶ ANTIQUE YELLOW HEART PINE. Flooring planks. ⅝" thick, 3"–12" wide; ¾" thick, 3"–12" wide; 6/4" thick, 3"–12" wide; 2'–12' random lengths. Special order.

CARLISLE RESTORATION LUMBER COMPANY

▶ SHIPLAP PINE BOARDS. 8"–12" wide, 8'–12' long. Special order.

▶ WIDE OAK BOARDS. 5"–10" wide, 8'–16' long. Special order

▶ WIDE PINE BOARDS. ⅞" and 1" thick, 14"–21" wide, 8'–16' long. Special order.

CASTLE BURLINGAME

Booklets on antique flooring selection, installation and finishing available ($5 each postpaid).

▶ ANTIQUE VIRGIN EASTERN WHITE PINE (KINGS PLANKS). Pumpkin pine with pit-sawn markings, double-tongue and double-groove edges. 1" thick, random widths and lengths. Special order.

▶ ANTIQUE VIRGIN SOUTHERN LONGLEAF YELLOW HEART PINE. Georgia pine with natural edges for later shiplap, butt joint or tongue-and-groove finish. ⅞" thick, random widths to 16", random lengths. Special order.

THE JOINERY COMPANY

▶ ANTIQUE SOUTHERN LONGLEAF YELLOW HEART PINE. Flooring, millwork, cabinetry, furniture and timber frames. Remilled from structures 100–200 years old. Quarter-sawn, edge-grain and original surfaces. Prime grade and antique original grade. $7/16''$ thick, to 20'' wide, 16' long. Installed at King's Arms Tavern, Colonial Williamsburg, Va. Stock items.

MOUNTAIN LUMBER COMPANY

▶ ANTIQUE SOUTHERN LONGLEAF YELLOW HEART PINE. Flooring, period moldings, paneling and trim. Milled from timbers taken from pre-1900 structures; graded and kiln dried. Tongue-and-groove planks. 3''–6'' and 6''–10'' random widths and lengths. Prime grade free of most knots and imperfections; cabin grade with knots, nail holes and some hairline cracks. Installed at Monticello, Charlottesville, Va. Stock items.

VINTAGE LUMBER AND CONSTRUCTION COMPANY

▶ ANTIQUE TIMBER. Random-width flooring. Remilled. Tongue-and-groove planks. Chestnut, $25/32''$ thick, 2''–10'' wide. Fir, $25/32''$ thick, 3''–8'' wide. Oak, $25/32''$ thick, 3''–8'' wide. Random lengths. Stock items.
▶ ANTIQUE YELLOW AND WHITE PINE. Random-width wide flooring. Tongue-and-groove planks. 4''–10'' wide, random lengths. Stock items.
▶ NEW OAK, WALNUT, CHERRY, MAPLE, POPLAR AND WHITE PINE. Random-width wide flooring. $3/4''$ thick, 3''–8'' wide, random lengths. Stock items.
▶ SOUTHERN LONGLEAF YELLOW HEART PINE. Random-width flooring. Remilled; kiln dried. Tongue-and-groove planks. 3''–10'' wide, random lengths. Stock items.

BRICK FLOORING

VICTOR CUSHWA AND SONS

▶ CALVERT COLONIAL PAVING BRICK. New brick. Suitable for brick floors and hearth treatments where appropriate. Formed in sand-coated wooden molds using Maryland shale clay. 4'' x $2^3/4''$ x $8^1/2''$. No. 30-200 (rose, full range); No. 103-200 (medium red, full range). Installed at National Park Service sites. Stock items.

COLONIAL WILLIAMSBURG FOUNDATION

▶ CORN HUSK MAT. Oval, handbraided corn husks. 18th to early 20th century. Approximately 26″ x 22″. No. 18024 (light cream). Stock item.

STARK CARPET CORPORATION

▶ CHINESE SEA GRASS MATTING. Basket-weave pattern of sea grass cords with braided bast fiber warp. Texture, scale and sheen resemble coarse 19th-century straw mattings. 13′2″ wide. Natural grass shades of pale gold, pale green and honey brown. Stock item.

ERNEST TREGANOWAN

▶ TATAMI GRASS MATTING. Japanese matting resembling Indian matting. Late 18th to 19th century. (Coarse Chinese straw mattings, 36″–54″, are no longer commercially made.) Period installation requires tacks or narrow U-shaped staples; fabric tape bindings must be removed before installation, and ends must be turned under. 36″ wide. No. 180 (natural greenish grass). Stock item.

W. A. G. (WAVENY APPLE GROWERS)

▶ DOORMATS. Used as early as 1766 in Virginia. Half-round, oval and rectangular (see description below). Custom sizes and shapes.
▶ HANDMADE RUSH CARPETS. Nine-ply weave made of nine strands of two or more rushes of even thickness, braided in strips 3″ wide and sewn together, forming carpets of various widths and lengths. Ends are bound with a fine rush binding. Installed at Agecroft Hall, Richmond, Va. Custom sizes and shapes.

GOOD AND COMPANY

Stencilled floorcloths on painted canvas also available in custom patterns, sizes and colors.
▶ DARTMOUTH. Adaptation of a floorcloth seen in 1793 painting of John Phillips by Joseph Steward. Various sizes, approximately 6″ repeat; fringe-motif border on all sizes larger than 2′ x 3′. Document color: dark green with brick red and tan; and other colors. Special order.
▶ EBENEZER. Small geometric rosette pattern. Various

MATTING

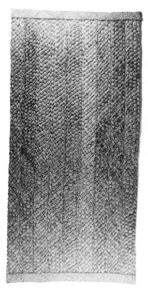

HANDMADE RUSH CARPET. Matting. W. A. G. (Waveny Apple Growers).

FLOORCLOTHS AND STENCILLING

sizes. Soldier blue with mustard gold and light blue; putty with Williamsburg blue and wine; light green with soldier blue and old yellow. Installed at the Ebenezer Waters House, West Sutton, Mass. Special order.

▶ TRADITIONAL CUBE. Tumbling-block pattern. Various sizes. Brick red with dark green and tan. Special order.

GRIGSBY/HALLMAN STUDIO

Produces a variety of stencilled floorcloths, some with marbleized finishes, including reproductions of documented English patterns from 1739 by John Carwitham, designer and engraver (suitable for the 19th century). Painted canvas. Sizes to 10' wide seamless, any length. Custom patterns, sizes and colors.

MARBLE AND DIA-MONDS. Floorcloth. Grigsby/Hallman Studio. Dark and light colors.

▶ COMPASS ROSE. Central compass on ground of marbleized diamonds. c. 1760. Based on London floorcloth painter's sign.

▶ MARBLE AND DIAMONDS. Marbleized diamonds in alternating dark and light colors.

▶ MASONIC ADAPTATION. Black and white squares with hexagonal lozenge border. 1720s. Adapted from a painted floorcloth made for an American Masonic temple.

▶ PLAIN ALTERNATING SQUARES. Large, alternating dark and light plain-colored squares.

▶ SIX-SIDED MARBLE. Hexagonal marbleized tiles separated by smaller dark squares.

▶ TUMBLING BLOCKS. Optical-illusion pattern of three-dimensional blocks.

MASONIC ADAPTATION. Floorcloth. Grigsby/Hallman Studio. Black and white.

HAND PAINTED STENCILS

Custom handcut patterns and colors stencilled directly onto the floor.

ISABEL O'NEIL STUDIO

Custom painted floors and painted and stencilled canvas floorcloths in various sizes.

PEMAQUID FLOORCLOTHS

▶ BORDERED FLORAL. Stencilled canvas floorcloth. Adaptation resembling late 18th-century patterns in print sources. 2' x 3', 2½' x 4', 4' x 6' and custom sizes. Custom colors. Special order.

▶ DIAGONAL SQUARES. Stencilled canvas floorcloth. Alternating dark and light squares. Based on period print sources. 2' x 3', 2½' x 4', 4' x 6' and custom sizes. Custom colors. Special order.

▶ MARINER'S COMPASS. Stencilled canvas floorcloth. Central compass on dark and light diamond ground. Based on 18th-century floor patterns. 2' x 3', 2½' x 4', 4' x 6' and custom sizes. Custom colors. Special order.

▶ WREATHS AND TULIPS. Stencilled canvas floorcloth. Adaptation resembling late 18th-century patterns in print sources, engravings and drawings. 2' x 3', 2½' x 4', 4' x 6' and custom sizes. Custom colors. Special order.

MARINER'S COMPASS. Floorcloth. Pemaquid Floorcloths. Custom colors.

SPECIAL EFFECTS BY SUE

Floorcloth designs duplicated on painted canvas in various sizes. Also available by special order are handpainted and stencilled canvas floorcloths in geometrics, wreaths and other patterns based on print sources, in various sizes and custom colors.

FLOORCLOTHS: BAIZE

THE DORR MILL STORE

▸ RUG WOOL. All wool. 57″ wide. No. 1313 (green); No. 6307 (dark blue); 32 other colors and color sample card available. Special order.

SUNFLOWER STUDIO

▸ CARPET BAIZE. All wool. 36″ wide. Handwoven. 14 oz. No. X18.12 (cream white) can be custom dyed 35 additional colors, including 7 shades of green. Special order.

RAG, LIST AND HANDMADE RUGS

THE GAZEBO OF NEW YORK

▸ HIT-AND-MISS. Rag rugs. All cotton rag weft; all linen warp. 27½″, 36″, 48″, 54″, 72″, 94″ and 132″ wide, any length. Multicolor. Reversible. Stock items; nonstandard widths and colors by special order.

HANDWOVEN

▸ HIT-AND-MISS. Rag rugs and stair runners. All cotton rag weft; strong polyester warp. Sizes to 10′ wide, any length. Multicolor; custom colors. Reversible. Special order.

IMPORT SPECIALISTS

▸ SPRINGFIELD TWILL PLAID. Cotton twill rugs. 2′ x 3′, 44″ x 72″ and 6′ x 9′. Similar to document in Smithsonian Institution collection. No. F 1044 (green and rust plaid). Reversible. Stock items.

PEERLESS IMPORTED RUGS

▸ COLONIAL. Hit-and-miss pattern woven mat and area rag rugs. All cotton. 2′ x 3½′, 2½′ x 4½′, 3½′ x 5½′, 5½′ x 8½′ and 8′ x 10′. No. 1117 (multicolor). Reversible. Stock items.

RASTETTER WOOLEN MILL

▶ HIT-AND-MISS. Handwoven rag rugs. All cotton or all wool; linen warps available. Sizes including 9′ x 12′ seamless; other custom sizes seamed together in the traditional manner. Multicolor. Stock items and custom made (e.g., will prepare rugs from cut-and-sewn carpet rags).

STARK CARPET CORPORATION

▶ HIT-AND-MISS. Rag rugs. All cotton. Custom sizes. Multicolor and monochromatic. Special order.

WEAVERS UNLIMITED

▶ HIT-AND-MISS. Rag rugs. All cotton. 2½′ x 4′, 2½′ x 5′, 2½′ x 6′, 3′ x 4′, 3′ x 5′, 3′ x 6′, 63″ x 60″, 63″ x 72″ and 63″ x 84″. Room-size rugs available using hand-sewn strips 24″, 30″, 36″ or 63″ wide. Multicolor or stripes. Special order.

▶ STENCILLED PATTERNS. Pineapples, flowers and custom designs applied to rag rugs above.

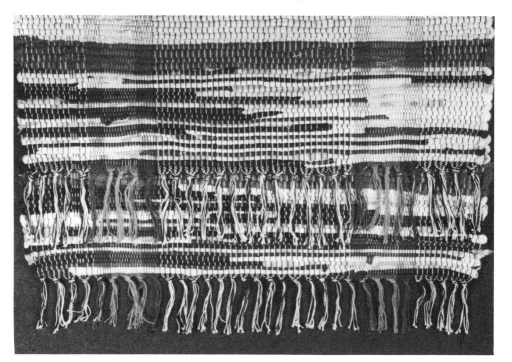

HIT-AND-MISS. Rag rug. Rastetter Woolen Mill. Multicolor.

THOS. K. WOODARD

▶ LANCASTER. Combination checked and striped rag rugs and stair runners. All cotton rag weft. Large rugs traditionally constructed from handsewn narrow widths: 9' x 12' seamless, 12' x 18' and 12' x 24'. Stair runners: 27" and 36" wide, 24' long. No. 23 (multicolor stripe on blue check); No. 23-B (multicolor stripe on burgundy check). Stock items and special order.

FLATWOVEN CARPETS: INGRAIN AND JERGA

BLOOMSBURG CARPET INDUSTRIES

▶ WILTON. Wilton adaptation of ingrain. Small geometric pattern. Late 18th to early 19th century. 80% wool, 20% nylon. 27" wide, 5" x 7" drop-match repeat. No. W 232 6C (olive green and black on cream); and custom colors. Special order.

COLEFAX AND FOWLER

▶ HIGFORD. Brussels adaptation of ingrain. Small geometric rosette pattern. Probably English, late 18th to early 19th century. Document found in the United States. 80% wool, 20% nylon. 27" wide, 5¼" repeat. Off-white, teal blues and dark brown. Special order.

LANGHORNE CARPET COMPANY

▶ CONGRESS HALL. Brussels adaptation of ingrain. Late 18th to early 19th century. Document at Congress Hall, Independence National Historical Park, Philadelphia. All wool pile. 36" wide. Document color: red and green. Special order.

MILLIKEN CONTRACT CARPETING

Contact company for a local representative.
▶ ALSACE. Printed adaptation of 1790s floorcloths or ingrain usable as a substitute for period carpeting. Suitable if installed so that the pattern is square to the walls. Not suitable where documentation is required. All nylon pile. 12' wide, 6" x 6" set-match repeat. No. 542 (hunt green); No. 544 (red). Stock items.

PATTERSON, FLYNN AND MARTIN

▶ DEL PEZZO. Wilton adaptation of a tessellated marbleized pattern; substitute for marble or floorcloths.

1790s; also appropriate for the 1820s because of the distinct diagonal pattern. Suitable where documentation is not required. 80% wool, 20% nylon. 27" wide, 27" repeat. Brick, cream, brown and black. Special order.

▶ HIGFORD. Brussels adaptation of ingrain. Small geometric rosette pattern. Probably English, late 18th to early 19th century. Document found in the United States. 80% wool, 20% nylon. 27" wide, 5¼" repeat. Off-white, teal blues and dark brown. Special order.

▶ INGRAIN. Brussels adaptation of ingrain. Small rosette pattern with borders. English, late 18th to early 19th century. Document a Scotch double-weave carpet in the Victoria and Albert Museum, London. All wool pile. 27" wide. No. 1814/7383 (brick, red brown and salmon center with black, maroon and ochre borders). Special order.

▶ INGRAIN. Brussels adaptation of ingrain. Small geometric pattern. English, late 18th to early 19th century. Document an ingrain in the Victoria and Albert Museum, London. English. All wool. 27" wide. No. 1815/7384 (black, cream, forest and olive green and gold); and custom colors. Special order.

▶ INGRAIN. Brussels adaptation of ingrain. Stepped geometric pattern with crosses and quatrefoils. Late 18th to early 19th century. Similar to floor patterns appearing in late 1790s–1820s paintings and print sources (which continued in longer use in less prosperous homes). 80% wool, 20% nylon. 27" wide. No. 1816/7385 (burgundy, red orange and cream on deep maroon). Special order.

SCALAMANDRE

▶ HADDONFIELD. Brussels adaptation of ingrain. Small geometric pattern. English, late 18th to early 19th century. Document an English double cloth (ingrain) in the Victoria and Albert Museum, London. All wool pile. 27" wide. Brick, brown, maize, red, apricot and olive green. Brittania Collection. Made for the Genesee Country Museum, Mumford, N.Y. Special order.

▶ INDEPENDENCE HALL. Ingrain reproduction. Geometric pattern with rosettes in centers of squares and at line crossings. Late 18th century to c. 1820. Document at Independence Hall, Independence National Histori-

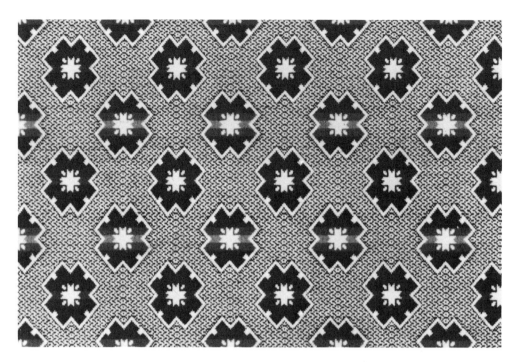

LEINSTER. Brussels adaptation of Scotch ingrain. Scalamandre. Cream, olive green and browns.

INDEPENDENCE HALL. Ingrain carpet. Scalamandre. Red, moss greens and cream.

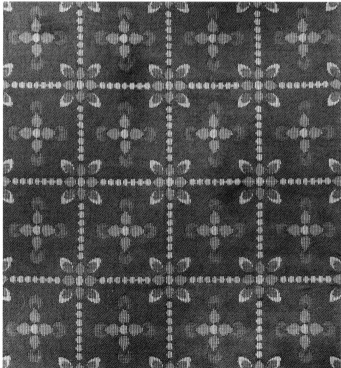

cal Park, Philadelphia. All wool. 36" wide, approximately 8½" repeat. Traditional two-ply construction. Document color: No. 97369-1 (red, moss greens and cream). Made for Independence Hall. Installed at the Gen. William Lenoir House, Fort Defiance, Lenoir, N.C., and Boscobel, Garrison, N.Y. Special order.
▶ LEINSTER. Brussels adaptation of Scotch ingrain. English, c. 1790–1820. Document in the Victoria and Albert Museum, London. All wool. 27" wide. Cream, olive green and browns. Made for Sunnyside (Washington Irving House), Tarrytown, N.Y. Special order.

SUNFLOWER STUDIO

▶ INGRAIN. Adaptation of period ingrain designs and illustrative materials. Geometric pattern. Early 19th century. All worsted wool. 36" wide. 20½ oz. Traditional two-ply construction. Brick, medium olive green, light yellow and tan. Reversible. Special order.
▶ JERGA. Durable woven twill carpet with 2" checks. Spanish colonial Southwest, 18th and 19th centuries. Similar to fabrics in the Museum of International Folk Art, Santa Fe, N.M. All wool. 24" wide. 26 oz. Natural sheep brown and cream white; and custom colors. Special order.

CRAIGIE STOCKWELL CARPETS

Also researches, designs and colors patterns to order. Ovals and shapes can be made to exact room configurations. Construction is handtufted or handknotted in the traditional 18th-century manner by Craigie Stockwell or its associated company, Stockwell Riley Hooley.
▶ CULZEAN CASTLE. Reproduction. Scotland, late 18th to early 19th century. Document an original Adam-style carpet. All wool pile. Room size. Handtufted. Brick red, cream, tan, brown, pale gold and apricot; and custom colors. Special order.
▶ LANCASTER HOUSE, LONDON. Reproduction. Deep borders with griffins, grapes and leaves. English, late 18th to early 19th century. Document a carpet from St. Petersburg. All wool. Approximately 20' x 32'. Handknotted. Red with beige, blue and cream. Special order.

PILE CARPETS: ROOM-SIZE MEDALLION PATTERNS

top left
TRINITY HOUSE.
Medallion pattern.
Craigie Stockwell Car-
pets. Beige with brown
and blue.

top right
LANCASTER HOUSE,
LONDON. Medallion
pattern. Craigie Stock-
well Carpets. Red with
beige, blue and cream.

right
CULZEAN CASTLE.
Medallion pattern.
Craigie Stockwell Car-
pets. Brick red, cream,
tan, brown, pale gold
and apricot.

▶ TRINITY HOUSE, LONDON. Reproduction. Ship and lighthouse motifs with central medallion. English, late 18th to early 19th century. Document a carpet made at the Royal Wilton Carpet Factory for Francis Millwork Company, specialists for 300–400 years in lighthouses and lightships. All wool. Approximately 20′ x 40′. Beige with brown and blue border. Handknotted. Special order.

SCALAMANDRE

Also duplicates historic patterns.
▶ NORMANDY. Adaptation. Oval central medallion pattern with a classical leaf border on a dark ground. c. 1790–1820. Suitable where documentation is not required. All wool pile. Room size. Handtufted. Custom colors and sizes.
▶ SAVANNAH PARLOR. Adaptation. Central large bordered rosette with leaf and urn medallions in the corners and deep borders. 1790–1820. Document a wallpaper in the Werms House, Savannah, Ga. All wool looped pile. Room size. Handtufted. Custom colors and sizes.

BLOOMSBURG CARPET INDUSTRIES

▶ WILTON. Central medallion with squared border. Late 18th to early 19th century. 80% wool, 20% nylon. 27″ wide, 28″ drop-match repeat. No. W 582 4C (custom colors). Special order.

J. R. BURROWS AND COMPANY

▶ OVERALL FLORAL WITH RED AND PINK ROSES. Brussels reproduction. English, c. 1800. Document a point paper in manufacturer's collection. 80% worsted wool, 20% nylon pile. 27″ wide. No. 87/0260 (black, yellow green, olive green and two shades of rose). Special order.
▶ OVERALL SERPENTINE VINE AND LEAF MOTIF ON VERMICELLI GROUND. Brussels reproduction. English, c. 1800. Document a point paper in manufacturer's collection. 80% worsted wool, 20% nylon pile. 27″ wide. No. 87-0220 (brown black, forest green, yellow gold and light yellow). Border available. ³/₄ (27″ wide) runner available. Special order.

SAVANNAH PARLOR. Medallion pattern. Scalamandre. Custom colors.

PILE CARPETS: REPEAT PATTERNS

OVERALL SERPENTINE VINE AND LEAF MOTIF. J. R. Burrows and Company.

PATTERNED OCTAGON MEDALLIONS. Brussels carpet (point paper). J.R. Burrows and Company. Cream, olive green, dark brown and lavender.

▶ PATTERNED OCTAGON MEDALLIONS. Brussels reproduction. English, 1797. Document a point paper in manufacturer's collection. 80% worsted wool, 20% nylon pile. 27″ wide, 13½″ set-match repeat. No. 87/0175 (cream, olive green, dark brown and lavender). Special order.

▶ QUATREFOIL WITH ALTERNATING FLORAL AND FOLIATE FILLINGS. Brussels reproduction. English, 1790s. Document a point paper in manufacturer's collection. 80% worsted wool, 20% nylon pile. 27″ wide. Cream, brown and gray brown with green patterned quatrefoils. Special order.

▶ WREATH MOTIF SEPARATED BY FOLIATE GARLANDS. Brussels reproduction. English, c. 1800. Document a point paper in manufacturer's collection. 80% worsted wool, 20% nylon pile. 27″ wide. Cream, brown and red on black. Special order.

CARPETS OF WORTH

▶ ADAM PANEL. Axminster adaptation. Alternating circles and bordered squares. English, 1790–1820. Appropriate for the late 18th to early 19th century. 80% wool, 20% nylon. 27″ and 36″ wide, approximately 13″ set-match repeat. Olympus Axminster No. 2/6002 (red orange, red, gold and black). Available colors not compatible with period coloring. Stock item.

▶ RUST ADELPHI. Axminster adaptation. English, 1790–1800. Based on Adam-style patterns. 80% wool, 20% nylon. 27″ and 36″ wide, approximately 18″ set-match repeat. Olympus Axminster No. 6/6008 (rust, gold, yellow cream and black). Stock item.

K. V. T. (PENNSYLVANIA WOVEN) CARPET MILLS

Also custom weaves Brussels and Wilton carpeting from historic documents in limited quantities.
▶ FLAME STITCH. Brussels. 1750–1800. Based on flame-stitch patterns appearing in embroidered fabrics and decorative items of the period. 80% wool, 20% nylon. 27″ wide. No. 9900-A-5584 (custom colors). Special order.

LACEY-CHAMPION CARPETS

Produces custom handtufted carpets and duplications of period patterns.

LANGHORNE CARPET COMPANY

Also duplicates and adapts historic documents. Contact company for a local representative.
▶ MEDALLION PATTERN CROSS. Brussels adaptation. c. 1792. Based on floor coverings in the paintings *Portrait of Chief Justice and Mrs. Oliver Ellsworth* and *Mrs. Noah Smith and Her Children*, both by Ralph Earl, in the

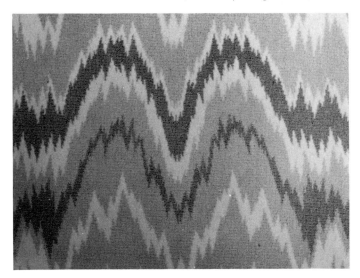

FLAME STITCH. Brussels carpet. K. V. T. (Pennsylvania Woven) Carpet Mills. Custom colors.

Metropolitan Museum of Art. 80% wool, 20% nylon. 27″ wide, 27″ repeat. Dark green, red, cream, tan and orange. Special order.

EDWARD MOLINA DESIGNS

▶ SHERATON DE LUXE. Contract Axminster. Alternating octagons and medallions with rosette centers. 1790s–1820s; 1840s. Suitable where documentation is not required. 80% wool, 20% nylon. 27″ wide, approximately 30″ repeat. 189 pitch/9 rpi. No. 412/4 (shades of gray, green and cream on dark olive green); No. 412/19 (shades of tan and honey brown on dark brown); No. 412/54 (white, blues, olive green and yellow on black). Special order.

ROBBINS BROTHERS

▶ ADAM FLORAL. Royal Seaton Axminster. Based on Adam motifs. Suitable for the late 18th to early 19th century. All wool pile or 80% wool, 20% nylon. 3′ and 12′ wide. No. 12/87501 (cardinal red); No. 40/87501 (cream). Special order.

▶ ADAM PANEL. Axminster. Large medallion. 1790–1820. 80% wool, 20% nylon. 27″, 3′ and 12′ wide, 36″ self-match repeat. No. 12/9001 (red, gold and fawn); No. 115/9001 (dark forest green, fawn and gold); and custom colors. Special order.

ROSECORE CARPETS

Some available Wilton and Brussels carpets are suitable where documentation is not required. Custom work also is provided, including development of patterns and duplication of carpeting from historic materials in the company's collection.

SAXONY CARPET COMPANY

Produces custom reproductions and adaptations in Brussels, Wilton and Axminster weaves, handtufted if required.

SCALAMANDRE

Also duplicates historic patterns.

▶ DEVONSHIRE. Wilton. Large-scale multibordered

square with rosette center. c. 1790–1820. Based on a mid-18th-century wall paneling designed by Charles Cameron. 80% wool, 20% nylon. 27″ wide, 27″ repeat. Cut or looped pile available. Greens, olive brown, apricot and shades of red. Made for the Old Merchant's House, New York City. Special order.

▶ EIFEL. Wilton. Alternating medallion and octagon on a diapered ground. 1790–1820. 80% wool, 20% nylon. 27″ wide, 54″ drop repeat. Red and green, blue and chrome yellow, yellow gold and black, brick, olive and cream with dark brown or black. Brittania Collection. Made for the Governor's Mansion, Jefferson City, Mo. Special order.

▶ MORRIS-JUMEL. Wilton adaptation. c. 1765. Document a photograph at the Morris-Jumel Mansion, New York City. 80% wool, 20% nylon. 27″ wide, 54″ repeat. Document color: brown, gray green, dark brown and lavender; and custom colors. Special order.

STARK CARPET CORPORATION

▶ GARBO AND GARBO BORDER. Wilton. Octagonal pattern. Late 18th century to 1820. All wool. 27″ wide. Red, olive green and gold; and custom colors. Special order.

▶ HUNTING ROOM. Wilton or Brussels reproduction. Wreath and leaf pattern. c. 1790. Suitable for the late

HUNTING ROOM. Wilton or Brussels carpet. Stark Carpet Corporation. Reds, gold, tan and black.

above left
SOUTHGATE. Wilton or Brussels carpet. Stark Carpet Corporation. Red with black, cream and gold.

above right
SYON. Wilton or Brussels carpet. Stark Carpet Corporation. Rose and blue with green.

18th to early 19th century. All wool. 27" wide. Reds, gold, tan and black; and custom colors. Special order.

▶ OCTOSET PETIT POINT. Brussels. Late 18th century. 80% wool, 20% nylon. 27" wide. Gold, green and rust; and custom colors. Special order.

▶ SALZBURG PETIT POINT AND BORDER. Brussels. c. 1788. Based on a design in Johann Eckstein's painting of the Samuels family of Philadelphia. 80% wool, 20% nylon. 27" wide. Black background with floral cluster in white, pale green and rose; and custom colors. Special order.

▶ SOUTHGATE. Wilton or Brussels. Alternating circles and octagonal medallions with leaf wreath and Greek-key banding. c. 1760. Document at Southgate House, England. All wool. 27" wide, 27" drop-match repeat. No. 9700 (red ground with black, cream and gold); and custom colors. Border No. 8116. 13½" wide. Special order.

▶ SYON. Wilton or Brussels. Floral pattern with rosettes. c. 1750. Document from the Long Gallery at Syon House, Middlesex, England. All wool. 27" wide. No. 9421 (rose and blue with ribbon trellis and soft green ground); and custom colors. Border No. 8383 (rose, green, pink, blue and brown); and custom colors. 18" wide. Special order.

CHARLES R. STOCK/V'SOSKE

▶ ADAM FLORAL. Royal Seaton Axminster adaptation. Based on Adam motifs. Suitable for the late 18th century. All wool pile or 80% wool, 20% nylon. 3′ and 12′ wide. Most suitable stock colors: No. 12/87501 (cardinal red); No. 182/87501 (zircon green). Stock items.

V'SOSKE
Provides custom reproductions and adaptations.

KARASTAN BIGELOW
COLONIAL WILLIAMSBURG REPRODUCTIONS

▶ CARTER'S GROVE RUG. Adaptation of a Feraghan rug. Overall Herati pattern. 1750–55. Document from the entrance hall of Carter's Grove, James City County, Va. Skein-dyed wool pile. Williamsburg No. 133389 (4′3″ x 5′9″); No. 133397 (5′8″ x 8′11″); No. 133405 (8′3″ x 11′7″). Karastan No. 554. Red with shades of blue and pale yellow. Stock items (small sizes) and special order (largest size).

▶ CHURCH MEDALLION RUG. Version of "Turkish Church Rug" with cream ground. Based on a 17th- or 18th-century Transylvanian prayer rug. All worsted wool pile. Williamsburg No. 133355 (3′10″ x 5′3″); No. 133363 (5′7″ x 8′8″); No. 133371 (8′2″ x 11′9″). Karastan No. 555. Cream, dark blue, tobacco and red. Stock items (small sizes) and special order (largest size).

ORIENTAL RUGS

CARTER'S GROVE RUG. Oriental rug. Karastan Bigelow, Colonial Williamsburg Reproductions. Red with blue and pale yellow.

USHAK RUG. Oriental rug. Karastan Bigelow, Colonial Williamsburg Reproductions. Red orange with gold and blue.

TURKISH CHURCH RUG. Oriental rug. Karastan Bigelow, Colonial Williamsburg Reproductions. Red, blue, tan and cream.

▶ TRANSYLVANIA CHURCH RUG. Adaptation of an antique "Turkey" carpet. Document at the Governor's Palace, Colonial Williamsburg, Va. All worsted wool. Williamsburg No. 10272 (5'2" x 4'1"). Karastan No. 550. Beige, red orange, gold and olive greens. Stock item.

▶ TURKISH BIRD RUG. Adaptation of a 17th-century antique. All worsted wool. Williamsburg No. 10629 (3'10" x 5'6"). Karastan No. 551. Red, light and dark blue, cream and tobacco. Stock item.

▶ TURKISH CHURCH RUG. Adaptation of a handknotted Transylvanian prayer rug. Balkans, 17th or 18th century. All worsted wool. Williamsburg No. 10777 (3'10" x 5'3"); No. 10801 (5'7" x 8'8"); No. 10272 (8'2" x 11'9"). Karastan No. 553. Red, blue, tan and cream. Stock items (small sizes) and special order (largest size).

▶ USHAK RUG. Adaptation of an antique rug. Document at the Brush-Everard House, Colonial Williamsburg, Va. All worsted wool. Williamsburg No. 10678 (4'3" x 5'9"); No. 10744 (5'8" x 8'11"); No. 10710 (8'3" x 11'7"). Karastan No. 552. Red orange with gold and patterned blue border. Stock item (small sizes) and special order (largest size).

TURKISH BIRD RUG. Oriental rug. Karastan Bigelow, Colonial Williamsburg Reproductions. Red, light and dark blue, cream and tobacco.

TRANSYLVANIA CHURCH RUG. Oriental rug. Karastan Bigelow, Colonial Williamsburg Reproductions. Beige, red orange, gold and olive greens.

1800 TO 1840:
THE LATE FEDERAL AND GRECIAN INTERIOR

A merica had gained its political independence from England, and spokesmen for the new nation often likened its government and people to those of ancient Greece or the Roman Republic. George Washington was hailed as a new Cincinnatus, and Thomas Jefferson, as statesman and amateur architect, was an influential advocate of neoclassical design. While minister to France (1785–89), Jefferson had become convinced of the perfection of ancient architecture and its power to impress not only Americans, but foreign visitors to the small, vulnerable nation as well. He modeled the Virginia State Capitol (1785–98) on the ruins of the Roman temple at Nîmes, France, and his own house, Monticello (1768–1809), on the publications of the 16th-century Italian architect Andrea Palladio. The earliest architects in America, such as Benjamin Latrobe, William Strickland and Robert Mills, followed this lead. And if Strickland in Philadelphia could base his design for the Second Bank of the United States (1818–24) on the Parthenon, then countless anonymous builders could fashion diminutive temples in wood, brick or stucco as homes for Americans. These houses dot the landscape of the original 13 states and the older settlements of the Midwest, upper South and Gulf Coast.

After the Revolution, Americans continued to look to European centers of fashion, specifically London and Paris, for inspiration. Not surprisingly, the style was neoclassical. By 1820 Americans called it Grecian (what we identify as Greek Revival)—a term more appropriate than Empire, which refers to the French Empire (1804–15) of Napoleon I. The plans of early 19th-century interiors

METROPOLITAN MUSEUM. Ingrain carpet. Scalamandre. Olive, moss, red and cream.

continued the general principles of symmetry and balance typical of the early Federal period at the end of the 18th century. However, the architectural detailing became bolder, with larger mantels, moldings and cornices and with taller windows. New styles of furniture first introduced in the Federal period by craftsmen such as Duncan Phyfe and émigrés such as Charles Honoré Lannuier and Michel Bouvier adopted forms based on classical antiquity, including *klismos* chairs, curule legs, pier tables, couches or *recamiers,* and French bedsteads whose ends swept up in graceful S curves. Fashionable upholstery, window coverings and carpeting employed intense shades of red, blue, green and yellow in highly contrasting schemes, such as red with green or blue with yellow.

The Industrial Revolution, begun in England during the last decades of the 18th century, spread to textile mills in New England in the early decades of the 19th century. The impetus for the American cotton industry had been the invention of the cotton gin in 1793, followed by trade blockades during the Napoleonic Wars that had prevented southern cotton from reaching foreign markets. The industrialization of floor covering manufacture developed more slowly because wool, unlike cotton, was dependent on foreign sources and was more difficult to prepare for use. Nevertheless, by 1830 advances in wool spinning and the enactment of two protectionist tariffs had encouraged the fledgling American carpet industry. By the mid-19th century, an increasing number of middle-class American households could purchase factory-produced floor coverings.

WOOD FLOORS. Houses built from 1800 to 1840 continued to have softwood floors of the type described in the previous chapter. The major difference was that narrower planks 4 to 6 inches wide became common, the result of second-growth timber and standardized milling practices. White pine was occasionally used, but increasingly floors were finished in harder, yellow pine just as they had been in the middle and southern colonies.

PAINTED FLOORS. Many homeowners continued to rely on paint, floorcloths and matting. Jefferson painted the entry-hall floor of Monticello a solid green and the floor of the dome room a gray blue. More decorative

Painted canvas floor-
cloth from the first half
of the 19th century,
reproduced by Good
and Company. (S. E.
Ekfelt)

treatments were also used. In 1830 Ruth Henshaw, wife
of a minister in Fitzwilliam, N.H., spent four days painting her parlor floor. The result, according to her diary,
was a floor "striped with red, green, blue, yellow and
purple—carpet like." At about the same date, the floor of
the library and dining room in the Vail House (c. 1830),
Morristown, N.J., was striped in less flamboyant colors of
fawn (tan) and drab (yellow brown).

FLOORCLOTHS. Floorcloths remained popular
although not inexpensive. In 1802 Jefferson considered a
floorcloth to protect the grass matting under the dining
room table of the Executive Mansion in Washington.
English floorcloths were apparently superior products,
because his assistant, Thomas Claxton, wrote, "The
English painted cloth costs about 3 dollars pr. square yd
and American I am told is scarcely ever used." While

Jefferson balked at the cost, he finally purchased one; an 1809 inventory of the White House included "a canvas floor cloth, painted green" in the south dining room.

The price of a good English floorcloth, according to Webster and Parkes in *The Encyclopedia of Domestic Economy* (1844), depended on the strength of the canvas, the number of coats of paint, the variety of colors making up the patterns and the time the product aged before it was sold. Factory-produced floorcloths were manufactured by first stretching canvas on a vertical frame, sizing it and then smoothing both sides to remove the small fibers raised during the sizing process. "Four coats of stiff oil paint are [then] laid on successively, on one side of the canvas, suffering each first to dry, and then three coats on the other side. After this paint is quite dry, the cloth is detached from the frame, in order to be printed in the manner of calico printing; for this purpose it is rolled up on a roller, and unrolled as required for the process. In giving the surface pattern stencilling was formerly employed; but printing with blocks is now generally practiced." A good floorcloth weighed $3\frac{1}{2}$ to $4\frac{1}{2}$ pounds per square yard. Presumably English products were superior to American ones because they had more layers of paint and were thus more durable. Aging also helped. As Miss (Eliza) Leslie explained in *The Lady's House Book* (1854), "We have seen an English oil-cloth that, not having been put down till five years after it was imported, looked fresh and new, though it had been ten years in constant use on an entry floor."

While Jefferson's purchase was apparently painted a single color, most floorcloths continued to be patterned. Geometric designs remained popular and early in the 19th century were joined by floral motifs set into square or diamond-shaped grids. John Claudius Loudon informed readers of *Cottage, Farm, and Villa Architecture and Furniture* (1833) that cottagers should select patterns imitating materials commonly used on floors such as tessellated pavement, colored stones or wood, while more prosperous householders might purchase floorcloths with patterns imitating carpets. These variations also explain why some floorcloths were used as rugs and others laid wall to wall, sometimes with a rug over them.

MATTING. Matting was also used wall to wall or as a carpet during the early decades of the 19th century. Loudon recommended "Indian matting" bound in either black or colored cotton tape for the floors of cottages. Generally woven in 36-inch widths, matting was laid in passages, or, for whole rooms, strips were abutted to cover the larger area. It was a cool alternative to carpeting in the summers and a year-round floor covering for a household whose budget did not permit carpets. It was highly recommended for bedchambers throughout the century as an easily cleaned, inexpensive finish. It was, however, easily damaged and soiled. Miss Leslie warned readers that matting should not be used on stairs because it "wears out very soon against the ledges of the steps and is, besides, too slippery to be safe for those that go up and down, particularly if they have to carry articles that may be broken."

Mats were also common in early 19th-century houses. Coarse ones were used near exterior doors while finer ones, of sheepskin or braided wool or cotton, were placed at the thresholds of rooms, in front of fireplaces and at the base of stairs. The value of carpeting and the difficulty of maintaining it before vacuum cleaners explain the abundance of mats in 19th-century houses.

MASONRY FLOORS. Tile floors remained a rarity in America, although English sources mentioned them. Loudon recommended six-inch square quarry tiles in blue, red, drab, black or tan for porches and entrance halls. However, regular shipments of such tiles did not reach America until the mid-19th century. A few homes, such as Gore Place (1801) near Boston and The Forest (1836) in Madison, N.J., had entrance halls of gray and white marble tiles laid in checkerboard patterns, but marble was simply too expensive for most American houses.

BRUSSELS AND WILTON CARPETS. Middle- and upper-class households bought increasing amounts of carpeting. In addition to the most expensive handknotted carpets (Orientals and Axminsters), Americans could choose from Brussels, Wilton, ingrain, list and Venetian. Brussels, Wilton and ingrain carpets required skilled weavers whose wages were comparatively high. A weaver had to manipulate the loom's harnesses to create the complex carpet pattern and also had to control the tension on the loom so that the patterns would match when the carpet strips were sewn together. Even with the invention of the Jacquard attachment about 1801, which automatically set the pattern and which was adapted for carpet looms in 1825, a skilled weaver could produce only about seven yards of carpeting a day. Furthermore, before the 1830s virtually all Brussels and Wilton carpets were imported to America from England, which added to their cost, as did the fact that they used more wool than ingrain, list or Venetian.

An 1801 inventory of the "President's House" in Washington, D.C., recorded Brussels carpeting in most rooms, including the dining room, where a "Green Baize Cover" was used as a drugget to protect the carpet from food spills. An inventory taken at the end of Jefferson's tenure in 1809 listed "elegant Brussels carpet" in several rooms including the president's sitting room, drawing room and bedroom. Certainly these carpets had been woven in England. Possibly the star-studded crimson Brussels carpet ordered for the Senate chamber in 1823 was a domestic product. But as these examples suggest, Brussels carpeting was beyond the reach of the vast majority of American households.

VENETIAN AND JERGA CARPETS. Most Americans could afford only less expensive carpets such as list, Venetian or ingrain. All three were flatwoven, meaning they had no pile, and consequently were reversible. Venetian carpeting was first woven in England and America about 1800 but its origin remains a mystery. *The Encyclopedia of Domestic Economy* informed readers, "It is not known that what we call Venetian carpeting was ever made in Venice." Venetian carpets were woven on narrow looms in strips varying from 18 to 36 inches wide. They were generally striped in distinct colors formed by wool warp threads so tightly packed that they totally covered the thicker weft threads; this filling traditionally was linen or a combination of whatever materials were at hand, including cotton, hemp and jute. Some checked patterns, known as Venetian damasks, were also woven. The English author of *The Workwoman's Guide* (1828) recommended "common Venetian" (striped) for servants' rooms and "Venetian damask" for stairs and sitting rooms. Webster and Parkes also recommended Venetian carpeting for bedrooms, where its flat, tightly woven surface was easy to sweep clean. It continued to be used throughout the 19th and early 20th centuries, although it lost popularity to ingrain and pile carpets by the second half of the 1800s.

Similar to Venetian carpeting were Jerga rugs woven about the same time in the Spanish Southwest. These wool, flat-pile coverings were produced on handlooms and usually contained two colors worked in a twill or herringbone weave. Like Venetian carpeting, Jergas were seamed together to form larger carpets. Their use was confined to the area around what is New Mexico today.

LIST CARPETS. Venetian carpeting is easily distinguished from list carpeting because the weft threads are not visible in Venetian carpeting, while the rag weft of list carpeting is its prominent feature. Both types of carpeting were woven in factories during the 19th century, but the simple construction of list made it easy to produce on home looms. *The New England Farmer* reported that the Essex Agricultural Show of October 1827 awarded "to Miss Rebecca Greenough, of Bradford, for 24 yards of handsome Rag Carpeting—made by hand, 4 yards wide, and without a seam, a gratuity of $3.00." List was also produced on narrower looms and the strips sewn together to create larger carpets. Its use continued into the 20th century, especially in Colonial Revival interiors.

INGRAIN CARPETS. Ingrain, the third type of flatwoven carpeting, was the most popular carpet until the last decades of the 19th century. Its complex patterns were woven on multiple-harness looms that produced two or three separate cloths joined only where the colors reversed from one side to the other, in the manner of woven coverlets. Like coverlets, ingrain carpets were woven in strips up to 54 inches wide (36 inches was standard) that were seamed together. Fairly small, geometric patterns were most common until the Jacquard attachment was adapted for carpet looms. This attachment freed carpet designs from the constraints of a weaver's memory and thus permitted incredibly complex patterns. Nonetheless, skilled weavers were still needed to operate the looms.

The earliest ingrains in America came from England and Scotland; consequently, the product was marketed by American merchants as Scotch, Kidderminster or English carpeting. Two American centers for weaving ingrain during the first half of the 19th century were Philadelphia and southern New England. Both employed a majority of weavers from Scotland. While Philadelphia's handweaving operations remained small, working mainly on the domestic "putting-out" system, the New England mills grew in size and increasingly turned to water-powered looms. American production of ingrain did not exceed British imports, however, until the 1840s. By then, Erastus Bigelow had perfected the first power looms for weaving two-ply and three-ply ingrains and the New England mills were prepared to supply this product for the domestic market.

The fledgling carpet industry in America could choose from several carpet types: ingrain, Venetian, Brussels, Wilton and Axminster. It chose to concentrate its efforts on ingrain and Venetian, thus supplying the majority of the American market. While Venetian was cheaper than ingrain, it was less popular because its patterns were limited. Ingrains offered more variation. After the adoption of the Jacquard attachment, the major constraint was that ingrain designs could not have large, unpatterned spaces. These spaces created "pockets" between the plies (layers) of the carpet that did not wear well. Consequently, before the Jacquard attachment, ingrain patterns were typically geometric designs with fairly small repeats of less than 12 inches. The Jacquard attachment made repeats of 24 to 36 inches fairly common; these designs were also complex, to avoid the problems of wear mentioned previously. Throughout the early 19th century geometric patterns in bright, highly contrasting colors were popular.

Brussels, Wilton and Axminster carpets did not share the design problem inherent with ingrains. However, they were expensive to weave and subject to strong competition from British imports so American mills made few of them. The Lowell Manufacturing Company in

Massachusetts, for example, produced 101,500 yards of ingrain but only 7,500 yards of Brussels in 1832. This situation prevailed throughout the industry. Paintings and surviving examples of early 19th-century Brussels and Wilton carpets suggest that geometric patterns employing squares, hexagons, octagons and wreaths, all embellished with neoclassical motifs, were preferred; the more complex the design, generally the larger the pattern repeat, with 60 inches not uncommon. Colors were bright and included golden yellows, blues, reds, greens and whites in highly contrasting schemes.

One final point should be mentioned concerning carpet installation. English mills wove decorative borders to match their carpet patterns, and paintings of English interiors often show bordered carpets covering most of the floor except the window reveals. Americans, however, apparently preferred to lay carpeting throughout a room, even into the recesses at windows and around fireplaces, and rarely used borders. Part of the explanation for this difference may lie in the fact that prosperous English houses often had oak floors while even the best American homes of the same date had floors of softwood.

AGED WOODS

WOOD FLOORING

▶ ANTIQUE CYPRESS. Flooring planks. 1/2″, 5/8″ and 3/4″ thick, 2″–11″ wide, 2′–12′ random lengths. Special order.

▶ ANTIQUE DISTRESSED AMERICAN CHESTNUT. Flooring planks. 5/8″ thick, 3″–7″ wide; 3/4″ thick, 3″–10″ wide; 1″ thick, 3″–10″ wide; 2′–12′ random lengths. Special order.

▶ ANTIQUE DISTRESSED OAK. Flooring planks. 5/8″ and 3/4″ thick, 3″–10″ wide; 6/4″ thick, 3″–12″ wide; 2′–12′ random lengths. Special order.

▶ ANTIQUE FIR. Flooring planks. 5/8″ thick, 3″–12″ wide; 3/4″ and 6/5″ thick, 3″–15″ wide; 2′–12′ random lengths. Special order.

▶ ANTIQUE MILLED AMERICAN CHESTNUT. Flooring planks. 5/8″, 3/4″ and 6/5″ thick, 3″–7″ wide; 2′–12′ random lengths. Special order.

▶ ANTIQUE MILLED OAK. Flooring planks. 5/8″ and

¾" thick, 3"–10" wide; ⁶⁄₄" thick, 3"–12" wide; 2'–12' random lengths. Special order.

▶ ANTIQUE POPLAR. Flooring planks. ⅝" thick, 3"–12" wide; ¾" thick, 3"–15" wide; ⁶⁄₄" thick, 3"–15" wide; 2'–12' random lengths. Special order.

▶ ANTIQUE WHITE PINE. Flooring planks. ⅝" thick, 3"–12" wide; ¾" thick, 3"–15" wide; ⁶⁄₄" thick, 3"–15" wide; 2'–12' random lengths. Special order.

▶ ANTIQUE YELLOW HEART PINE. Flooring planks. ⅝" thick, 3"–12" wide; ¾" thick, 3"–12" wide; ⁶⁄₄" thick, 3"–12" wide; 2'–12' random lengths. Special order.

CARLISLE RESTORATION LUMBER COMPANY

▶ SHIPLAP PINE BOARDS. 8"–12" wide, 8'–12' long. Special order.

▶ WIDE OAK BOARDS. 5"–10" wide, 8'–16' long. Special order.

▶ WIDE PINE BOARDS. ⅞" and 1" thick, 14"–21" wide, 8'–16' long. Special order.

CASTLE BURLINGAME

Booklets on antique flooring selection, installation and finishing available ($5 each postpaid).

▶ ANTIQUE VIRGIN EASTERN WHITE PINE (KINGS PLANKS) Pumpkin pine with pit-sawn markings, double-tongue and double-groove edges. 1" thick, random widths and lengths. Special order.

▶ ANTIQUE VIRGIN SOUTHERN LONGLEAF YELLOW HEART PINE. Georgia pine with natural edges for later shiplap, butt joint or tongue-and-groove finish. ⅞" thick, random widths to 16", random lengths. Special order.

THE JOINERY COMPANY

▶ ANTIQUE SOUTHERN LONGLEAF YELLOW HEART PINE. Flooring, millwork, cabinetry, furniture and timber frames. Remilled from structures 100–200 years old. Quarter-sawn, edge-grain and original surfaces. Prime grade and antique original grade. ⁷⁄₁₆" thick, to 20" wide, 16' long. Installed at King's Arms Tavern, Colonial Williamsburg, Va. Stock items.

Mountain Lumber Company

▶ ANTIQUE SOUTHERN LONGLEAF YELLOW HEART PINE. Flooring, period moldings, paneling and trim. Milled from timbers taken from pre-1900 structures; graded and kiln dried. Tongue-and-groove planks. 3"–6" and 6"–10" random widths and lengths. Prime grade free of most knots and imperfections; cabin grade with knots, nail holes and some hairline cracks. Installed at Monticello, Charlottesville, Va. Stock items.

SOUTHERN LONG-LEAF YELLOW HEART PINE. Wood flooring. Vintage Lumber and Construction Company.

VINTAGE LUMBER AND CONSTRUCTION COMPANY

▶ ANTIQUE TIMBER. Random-width flooring. Re-milled. Tongue-and-groove planks. Chestnut, $^{25}/_{32}''$ thick, 2″–10″ wide. Fir, $^{25}/_{32}''$ thick, 3″–8″ wide. Oak, $^{25}/_{32}''$ thick, 3″–8″ wide. Random lengths. Stock items.

▶ ANTIQUE YELLOW AND WHITE PINE. Random-width wide flooring. Tongue-and-groove planks. 4″–10″ wide, random lengths. Stock items.

▶ NEW OAK, WALNUT, CHERRY, MAPLE, POPLAR AND WHITE PINE. Random-width wide flooring. $^{3}/_{4}''$ thick, 3″–8″ wide, random lengths. Stock items.

▶ SOUTHERN LONGLEAF YELLOW HEART PINE. Random-width flooring. Remilled; kiln dried. Tongue-and-groove planks. 3″–10″ wide, random lengths. Stock items.

BRICK FLOORING

VICTOR CUSHWA AND SONS

▶ CALVERT COLONIAL PAVING BRICK. New brick. Suitable for brick floors and hearth treatments where appropriate. Formed in sand-coated wooden molds using Maryland shale clay. 4″ x 2¾″ x 8½″. No. 30-200 (rose, full range); No. 103-200 (medium red, full range). Installed at National Park Service sites. Stock items.

MATTING

COLONIAL WILLIAMSBURG FOUNDATION

▶ CORN HUSK MAT. Oval, handbraided corn husks. 18th to early 20th century. Approximately 26″ x 22″. No. 18024 (light cream). Stock item.

STARK CARPET CORPORATION

▶ CHINESE SEA GRASS MATTING. Basket-weave pattern of sea grass cords with braided bast fiber warp.

CORN HUSK MAT. Matting. Colonial Williamsburg Foundation. Light cream.

Texture, scale and sheen resemble coarse 19th-century straw mattings. 13'2" wide. Natural grass shades of pale gold, pale green and honey brown. Stock item.

ERNEST TREGANOWAN

▶ TATAMI GRASS MATTING. Japanese matting resembling Indian matting. Late 18th to 19th century. (Coarse Chinese straw mattings, 36"–54", are no longer commercially made.) Period installation requires tacks or narrow U-shaped staples; fabric tape bindings must be removed before installation, and ends must be turned under. 36" wide. No. 180 (natural greenish grass). Stock item.

W. A. G. (WAVENY APPLE GROWERS)

▶ DOORMATS. Used as early as 1766 in Virginia. Half-round, oval and rectangular (see description below). Custom sizes and shapes.
▶ HANDMADE RUSH CARPETS. Nine-ply weave made of nine strands of two or more rushes of even thickness, braided in strips 3" wide and sewn together, forming carpets of various widths and lengths. Ends are bound with a fine rush binding. Installed at Agecroft Hall, Richmond, Va. Custom sizes and shapes.

BRINTONS LIMITED

▶ ZENITH CONTRACT AXMINSTER. Ingrain and floorcloth adaptation. Small-scale Gothic pattern. 1800–20. Also available in Super Zenith and Zenith Jr. grades. 80% wool, 20% nylon. 27" wide, 3½" set-match repeat. Most appropriate stock colors: No. 3/5251 (golden tan and red on dark blue); No. 4/5251 (red and orange on dark green). Stock items.

GOOD AND COMPANY

Stencilled floorcloths on painted canvas also available in custom patterns, sizes and colors.
▶ DARTMOUTH. Adaptation of a floorcloth seen in 1793 painting of John Phillips by Joseph Steward. Various sizes, approximately 6" repeat; fringe-motif border on all sizes larger than 2' x 3'. Document color: dark green with brick red and tan; and other colors. Special order.

FLOORCLOTHS AND STENCILLING

▶ EBENEZER. Small geometric rosette pattern. Various sizes. Soldier blue with mustard gold and light blue; putty with Williamsburg blue and wine; light green with soldier blue and old yellow. Installed at the Ebenezer Waters House, West Sutton, Mass. Special order.

▶ STURBRIDGE. Alternating dark and light blocks with rosette. Based on an illustration in Nina Fletcher Little's *Floor Coverings in New England Before 1850*, p. 60. Various sizes. Special order.

▶ TRADITIONAL CUBE. Tumbling-block pattern. Various sizes. Brick red with dark green and tan. Special order.

GRIGSBY/HALLMAN STUDIO

Produces a variety of stencilled floorcloths, some with marbleized finishes, including reproductions of documented English patterns from 1739 by John Carwitham, designer and engraver (suitable for the 19th century). Painted canvas. Sizes to 10′ wide seamless, any length. Custom patterns, sizes and colors.

▶ MARBLE AND DIAMONDS. Marbelized diamonds in alternating dark and light colors.

▶ PLAIN ALTERNATING SQUARES. Large, alternating dark and light plain-colored squares.

PLAIN ALTERNATING SQUARES. Floorcloth. Grigsby/Hallman Studio. Dark and light colors.

▶ SIX-SIDED MARBLE. Hexagonal marbleized tiles separated by smaller dark squares.

▶ TUMBLING BLOCKS. Optical-illusion pattern of three-dimensional blocks.

HAND PAINTED STENCILS

Custom handcut patterns and colors stencilled directly onto the floor.

ISABEL O'NEIL STUDIO

Custom painted floors and stencilled and marbleized canvas floorcloths in various sizes.

PEMAQUID FLOORCLOTHS

▶ BORDERED FLORAL. Stencilled canvas floorcloth. Adaptation resembling late 18th-century patterns in print sources. 2' x 3', 2½' x 4', 4' x 6' and custom sizes. Custom colors. Special order.

▶ DIAGONAL SQUARES. Stencilled canvas floorcloth. Alternating dark and light squares. Based on period print sources. 2' x 3', 2½' x 4', 4' x 6' and custom sizes. Custom colors. Special order.

▶ MARINER'S COMPASS. Stencilled canvas floorcloth. Central compass on dark and light diamond ground. Based on 18th-century floor patterns. 2' x 3', 2½' x 4', 4' x 6' and custom sizes. Custom colors. Special order.

▶ SNOWFLAKE. Stencilled canvas floorcloth. Center pattern suitable for the 19th century if period colors are

above left
STENCILLED FLOOR WITH BORDER. Stencilling. Hand Painted Stencils.

above right
STENCILLED FLOOR BORDER. Stencilling. Hand Painted Stencils.

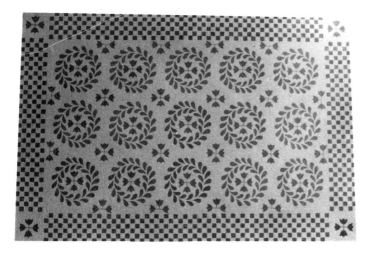

used. Painted canvas. 2' x 3', 2½'·x 4', 4'x 6' and custom sizes. Custom colors. Special order.

▶ WREATHS AND TULIPS. Stencilled canvas floorcloth. Adaptation resembling late 18th-century patterns in print sources. 2' x 3', 2½' x 4', 4 'x 6' and custom sizes. Custom colors. Special order.

SPECIAL EFFECTS BY SUE

Floorcloth designs duplicated on painted canvas in various sizes. Also available by special order are handpainted and stencilled canvas floorcloths in geometrics, wreaths and other patterns based on print sources, in various sizes and custom colors.

THE DORR MILL STORE

▶ RUG WOOL. All wool. 57" wide. No. 1313 (green); No. 6307 (dark blue); 32 other colors and color sample card available. Special order.

SUNFLOWER STUDIO

▶ CARPET BAIZE. All wool. 36" wide. Handwoven. 14 oz. No. X18.12 (cream white) can be dyed 35 additional colors, including 7 shades of green. Special order.

THE GAZEBO OF NEW YORK

▶ HIT-AND-MISS. Rag rugs. All cotton rag weft; all linen warp. 27½", 36", 48", 54", 72", 94" and 132" wide,

FLOORCLOTHS:
BAIZE

RAG, LIST AND
HANDMADE
RUGS

any length. Multicolor. Reversible. Stock items; nonstandard widths and colors by special order.

HANDWOVEN

▶ HIT-AND-MISS. Rag rugs and stair runners. All cotton rag weft; strong polyester warp. Sizes to 10′ wide, any length. Multicolor; custom colors. Reversible. Special order.

IMPORT SPECIALISTS

▶ SPRINGFIELD TWILL PLAID. Cotton twill rugs. 2′ x 3′, 44″ x 72″ and 6′ x 9′. Similar to document in Smithsonian Institution collection. No. F 1044 (green and rust plaid). Reversible. Stock items.

PEERLESS IMPORTED RUGS

▶ COLONIAL. Hit-and-miss pattern woven mat and area rag rugs. All cotton. 2′ x 3½′, 2½′ x 4½′, 3½′ x 5½′, 5½′ x 8½′ and 8′ x 10′. No. 1117 (multicolor). Reversible. Stock items.

RASTETTER WOOLEN MILL

▶ HIT-AND-MISS. Handwoven rag rugs. All cotton or all wool; linen warps available. Sizes including 9′ x 12′ seamless; other custom sizes seamed together in the traditional manner. Multicolor. Stock items and custom made (e.g., will prepare rugs from cut-and-sewn carpet rags).

STARK CARPET CORPORATION

▶ HIT-AND-MISS. Rag rugs. All cotton. Custom sizes. Multicolor and monochromatic. Special order.

WEAVERS UNLIMITED

▶ HIT-AND-MISS. Rag rugs. All cotton. 2½′ x 4′, 2½′ x 5′, 2½′ x 6′, 3′ x 4′, 3′ x 5′, 3′ x 6′, 63″ x 60″, 63″ x 72″ and 63″ x 84″. Room-size rugs available using handsewn strips 24″, 30″, 36″ or 63″ wide. Multicolor or stripes. Special order.

▶ STENCILLED PATTERNS. Pineapples, flowers and custom designs applied to rag rugs above.

THOS. K. WOODARD

Variety of traditional rag patterns based on 19th-century striped and patterned handwoven carpeting. Documents in Thos. K. Woodard collection. All cotton rag weft. All patterns available as runners 27″ and 36″ wide, to 24′ long. Rugs 4′ and 6′ wide, to 24′ long. Large sizes, 12′ x 18′ and 18′ x 24′, constructed from narrower widths sewn together in the traditional manner. Seamless 9′ x 12′ room-size rugs also available. Stock items.

Striped and plaid patterns include:

▶ ESSEX. No. 3 (blue, burgundy and tan plaid).

▶ JEFFERSON STRIPES. No. 22-A (rose, mustard, blue, green and beige); No. 22-B (blue, green, lavender and beige).

▶ LANCASTER. No. 23 (multicolor stripe on blue check); No. 23-B (multicolor stripe on burgundy).

▶ PENNSYLVANIA BARS. No. 1-A-6 (natural stripes on blue); No. 1-E-1 (slate blue on neutral); No. 21 (natural on red).

▶ PENNSYLVANIA STRIPES. No. 2-A-1 (multicolor stripes on neutral).

▶ READING. No. 19 (red stripes on natural); No. 19-D (natural on blue); No. 24 (natural on red).

▶ RITTENHOUSE SQUARE. No. 130-A (blue and white check); No. 130-BT (green and white); No. 130-CT (red and white).

above left
SPRINGFIELD TWILL PLAID. Rag rug. Import Specialists. Green and rust.

above right
HIT-AND-MISS and PATTERN BANDED. Rag rugs. Rastetter Woolen Mill. Multicolor.

▶ ROXBURY. No. 7 (red, black, tan, blue, green and yellow mix).

▶ SHAKER. No. 130 (teal, tan and brown plaid).

▶ WAINSCOTT. No. 11 (blue and tan plaid).

FLATWOVEN CARPETS: INGRAIN, JERGA AND VENETIAN

BLOOMSBURG CARPET INDUSTRIES

▶ WILTON. Wilton adaptation of ingrain. Small geometric pattern. Late 18th to early 19th century. 80% wool, 20% nylon. 27" wide, 5" x 7" drop-match repeat. No. W 232 6C (olive green and black on cream); and custom colors. Special order.

COLEFAX AND FOWLER

▶ HIGFORD. Brussels adaptation of ingrain. Small geometric rosette pattern. Probably English, late 18th to early 19th century. Document found in the United States. 80% wool, 20% nylon. 27" wide, 5¼" repeat. Off-white, teal blues and dark brown. Special order.

COLONIAL WILLIAMSBURG FOUNDATION

▶ FOLK ART FAVORITES NO. 1. Reproduction Venetian carpeting. Document is Deborah Goldsmith's 1832 portrait of the Talcott family. All cotton. "Abigail": No. 148627 (3' x 5'); No. 152363 (6' x 9'); No. 101014 (7' x 10'). Green and yellow. "Betsey": No. 148619 (3' x 5'); No. 149708 (6' x 9'); No. 10918 (7' x 10'). Red and blue. Stock items.

below left
RAG RUGS. Thos. K. Woodard. Various colors.

below right
LANCASTER, ESSEX and ROXBURY STAIR RUNNERS. Rag rugs. Thos. K. Woodard. Various colors.

▶ FOLK ART FAVORITES NO. 2. Reproduction checked rug with fringed edges. Document a 19th-century sample in the Abby Aldrich Rockefeller Folk Art Center. No. 116624 (4' x 6'); No. 104940 (6' x 9'); 105932 (9' x 12'). Gray and cream. Stock items (small sizes) and special order (large size).

FAMILY HEIR-LOOM WEAVERS

▶ GEOMETRIC AND FLORAL. Ingrain reproduction. Foliate medallion surrounded by geometric banding. 1825–50. Document in a private collection. All worsted wool. 36" wide, 42" repeat. Document colors: red, brown and olive green. Traditional two-ply construction. Made for the National Park Service. Special order.
▶ MAPLE LEAF. Ingrain. Alternating floral cartouche design with finely patterned ground. 1825–50. Documents in a private collection. All worsted wool. 36" wide, 52" repeat. Traditional two-ply construction. Red, brown and shades of olive green; and custom colors. Installed at National Park Service sites. Special order.

LANGHORNE CARPET COMPANY

▶ CONGRESS HALL. Brussels adaptation of ingrain. Late 18th to early 19th century. Document at Congress Hall, Independence National Historical Park, Philadelphia. All wool pile. 36" wide. Document color: red and green. Special order.

HIGFORD. Brussels adaptation of ingrain. Colefax and Fowler. Off-white, teal blues and dark brown.

above left
FOLK ART FAVORITES
NO. 2. Checked rug.
Colonial Williamsburg
Foundation. Gray and
cream.

above right
FOLK ART FAVORITES
NO. 1: ABIGAIL. Vene-
tian carpet. Colonial
Williamsburg Founda-
tion. Green and yellow.

opposite
FOLK ART FAVORITES
NO. 1: BETSEY. Vene-
tian carpet. Colonial
Williamsburg Founda-
tion. Red and blue.

PATTERSON, FLYNN AND MARTIN

▶ DEL PEZZO. Wilton adaptation of a tessellated marbleized pattern; substitute for marble or floorcloths.
1790s; also appropriate for the 1820s because of the
distinct diagonal pattern. Suitable where documentation
is not required. 80% wool, 20% nylon. 27" wide, 27"
repeat. Brick, cream, brown and black. Special order.

▶ HIGFORD. Brussels adaptation of ingrain. Small geometric rosette pattern. Probably English, late 18th to
early 19th century. Document found in the United
States. 80% wool, 20% nylon. 27" wide, 5¼" repeat.
Off-white, teal blues and dark brown. Special order.

▶ INGRAIN. Brussels adaptation of ingrain. Small
rosette pattern with borders. English, late 18th to early
19th century. Document a Scotch double-weave carpet in
the Victoria and Albert Museum, London. All wool pile.
27" wide. No. 1814/7383 (brick, red brown and salmon
center with black, maroon and ochre borders). Special
order.

▶ INGRAIN. Brussels adaptation of ingrain. Small geo-

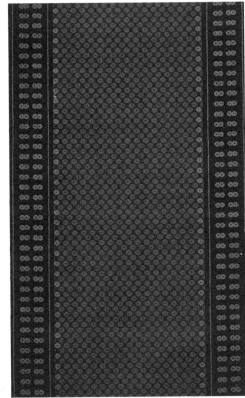

above left
GEOMETRIC AND
FLORAL. Ingrain car-
pet. Family Heir-Loom
Weavers. Red, brown
and olive green.

above right
INGRAIN. No. 1814/
7383. Brussels adapta-
tion of ingrain. Patter-
son, Flynn and Martin.
Brick, red brown, salmon,
black, maroon and ochre.

right
INGRAIN. No. 1816/
7385. Brussels adapta-
tion of ingrain. Patter-
son, Flynn and Martin.
Burgundy, red orange,
cream and maroon.

metric pattern. English, late 18th to early 19th century. Document an ingrain in the Victoria and Albert Museum, London. English. All wool. 27″ wide. No. 1815/7384 (black, cream, forest and olive green and gold); and custom colors. Special order.

▶ INGRAIN. Brussels adaptation of ingrain. Stepped geometric pattern with crosses and quatrefoils. Late 18th to early 19th century. Similar to floor patterns appearing in late 1790s–1820s paintings and print sources (which continued in longer use in less prosperous homes). 80% wool, 20% nylon. 27″ wide. No. 1816/7385 (burgundy, red orange and cream on deep maroon). Special order.

SAXONY CARPET COMPANY

Also custom duplicates and adapts period patterns.

▶ INGRAIN. Brussels adaptation of ingrain or floorcloth. Overall diamond pattern with central geometric motif. 1815–30. Document in the Victoria and Albert Museum, London. 80% wool, 20% nylon. 27″ wide, 9″ repeat. No. 1816/4 (dark gold, brick red and cream). V&A No. 7385. Special order.

SCALAMANDRE

Also duplicates historic patterns.

▶ HADDONFIELD. Brussels adaptation of ingrain. Small geometric pattern. English, late 18th to early 19th century. Document an English double cloth (ingrain) in the Victoria and Albert Museum, London. All wool pile. 27″ wide. Brick, brown, maize, red, apricot and olive green. Brittania Collection. Made for the Genesee Country Museum, Mumford, N.Y. Special order.

▶ INDEPENDENCE HALL. Ingrain reproduction. Geometric pattern with rosettes in centers of squares and at line crossings. Late 18th century to c. 1820. Document at Independence Hall, Independence National Historical Park, Philadelphia. All wool. 36″ wide, approximately 8½″ repeat. Traditional two-ply construction. Document color: No. 97369-1 (red, moss greens and cream). Made for Independence Hall. Installed at the Gen. William Lenoir House, Fort Defiance, Lenoir, N.C., and Boscobel, Garrison, N.Y. Special order.

▶ LEINSTER. Brussels adaptation of Scotch ingrain. English, c. 1790–1820. Document in the Victoria and Albert Museum, London. All wool. 27″ wide. Cream, olive green and browns. Made for Sunnyside (Washington Irving House), Tarrytown, N.Y. Special order.

▶ METROPOLITAN MUSEUM. Ingrain reproduction. Alternating bordered squares and diamonds with rosette centers. 1830–50. Document at the Metropolitan Museum of Art, New York City. 90% wool, 10% nylon. 36″ wide, 40″ repeat. No. 97223-1 (olive, moss, red and cream). Made for the Metropolitan Museum of Art. Installed at the Richard Owens House, New Harmony, Ind. Special order.

▶ VENETIAN. Warp-face striped carpet. 19th century. Document in manufacturer's collection. 54% wool, 46% cotton. 36″ wide. Pink, red, mauve, olive greens, black, melon, blue green or gray beige. Installed at the Custom House, Sag Harbor, N.Y. Stock item.

▶ WICKFIELD. Brussels adaptation of ingrain. Four-color pattern of crosses. c. 1800–20. Suitable also as a mid-19th-century Brussels pattern. All wool. 27″ wide, 6″ set-match repeat. Custom colors. Special order.

SUNFLOWER STUDIO

▶ INGRAIN. Adaptation of period ingrain designs and illustrative materials. Geometric pattern. Early 19th century. All worsted wool. 36″ wide. 20½ oz. Traditional two-ply construction. Brick, medium olive green, light yellow and tan. Reversible. Special order.

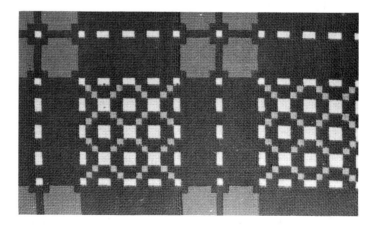

INGRAIN. Ingrain carpet. Sunflower Studio. Brick, medium olive green, light yellow and tan.

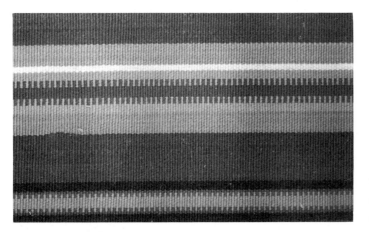

VENETIAN. Venetian carpet. Sunflower Studio. Custom colors.

▶ JERGA. Durable woven twill carpet with 2″ checks. Spanish colonial Southwest, 18th and 19th centuries. Similar to fabrics in the Museum of International Folk Art, Santa Fe, N.M. All wool. 24″ wide. 26 oz. Natural sheep brown and cream white; and custom colors. Special order.

▶ VENETIAN. Warp-face striped carpet. 19th century. Based on paintings of the period. 55% worsted wool, 45% linen. 30″ wide. Custom striped patterns and colors.

THOS. K. WOODARD

▶ THE TALCOTT COLLECTION. Reproduction Venetian rugs and stair runners. Document is Deborah Goldsmith's 1832 portrait of the Talcott family. All cotton. 27″ wide, 3′ x 5′, 9′ x 12′ and 6′ wide, any length. "Abigail Talcott": No. 28-A (green, blue, yellow, tan, rust and black). "Betsey Talcott": No. 28-B (brick red, blue, tan, green and black). "Charles Talcott": No. 28-C (gray, blue, tan, pink and black). Stock items.

THE TALCOTT COLLECTION. Venetian carpet. Thos. K. Woodard. Various colors.

CRAIGIE STOCKWELL CARPETS

Also researches, designs and colors patterns to order. Ovals and shapes can be made to exact room configurations. Construction is handtufted or handknotted in the traditional 18th-century manner by Craigie Stockwell or its associated company, Stockwell Riley Hooley.

▶ BRIGHTON PAVILION MUSIC ROOM. Reproduction. c. 1817. Document a carpet for the music room, Royal

PILE CARPETS: ROOM-SIZE MEDALLION PATTERNS

above left
CHATSWORTH
HOUSE. Medallion pat-
tern. Craigie Stockwell
Carpets. Dark red with
56 colors.

above right
BRIGHTON PAVILION
MUSIC ROOM. Medal-
lion pattern. Craigie
Stockwell Carpets.
Golds and turquoise.

right
17 HILL STREET,
MAYFAIR, LONDON.
Medallion pattern.
Craigie Stockwell Car-
pets. Beige, Adam
blue, rust and gold.

Pavilion, Brighton, England, later used by Queen Victoria. All wool pile. 40′ x 70′. Handknotted. Bright golds and turquoise; and custom colors. Special order.

▶ CHATSWORTH HOUSE. Reproduction. c. 1820. Document a scroll-pattern carpet for a private dining room. All wool. 19′7″ x 35′8″. Dark red with 56 colors. Special order.

▶ CULZEAN CASTLE. Reproduction. Scotland, late 18th to early 19th century. Document an Adam-style carpet. All wool pile. Room size. Handtufted. Brick red, cream, tan, brown, pale gold and apricot; and custom colors. Special order.

▶ LANCASTER HOUSE, LONDON. Reproduction. Deep borders with griffins, grapes and leaves. English, late 18th to early 19th century. Document a carpet from St. Petersburg. All wool. Approximately 20′ x 32′. Handknotted. Red with beige, blue and cream. Special order.

▶ 17 HILL STREET, MAYFAIR, LONDON. Reproduction. English, late 18th to early 19th century. Document an original carpet matching Adam-style ceiling in Sir John Soane's Museum. All wool pile. 24′ x 40′. Handtufted. Beige with Adam blue, rust, gold and lighter tones; and custom colors. Special order.

LACEY-CHAMPION CARPETS

Produces custom handtufted carpets and duplications of period patterns.

SCALAMANDRE

Also duplicates historic patterns.

▶ CAMPBELL-WHITTLESEY. Brussels adaptation. Medallion-style pattern. 1835–50. Document at the Campbell-Whittlesey House, Rochester, N.Y. All wool. Handtufted. Document colors: red, maroon, cream, tan, rust, yellow and blue. Made for the Campbell-Whittlesey House. Speical order.

▶ NORMANDY. Adaptation. Oval central medallion pattern with a classical leaf border on a dark ground. c. 1790–1820. Suitable where documentation is not required. All wool pile. Room size. Handtufted. Custom colors and sizes.

WILTON. Wilton adaptation of ingrain. Bloomsburg Carpet Industries. Red, burgundy, cream and black.

PILE CARPETS: REPEAT PATTERNS

▶ SAVANNAH PARLOR. Adaptation. Central large bordered rosette with leaf and urn medallions in the corners and deep borders. 1790–1820. Document a wallpaper in the Werms House, Savannah, Ga. All wool looped pile. Room size. Handtufted. Custom colors and sizes.

BLOOMSBURG CARPET INDUSTRIES

▶ WILTON. Wilton adaptation of ingrain. 1825–50. Alternating squares and diamonds. 80% wool, 20% nylon. 27″ wide, 13″ set-match repeat. WB 422 3C (red, burgundy, cream and black); and custom colors. Special order.

J. R. BURROWS AND COMPANY

▶ GEOMETRIC FLORAL. Brussels or Wilton reproduction. Alternating stylized geometric flowers and small four-petal flower. English, 1825. Document a point paper in manufacturer's collection. All wool. 27″ wide, 13″ repeat. No. 87/1405 (red, yellow, white, blue, green and black). Border available. ¾ (27″ wide) and 4/4 (36″ wide) runners available. Special order.

▶ HEXAGON FLORAL. Brussels reproduction. Concentric hexagonal rings inset with floral motifs and patterns resembling dress fabrics of the period. English, c. 1810. Document a point paper in manufacturer's collection.

80% worsted wool, 20% nylon pile. 27″ wide. No. 87/ 0159 (forest greens, roses, red, yellow gold and cream). Special order.

▶ HIEROGLYPHIC. Brussels or Wilton reproduction. Birds, animals, geometric figures and serpents representing hieroglyphics. English, c. 1805–06. Document an undated point paper by an artist known through initials and dates on other contemporaneous design papers for neo-Pompeiian and neo-Egyptian designs. 80% worsted wool, 20% nylon. 27″ wide. No. 87/0400 (red, black and tan). Special order.

▶ HORIZONTAL DIAMONDS WITH FLOWERS AND LEAVES. Brussels or Wilton reproduction. Horizontal diamonds, split crosswise, with alternating floral and leaf patterns. English, 1807. Document a point paper in manufacturer's collection. 80% worsted wool, 20% nylon. 27″ wide, 16″ set-match repeat. No. 49/6836 (tan and white ground with naturalistic-colored flowers). Special order.

▶ INTERLOCKING MEDALLION AND SQUARES WITH FLOWERS. Brussels reproduction. Interlocking medallion and square pattern with naturalistic floral centers. English, 1807. Document a point paper in manufacturer's collection. 80% worsted wool, 20% nylon pile. 27″ wide. No. 87/0131 (greens, black, reds, yellow orange

HEXAGON FLORAL. Brussels carpet (point paper). J. R. Burrows and Company. Forest greens, roses, red, yellow gold and cream.

on ground of cream, browns and tans). Special order.

▶ LAUREL WREATH, MEDALLION AND URN. Brussels or Wilton reproducion. Diaper rosettes overlaid with large medallions and laurel wreaths encircling urns. English, 1815. Document a point paper in manufacturer's collection. 80% worsted wool, 20% nylon. 27" wide. No. 87/6941 (blue, yellow gold, red and orange). Runner available. Special order.

▶ MOSAIC WITH ROSETTES. Brussels reproduction. Irregular mosaic pattern with rosettes in center of each "tile" and small leaves. English, c. 1810. Document a point paper in manufacturer's collection. 80% worsted wool, 20% nylon pile. 27" wide, 23" repeat. 87/0370 (tan, dark brown and black, with leaves in green, gold and white). Special order.

▶ OVERALL FLORAL WITH RED AND PINK ROSES. Brussels reproduction. English, c. 1800. Document a point paper in manufacturer's collection. 80% worsted wool, 20% nylon pile. 27" wide. No. 87/0260 (black, yellow green, olive green and two shades of rose). Special order.

▶ OVERALL SERPENTINE VINE AND LEAF MOTIF ON VERMICELLI GROUND. Brussels reproduction. English, c. 1800. Document a point paper in manufacturer's collection. 80% worsted wool, 20% nylon pile. 27" wide. No. 87/0220 (brown black, forest green, yellow gold and light yellow). Border available. ¾ (27" wide) runner available. Special order.

▶ RED MEDALLION. Brussels or Wilton reproduction. Red ground with deeper red medallions inset in squares of yellow gold. 1828. Document a point paper in manufacturer's collection. 80% worsted wool, 20% nylon. 27" wide. 87/1659 (reds with yellow gold). Special order.

▶ ROSETTES AND QUATREFOIL TRELLIS. Brussels or Wilton reproduction. Alternating octagonal rosettes on a ground diapered with a quatrefoil trellis. 1829. Document in manufacturer's collection. 80% worsted wool, 20% nylon pile. 27" wide, 25" repeat. No. 87/0644 (red, white, yellow gold, black and pink). Special order.

▶ TURKEY FLORAL. Brussels or Wilton reproduction. Alternating stylized geometric flowers and small four-petal flowers in the Turkish style; border includes clusters of geometric flowers and pattern bands. English, 1825. Document a point paper in manufacturer's collection. 80% worsted wool, 20% nylon. 27″ wide. No. 87/1405 (red, white, blue, green and black). ¾ (27″ wide) and 4/4 (36″ wide) runners available. Special order.

▶ TURKEY PATTERN. Brussels or Wilton reproduction. One of the first documented Brussels-Wilton construction "Turkey" rugs, with a large repeat and colors characteristic of Turkish rugs of the period. 1812. Document a point paper in manufacturer's collection. 80% worsted wool, 20% nylon pile. 27″ wide. No. 87/0524 (deep blue, red, yellow and celadon green). Special order.

▶ WREATH MOTIF SEPARATED BY FOLIATE GARLANDS. Brussels reproduction. c. 1800. Document a point paper in manufacturer's collection. 80% worsted wool, 20% nylon. 27″ wide. Cream, brown, red and black. Special order.

CARPETS OF WORTH

▶ ADAM PANEL. Axminster adaptation. Alternating circles and bordered squares. English, 1790–1820. Appropriate for the late 18th to early 19th century. 80% wool, 20% nylon. 27″ and 36″ wide, approximately 13″ set-match repeat. Olympus Axminster No. 2/6002 (red orange, red, gold and black). Available colors not compatible with period coloring. Stock item.

▶ RUST ADELPHI. Axminster adaptation. English, 1790–1800. Based on Adam-style patterns. 80% wool, 20% nylon. 27″ and 36″ wide, approximately 18″ set-match repeat. Olympus Axminster No. 6/6008 (rust, gold, yellow cream and black). Stock item.

COLEFAX AND FOWLER

▶ BYWELL. Brussels or Wilton. Scattered star pattern. English, 1800–15. Document in manufacturer's collection. 80% wool, 20% nylon. 27″ wide, 13½″ set-match repeat. Red orange, olive and tan. Border available. Special order.

▶ MEDALLION. Brussels adaptation. Gothic-cross pattern. English, late 1830s on. Based on patterns found in

BYWELL. Brussels or Wilton carpet. Colefax and Fowler. Red orange, olive and tan.

English country houses. 80% wool, 20% nylon. 27"
wide, 6" repeat. Dark brick red, dark brown and tan.
Border available. Special order.

K. V. T. (PENNSYLVANIA WOVEN) CARPET MILLS

Also custom weaves Brussels and Wilton carpeting from
historic documents in limited quantities.

▶ BRUSSELS. Small diamond geometric pattern with
quatrefoils. 1800–40. Suitable where documentation is
not required. All wool. 27" wide, approximately 4½"
set-match repeat. No. 9858-A-5416 (olive green and
black on cream); and custom colors. Special order.

▶ WILTON. Octagonal design with patterned center and
rosette in square at corners. 1830–50. Suitable where
documentation is not required. 80% wool, 20% nylon.
27" wide, approximately 13½" x 13½" repeat. No.
6329-A-6053 (red, dark green and brick on black); and
custom colors. Special order.

▶ WILTON. Moiré pattern. 1800–40. Suitable where
documentation is not required. 80% wool, 20% nylon
pile. 27" wide. No. 9456-A-5472 (olive green shades);
and custom colors. Special order.

LANGHORNE CARPET COMPANY

Also duplicates and adapts historic documents. Contact
company for a local representative.

JAMES LORAH HOUSE
PARLOR. Brussels or
Wilton carpet. Lang-
horne Carpet Com-
pany. Burgundy, cream,
rose and green.

▶ JAMES LORAH HOUSE PARLOR. Brussels or Wilton adaptation of tapestry carpet. Large-scale leaf and floral pattern with cartouches and wreaths. 1830–50. Document at the James Lorah House, Doylestown, Pa. 80% wool, 20% nylon. 27″ wide, 62″ drop-match repeat. Burgundy, cream, rose and green. Made for the Lorah House. Special order.

▶ OLD MERCHANT'S HOUSE. Brussels or Wilton reproduction. Large-scale cartouche and medallion pattern. 1830–50. Document at the Old Merchant's House, New York City. 80% wool, 20% nylon. 27″ wide, 55½″ drop-match repeat. No. 5294 (golds, red, black, blue and lavender). Border available: 13½″. Made for the Old Merchant's House. Special order.

above left
WILTON. No. 9456–A–5472. Wilton carpet. K. V. T. (Pennsylvania Woven) Carpet Mills. Olive green.

above right
OLD MERCHANT'S HOUSE. Brussels or Wilton carpet. Langhorne Carpet Company. Golds, red, black, blue and lavender.

MILLIKEN CONTRACT CARPETING

▶ ALSACE. Adaptation of floorcloth and ingrain. Tufted carpet with printed pattern. 1800–40. Suitable where documentation is not required. All nylon pile. 12′ wide, 6″ x 6″ set-match repeat. No. P/1685. Most suitable available colors: No. 542 (hunt green); No. 544 (red); No. 547 (blue and taupe). Stock items.

▶ EMPIRE PLATE. Adaptation of floorcloth and Brussels. Tufted carpet with printed pattern. 1800–40. Suitable where documentation is not required. All nylon pile. 12′ wide, 30″ x 30″ set-match repeat. No. P/1691. Color No. 83 (brown); No. 84 (hunter green); No. 86 (burgundy). Stock items.

EDWARD MOLINA DESIGNS

▶ SHERATON DE LUXE. Contract Axminster adaptation. Alternating octagons and medallions with rosette centers. 1790s–1820s; 1840s. Suitable where documentation is not required. 80% wool, 20% nylon. 27″ wide, approximately 30″ repeat, 189 pitch/9 rpi. No. 412/4 (shades of gray, green and cream on dark olive green); No. 412/19 (shades of tan and honey brown on dark brown); No. 412/54 (white, blues, olive green and yellow on black). Special order.

▶ SPANISH TILE. Contract Axminster adaptation. Square pattern with strong borders and alternating rosette and square centers, with a diapered ground. Similar to ingrain patterns of the period. c. 1830. Suitable where documentation is not required. 80% wool, 20% nylon. 27″ wide. Royal Court No. 525/16 (brick, cream, dark maroon, brown and tan). Stock item.

PATTERSON, FLYNN AND MARTIN

▶ BRUSSELS. Documented reproduction. Alternating cartouche patterns. 1840–70. 80% wool, 20% nylon. 27″ wide, 31″ repeat. No. 1812/7381 (dark brown ground with white, tan, maroon and dark red). Special order.

▶ BYWELL. Brussels or Wilton. Scattered star pattern. English, 1800–15. Document in manufacturer's collection. 80% wool, 20% nylon. (Wilton available in all wool pile.) 27″ wide, 13½″ set-match repeat. Red orange, olive and tan. Border available. Special order.

▶ MEDALLION. Brussels. Gothic-cross pattern. English, late 1830s on. Based on patterns found in English country houses. 80% wool, 20% nylon. 27″ wide, 6″ repeat. Dark brick red, dark brown and tan. Border available. Special order.

▶ MELROSE DINING ROOM. Wilton or Brussels adaptation. Cross pattern with feathered central medallion and formal block and leaf motif. Natchez, Miss., c. 1845. Based on mid-19th-century furniture designs. 80% wool, 20% nylon. 27″ wide. Cream, gold and black. Special order.

▶ MELROSE DRAWING ROOM. Brussels or Wilton adaptation. Large-scale floral and scroll pattern.

MELROSE DINING ROOM. Wilton or Brussels carpet. Patterson, Flynn and Martin. Cream, gold and black.

WATTEAU. Brussels or Wilton carpet. Patterson, Flynn and Martin. Beige with pale lavender, gray, tan, rose, deep rose and blue.

Natchez, Miss., c. 1845. Based on a mid-19th-century tapestry or Wilton carpet. 80% wool, 20% nylon. 27" wide, large-scale repeat. Cream ground with rust brown, reds and greens. Special order.

▶ WADSWORTH HOUSE. Wilton. Large-scale pattern of naturalistic floral clusters with leaf, scroll and cartouche surrounds. 1830–60. Suitable where documentation is not required. 80% wool, 20% nylon. 27" wide. Beige background with dark brown, honey, rose, pink and blue. Installed at San Francisco Plantation, Reserve, La. Special order.

▶ WATTEAU. Brussels or Wilton. Large-scale floral cartouche pattern. 1835–50. Suitable where documentation is not required. 80% wool, 20% nylon. 27" wide, approximately 54" repeat. Beige with pale lavender, gray, tan, rose, deep rose and blue. Installed at San Francisco Plantation, Reserve, La. Special order.

ROSECORE CARPETS

Some available Wilton and Brussels carpets are suitable where documentation is not required. Custom work also

DEVONSHIRE. Wilton carpet. Scalamandre. Greens, olive brown, apricot and red.

is provided, including development of patterns and duplication of carpeting from historic materials in the company's collection.

SCALAMANDRE

Also duplicates historic patterns.

▶ BERNARD. Wilton. Medallion with Empire-style laurel leaf surround. 18th century; 1800–25. 80% wool, 20% nylon. 27″ wide, 54″ drop-match repeat. Olive ground with brown, ochre, yellow and red. Special order.

▶ DE GAULLE. Wilton. Wreath motif with ground of small rosettes and stylized leaves. French, c. 1832. 80% wool, 20% nylon. 27″ wide, 18″ drop-match repeat. Red and gold; green and gold; blue and gold. Made for The Georgian (MacCracken-Huffman House), Lancaster, Ohio. Special order.

▶ DEVONSHIRE. Wilton. Large-scale multibordered square with rosette center. c. 1790–1820. Based on a mid-18th-century wall paneling designed by Charles Cameron. 80% wool, 20% nylon. 27″ wide, 27″ repeat. Cut or looped pile available. Greens, olive brown, apricot and shades of red. Made for the Old Merchant's House, New York City. Special order.

▶ EIFEL. Wilton. Alternating medallion and octagon on a diapered ground. 1790–1820. 80% wool, 20% nylon. 27″ wide, 54″ drop-match repeat. Red and green, blue and chrome yellow, yellow gold and black, brick, olive and cream with dark brown or black. Brittania Collection. Made for the Governor's Mansion, Jefferson City, Mo. Special order.

▶ FRENCH LAUREL. Wilton. Empire-style medallions with laurel-leaf surround and scattered rosette motifs. French, 1800–40. 80% wool, 20% nylon. 27″ wide, 18″ drop-match repeat. 2 colors. Made for Maplewood, Columbia, Mo. Special order.

▶ LORENZO. Brussels. Alternating cartouche and leaf field. c. 1840–70. Document at Lorenzo, Cazenovia, N.Y. All wool pile. 27″ wide, 31″ repeat. Dark and medium brown, tan, red and yellow tan. Border available: 14″ repeat. Special order.

▶ LYON. Wilton. Laurel medallions with patterned ground. French, c. 1840. 80% wool, 20% nylon. 27″

LYON. Wilton carpet. Scalamandre. Maroon with cranberry red, yellow, ochre and dark red.

opposite
CHINESE GALLERY. Wilton or Brussels carpet. Stark Carpet Corporation. Red, rose, black and gold.

wide, 18″ drop-match repeat. Maroon ground with cranberry red, yellow, ochre and dark red. Made for the Judge Flanagan Residence, Peoria, Ill., and The Georgian (MacCracken-Huffman House), Lancaster, Ohio. Special order.

▶ MAGINOT. Wilton. Alternating large and small rosette medallions. French, 1800–30. 80% wool, 20% nylon. 27″ wide, 9″ set-match repeat. Document color: yellow green with yellow. Special order.

▶ ORLEANS. Wilton or Brussels. Overall fleur-de-lis pattern. French, c. 1820. 80% wool, 20% nylon. 27″ wide, 9″ set-match repeat. 2 colors. Special order.

▶ PERCIER. Wilton. Overall rosette pattern. French, 1800–20. 80% wool, 20% nylon. 27″ wide, 3½″ set-match repeat. Document color: red ground with yellow gold. Made for the Price Gallery, Chicago Historical Society. Special order.

▶ ROXANNE. Wilton. Rosette with leaf diaper ground. French, 1800–35. 80% wool, 20% nylon. 27″ wide, 10″ set-match repeat. 2 colors. Special order.

STARK CARPET CORPORATION

▶ CHINESE GALLERY. Wilton or Brussels. Striped Oriental-style pattern. c. 1820. Based on pattern in the long corridor, Royal Pavilion, Brighton, England. All wool. 27″ wide, 27″ repeat. No. 9801 (shades of red and rose, black and gold). Border No. 8368: 12″ wide. Special order.

▶ HUNTING ROOM. Wilton or Brussels. Wreath and leaf pattern. c. 1790. Suitable for the late 18th to early 19th century. All wool. 27″ wide. Reds, gold, tan and black; and custom colors. Special order.

▶ LAYCOCK. Wilton or Brussels. Rose bunches tied with ribbons. English, c. 1840. Document at Lacock Abbey, Wiltshire, England. All wool pile. 27″ wide, 48″ repeat. No. 9385 (red, shades of tan, beige and green brown). Border No. 8369: 12″ wide. Special order.

U.S. AXMINSTER

▶ REGAL SPLENDOR. Palladium II Contract Axminster. 1800–40. Scale slightly small for the period. Suitable where documentation is not required. All nylon pile. 27″–15′ wide, 18″ x 18″ set-match repeat, 189 pitch/7 rpi. Red and green. Stock item.

▶ ROYAL BOXWOOD. Contract Axminster. 1800–40. Suitable where documentation is not required. All nylon pile. 27″–15′ wide, 18″ x 18″ set-match repeat. No. 39 (10 colors). Design Inspiration Collection. Stock item (500-yard minimum).

▶ SARATOGA. Contract Axminster. Hexagonal pattern with rosettes. 1800–40. Suitable where documentation is not required. 80% wool, 20% nylon. 27″–15′ wide, 18″ x 18″ set-match repeat, 189 pitch/8, 9 or 10 rpi. No. 41 (150 colors). Design Inspiration Collection. Stock item (500-yard minimum)

LAYCOCK. Wilton or Brussels carpet. Stark Carpet Corporation. Red, tan, beige and green brown.

1840 TO 1875:
THE EARLY VICTORIAN INTERIOR

The decades spanning the mid-19th century mark the beginning of the modern American domestic interior. The shift from a commercial to an industrial economy altered the composition of American society by creating an enormous middle-class population. This group, previously quite small, almost overnight became the dominant class in America. Despite serious economic downturns and a bitter civil war in which more Americans died than in any war in our history, an increasing percentage of the population was able to enjoy the seemingly endless array of products made possible by industrialization. Factories produced wallpapers, fabrics, suites of Rococo and Renaissance Revival furniture, gas-burning lighting fixtures and floor coverings as well as small objects and artwork. These products proliferated in all the rooms of houses that, after mid-century, were increasingly built around the peripheries of cities in suburban developments made possible by streetcars. The quantity of furnishings and the stationary character of gas lighting created more static room arrangements. Chairs, for example, ceased daily gravitations toward the best light source and remained fixed, near sofas, hearths or center tables in much the manner they are today.

WOOD FLOORS. Also like today, wall-to-wall carpeting was preferred by households that could afford it. By mid-century, architects and critics complained that the use of floor coverings was so widespread that few carpenters bothered to lay wood floors well, knowing that their work would only be covered. Yellow pine remained the most common wood flooring, and sawmills produced planks in

FLORAL SQUARES. Axminster adaptation of needlepoint rug. U.S. Axminster. Black and multicolor.

standard widths. The best floors were the tongue-and-groove type. These were not varnished but were occasionally painted, particularly in kitchens, halls and bedrooms, where other types of floor coverings were less common.

FLOORCLOTHS. Floorcloths, generally called oilcloths by mid-century, continued in use but were rarely found in more formal rooms such as parlors. While two American manufacturers displayed their products at the Crystal Palace Exhibition in London in 1851, most critics believed that English floorcloths were more durable and attractive. Miss Leslie told readers of *The Lady's House Book* (1854), "There is no better covering [for kitchen floors] than a coarse, stout, plain oil-cloth, unfigured, or all one color; for instance, dark red, blue, brown, olive, or ochre yellow." They were easy to wipe clean, kept the kitchen warm and, Leslie advised, "have the advantage of collecting and retaining no dust or grease." Catharine Beecher and Harriet Beecher Stowe included directions for making kitchen oilcloths in *The American Woman's Home* (1869).

TILE FLOORS. Oilcloths were also used in entry halls, where their designs continued to imitate more expensive and durable materials such as ceramic or marble tiles. However, America's first great architecture critic, Andrew Jackson Downing, recommended patterned ceramic tiles in "brown, enriched with patterns and figures of fawn or blue." Downing told readers of *Country Houses* (1850) that these tiles, while more expensive, were "far more durable . . . and, in the end, much more economical" than carpets or floorcloths for vestibules and entry halls. Downing's description of encaustic tiles is one of the earliest by an American writer. Two types of tiles were imported from England during these decades. The patterned type was produced by impressing a design into a newly formed tile and filling it with liquid clay of a different color before firing. The English designated these as encaustic tiles, a term describing impressed designs fixed by heat. The plain type was produced in a variety of shapes and colors, such as buff, red, brown, blue and black, and then laid in patterns. The English called these tiles geometrics. Americans ignored the distinction and identified both types as encaustic tiles during the 19th century.

Tile patterns illustrated in Samuel Sloan's *Homestead Architecture* (1861). While Americans called these tiles "encaustics," the English termed them "geometrics" to distinguish them from their encaustic patterned tiles. (The Athenaeum of Philadelphia)

ENGLISH ENCAUSTIC FLOORING TILE.

Imported & For Sale by S. A. HARRISON, 1010 Chestnut St. Philadelphia.

No. 1.

Tile 40 cts. per Square Foot – laid 50 cts.

No. 2.

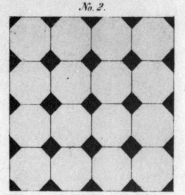

Tile 32 cts. per Square Foot — laid 42 cts.

No. 3.

Tile 32 cts. per Square Foot – laid 42 cts.

No. 4.

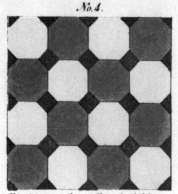

Tile 34 cts. per Square Foot – laid 44 cts.

No. 5.

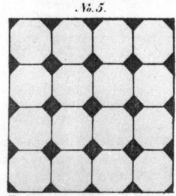

Tile 36 cts. per Square Foot — laid 46 cts.

No. 6.

Tile 32 cts. per Square Foot — laid 42 cts.

The Price for laying is estimated for floors of 100 Square Feet or over.

While the cost of these tiles precluded their immediate adoption in most homes, wealthy Americans throughout the country used them. Philadelphia architect John Notman chose encaustic tiles manufactured by Minton and Company for the floor of the octagonal stair hall of Fieldwood (c. 1855), a house in Princeton, N.J. The entry hall of the McDonnell House (1858) in Madison, Wis., also was finished with them, as were the floors of Thomas Ustick Walter's additions (1851–65) to the United States Capitol. Architect Samuel Sloan recommended them for libraries and conservatories as well as vestibules. He intended to use them on the floor of the rotunda at Longwood (1860–62), the ill-fated octagon house begun on the eve of the Civil War for Dr. Haller Nutt of Natchez, Miss., but left unfinished.

MATTING. Grass matting remained in use as a seasonal or year-round floor covering. While shops continued to advertise checked matting, Miss Leslie informed her readers that the effect was "common and ungenteel"; she recommended the plain sort. When used over wall-to-wall carpeting as a summer treatment, the strips were sewn together and the edges bound with tape, harmonizing with the color scheme of the room. When used as the only floor covering, matting was simply laid with the edges of the strips abutting and tacked to the floorboards as it had been in the 18th century. Beecher and Stowe praised matting as an attractive and inexpensive floor covering; they estimated it cost 50 cents a yard. Acknowledging its lack of durability they told readers, "We humbly submit that it is precisely the thing for a parlor, which is reserved for the reception-room of friends, and for our own dressed leisure hours." They admitted, however, "Matting is not good economy in a dining-room or a hard-worn sitting room." Matting also remained popular for bedroom floors throughout the century because it was so easy to sweep clean.

THE CARPETING REVOLUTION. During the mid-19th century, carpeting came to be viewed as an essential part of middle-class interior decoration. C. P. Dwyer told readers of *The Economic Cottage Builder* (1856), "As it is customary to carpet every room in the house, flooring need not be laid with a view to appearance. It is cheap to

lay down an undressed floor, covering the joints with slips of brown paper, and then spreading old newspapers, instead of straw, under the carpet." During the 1850s and 1860s, ingrain carpeting accounted for 80 to 90 percent of all the carpeting manufactured in the United States. Critics relegated cheaper carpets, such as list and Venetian, to inferior spaces such as stairs and hallways. Improved manufacturing techniques brought about these changes in carpeting use.

The Jacquard attachment, first used to produce American carpets in 1825, marked the beginning of the revolution in the carpet industry. The second great advance was Erastus Bigelow's invention of a steam-powered loom for weaving ingrain carpets. By 1841, with continued improvements, Bigelow's looms were producing 25 yards of carpeting a day, a fourfold increase over handlooms. Improved manufacturing techniques increased the supply while lowering the cost to the consumer. In 1833 the Thompsonville Carpet Manufacturing Company of Con-

Encaustic tile floor in The Willows (1854), Morristown, N.J. (Morris County Park Commission)

necticut sold three-ply ingrains at $1.68 a yard; by 1847 the same carpet sold at $1.25 a yard, and the cost continued to drop throughout the century. American mills using steam-powered ingrain looms dominated the domestic market by 1850, thus setting the stage for the appearance of carpeting in the majority of middle-class households.

BRUSSELS AND WILTON CARPETS. For wealthier households, Brussels and Wilton carpets were the alternatives. The Jacquard attachment had been used on Brussels looms as early as the 1820s. However, skilled weavers working on handlooms could produce only seven yards a day. Furthermore, these carpets used more wool than ingrains, which increased their cost. While most of the wool yarns of ingrain carpeting appear on the surface as part of the design, in Brussels and Wilton carpets they do not. The warp threads, which create the pattern, are composed of as many as five separate strands of colored wool, only one of which can appear on the surface of a given row at any one time; the others are carried along under the surface as part of the body of the carpet. This additional wool plus the salaries commanded by skilled weavers kept Brussels and Wiltons beyond the reach of most middle-class households. In 1847 the Thompsonville Carpet Manufacturing Company sold Brussels carpeting for $1.50 a yard, nearly twice the price of its two-ply ingrain, which was priced at 87 cents a yard. American Brussels also faced stiff competition from British imports, which continued to cater to a discriminating American market able to afford higher-priced goods.

In 1846 Erastus Bigelow began to perfect a power loom for weaving Brussels. By 1849, along with his brother, Horatio, he began production in Clinton, Mass., and exhibited the products at the Crystal Palace Exhibition in London two years later. The early designs were simple geometrics in plain red, green, blue or black with little color shading. By 1854 the Bigelow Carpet Company produced 167,700 yards of 27-inch wide, five-frame Brussels, most of which was sold through W. and J. Sloane in New York City. The Bigelows' success notwithstanding, few other domestic mills produced large amounts of Brussels; British imports through mid-century continued to supply two-thirds of the American market.

TAPESTRY CARPETS. Even with Bigelow's invention, Brussels and Wilton carpets remained expensive and the patterns were limited to five colors in most designs. As explained earlier, the weaving process carried the multicolored warp threads throughout the carpet, although only one color could appear on the surface at any given time. The others formed the body of these exceptionally durable carpets. Thus, Brussels and Wilton carpets used a great deal of wool and were commensurately higher priced. Both problems were solved in 1831 by Richard Whytock of Edinburgh, Scotland, who developed a patterning system that employed preprinted warp threads wound on large drums. The woolen warp threads appeared only as the surface pile of the carpet; less expensive structural yarns were used for the warp and weft threads that formed the body. Furthermore, because the warp was preprinted, a virtually limitless number of colors could be used to create the patterns of these tapestry Brussels and velvet carpets. Because the tension was not always consistent during weaving, tapestry carpets generally had a slightly out-of-focus appearance. Like body Brussels and Wiltons, tapestry carpets were originally woven in 27-inch widths that were seamed together to cover entire floors.

Drum printing, as Whytock's invention was called, was introduced to America in the 1840s. The Higgins Company of New York City was one of the few American firms to specialize in weaving tapestry carpets during the 1850s and 1860s; British imports supplied the rest. Most American mills concentrated on ingrain carpets for the large, middle-class market even though tapestry carpets cost less than body Brussels or Wiltons and only a little more than the best three-ply ingrains. Furthermore, the invention of the tapestry drum coincided with a growing taste for naturalistic design as evidenced in Rococo Revival furniture. Tapestry carpets could employ endless colors to create floral patterns with incredibly realistic shading.

While tapestry carpets appealed to homeowners, the

critics despised them. In *Rural Homes* (1851), architect Gervase Wheeler grumbled, "Carefully shaded flowers, wreaths, and other vegetative decoration always appear out of place upon the floor to be trodden on; crushing living flowers under foot, even to inhale their odor, is a barbarity, but to tread on worsted ones, odorless, and without form, certainly seems senseless." Other critics condemned their lack of durability because, using less wool, they wore out sooner than body Brussels and Wiltons. Nonetheless, by the end of the century tapestry carpets had replaced ingrains on the floors of most middle-class homes.

Miss Leslie, author of *The Lady's House Book*, praised the less flamboyant patterns of true Brussels and Wilton carpets. She urged her readers to avoid gaudy colors and suggested, "Two colors only, with the dark and light shades of each, will make a very handsome carpet." Her recommendations included light blue grounds with figures of crimson or purple, salmon or buff colors with deep green, or carpets of various shades of green or red. The simpler the design, the smaller the size of the repeat, with 12 to 18 inches being common. Plain diagonal bands encircling quatrefoils were popular, as were trellis patterns composed of stylized flowers or stripes alternating with simple clusters of flowers. Mills also continued to weave complex patterns borrowed from Oriental carpets, which were generally far larger in scale, as were the realistic floral patterns of tapestry carpets. In all cases, small hearth rugs in designs complementing the various carpet patterns were also popular.

WOOD FLOORING

CARLISLE RESTORATION LUMBER COMPANY

▶ SHIPLAP PINE BOARDS. 8"–12" wide, 8'–12' long. Special order.

▶ WIDE OAK BOARDS. 5"–10" wide, 8'–16' long. Special order.

▶ WIDE PINE BOARDS. 7/8" and 1" thick, 14"–21" wide, 8'–16' long. Special order.

CASTLE BURLINGAME

Booklets on antique flooring selection, installation and finishing available ($5 each postpaid).

▶ ANTIQUE VIRGIN EASTERN WHITE PINE (KINGS PLANKS). Pumpkin pine with pit-sawn markings, double-tongue and double-groove edges. 1″ thick, random widths and lengths. Special order.

▶ ANTIQUE VIRGIN SOUTHERN LONGLEAF YELLOW HEART PINE. Georgia pine with natural edges for later shiplap, butt joint or tongue-and-groove finish. 7/8″ thick, random widths to 16″, random lengths. Special order.

THE JOINERY COMPANY

▶ ANTIQUE SOUTHERN LONGLEAF YELLOW HEART PINE. Flooring, millwork, cabinetry, furniture and timber frames. Remilled from structures 100–200 years old. Quarter-sawn, edge-grain and original surfaces. Prime grade and antique original grade. 7/16″ thick, to 20″ wide, 16′ long. Installed at King's Arms Tavern, Colonial Williamsburg, Va. Stock items.

ANTIQUE SOUTHERN LONGLEAF YELLOW HEART PINE. Wood flooring. The Joinery Company.

HERRINGBONE. Parquet flooring. Kentucky Wood Floors.

KENTUCKY WOOD FLOORS

Custom parquet borders and floor patterns also duplicated and designed.

▶ CUSTOM BORDER. Parquet flooring. Elaborate interlaced border suitable for parlors. Mixed-species hardwoods. Unfinished surface. $5/16''$ thick, 12" wide, 22" long. Special order.

▶ FEATURE STRIP. Parquet border. Light and dark banded strip used as a decorative border in rooms and halls. Plain oak, quartered oak, ash, walnut and cherry. $3/4''$ thick, random widths and lengths. Stock item.

▶ HERRINGBONE I. Parquet flooring. Red oak, tropical walnut and cherry. Unfinished surface; paper faced. $5/16''$ thick, 14" wide, 17" long. Packaged 25 square feet per carton. Stock item.

▶ HERRINGBONE II. Parquet flooring. Plain oak, quartered oak, ash, walnut and cherry. Unfinished surface. $3/4''$ thick, $2 1/4''$ wide, $6 3/4''$–18" long. Individual pieces bundled as ordered. Stock item.

▶ SIMPLICITY. Parquet flooring. Four-strip alternating vertical-horizontal pattern. Red oak, tropical walnut and cherry. Prefinished surface. $5/16''$ thick, 9" wide, 9" long. Stock item.

▶ STRIP. Parquet flooring. Plain oak, quartered oak and maple. Unfinished surface; square edge. $3/4''$ thick, $2 1/2''$ wide, random lengths. Stock item.

MOUNTAIN LUMBER COMPANY

▶ ANTIQUE SOUTHERN LONGLEAF YELLOW HEART PINE. Flooring, period moldings, paneling and trim. Milled from timbers taken from pre-1900 structures; graded and kiln dried. Tongue-and-groove planks. 3″–6″ and 6″–10″ random widths and lengths. Prime grade free of most knots and imperfections; cabin grade with knots, nail holes and some hairline cracks. Installed at Monticello, Charlottesville, Va. Stock items.

JANOS P. SPITZER FLOORING COMPANY

Parquet floor borders (after 1870) in mixed-species hardwoods available as stock items and custom made.

VINTAGE LUMBER AND CONSTRUCTION COMPANY

▶ ANTIQUE TIMBER. Random-width flooring. Remilled. Tongue-and-groove planks. Chestnut, $^{25}/_{32}$″ thick, 2″–10″ wide. Fir, $^{25}/_{32}$″ thick, 3″–8″ wide. Oak, $^{25}/_{32}$″ thick, 3″–8″ wide. Random lengths. Stock items.
▶ ANTIQUE YELLOW AND WHITE PINE. Random-width wide flooring. Tongue-and-groove planks. 4″–10″ wide, random lengths. Stock items.
▶ NEW OAK, WALNUT, CHERRY, MAPLE, POPLAR AND WHITE PINE. Random-width wide flooring. $^{3}/_{4}$″ thick, 3″–8″ wide, random lengths. Stock items.
▶ SOUTHERN LONGLEAF YELLOW HEART PINE. Random-width flooring. Remilled; kiln dried. Tongue-and-groove planks. 3″–10″ wide, random lengths. Stock items.

TILE FLOORING

AMERICAN OLEAN TILE COMPANY

▶ 1″ HEX. Porcelain ceramic hexagonal mosaic tiles. Late 1870s–1930s. Used for bathrooms, foyers, stores and restaurants. $^{1}/_{4}$″ thick, 1″ wide. Overall patterns and bordered designs prearranged on 1′ x 2′ sheets for installation. Unglazed. Black, white and various colors. Stock items.

DESIGNS IN TILE

Also reproduces and adapts historic patterns; develops encaustic tile designs in brick, white, black and green; and provides installation.

ENCAUSTIC and CUT
GEOMETRIC TILES.
Tile flooring. L'Esper-
ance Tileworks.

CUT GEOMETRIC
FLOOR TILES. Tile
flooring. Designs in
Tile.

▶ GEOMETRIC AND CUT TILE PAVEMENTS. Encaustic
ceramic tile. Brick red, white, black and green. Stock
items.

▶ HEXAGONAL ENCAUSTIC TILES. Porcelain ceramic
tiles. Used for bathrooms, foyers and stores. 1″ square.
Unglazed. Brick red, white, black and green. Special
order.

H AND R JOHNSON TILES

Restores, replaces and duplicates geometric cut tiles
used for solariums, foyers, halls and public spaces,
1850–1920; available in period colors. Johnson Tiles
also provides patterned two-color decorative encaustic
tiles for use with its geometric tiles, suitable for solariums, foyers, halls and public spaces of the period 1850–
1900. Custom made and special order.

L'ESPERANCE TILEWORKS

Duplicates cut geometric and two-color patterned encaustic patterns of 1860–1930 in a variety of period colors. Custom made and special order.

STARK CARPET CORPORATION

▶ CHINESE SEA GRASS MATTING. Basket-weave pattern of sea grass cords with braided bast fiber warp. Texture, scale and sheen resemble coarse 19th-century straw mattings. 13'2" wide. Natural grass shades of pale gold, pale green and honey brown. Stock item.

ERNEST TREGANOWAN

▶ TATAMI GRASS MATTING. Japanese matting resembling Indian matting. Late 18th to 19th century. (Coarse Chinese straw mattings, 36"–54", are no longer commercially made.) Period installation requires tacks or narrow U-shaped staples; fabric tape bindings must be removed before installation, and ends must be turned under. 36" wide. No. 180 (natural greenish grass). Stock item.

GOOD AND COMPANY

Stencilled floorcloths on painted canvas also available in custom patterns, sizes and colors.
▶ EBENEZER. Small geometric rosette pattern. Various sizes. Soldier blue with mustard gold and light blue; putty with Williamsburg blue and wine; light green with soldier blue and old yellow. Installed at the Ebenezer Waters House, West Sutton, Mass. Special order.
▶ STURBRIDGE. Alternating dark and light blocks with rosette. Based on an illustration in Nina Fletcher Little's *Floor Coverings in New England Before 1850*, p. 60. Various sizes. Special order.
▶ TRADITIONAL CUBE. Tumbling-block pattern. Various sizes. Brick red with dark green and tan. Special order.

GRIGSBY/HALLMAN STUDIO

Produces a variety of stencilled floorcloths, some with marbleized finishes, including reproductions of documented English patterns from 1739 by John Carwitham,

MATTING

FLOORCLOTHS
AND
STENCILLING

above left
STENCILLED FLOOR.
Floorcloth. Hand
Painted Stencils.

above right
STENCILLED CANVAS
FLOORCLOTH. Floor-
cloth. Hand Painted
Stencils.

right
BORDERED FLORAL.
Floorcloth. Pemaquid
Floorcloths. Custom
colors.

designer and engraver (suitable for the 19th century). Sizes to 10' wide seamless, any length. Custom patterns, sizes and colors.

▶ MARBLE AND DIAMONDS. Marbleized diamonds in alternating dark and light colors.

▶ PLAIN ALTERNATING SQUARES. Large, alternating dark and light plain-colored squares.

▶ SIX-SIDED MARBLE. Hexagonal marbleized tiles separated by smaller dark squares.

130

▶ TUMBLING BLOCKS. Optical-illusion pattern of three-dimensional blocks.

HAND PAINTED STENCILS

Custom handcut patterns and colors stencilled directly onto the floor.

ISABEL O'NEIL STUDIO

Custom painted floors and stencilled and marbleized canvas floorcloths in various sizes.

PEMAQUID FLOORCLOTHS

▶ BORDERED FLORAL. Stencilled canvas floorcloth. Adaptation resembling late 18th-century patterns in print sources. 2' x 3', 2½' x 4', 4' x 6' and custom sizes. Custom colors. Special order.

▶ DIAGONAL SQUARES. Stencilled canvas floorcloth. Alternating dark and light squares. Based on various print sources. 2' x 3', 2½' x 4', 4' x 6' and custom sizes. Custom colors. Special order.

▶ SNOWFLAKE. Stencilled canvas floorcloth. Center pattern suitable for the 19th century if period colors are used. 2' x 3', 2½' x 4', 4' x 6' and custom sizes. Custom colors. Special order.

SPECIAL EFFECTS BY SUE

Floorcloth designs duplicated on painted canvas in various sizes. Also available by special order are handpainted and stencilled canvas floorcloths in geometrics, wreaths and other patterns based on print sources, in various sizes and custom colors.

THE DORR MILL STORE

▶ RUG WOOL. All wool. 57" wide. No. 1313 (green); No. 6307 (dark blue); 32 other colors and color sample card available. Special order.

SUNFLOWER STUDIO

▶ CARPET BAIZE. All wool. 36" wide. Handwoven. 14 oz. No. X18.12 (cream white) can be custom dyed 35 additional colors, including 7 shades of green. Special order.

FLOORCLOTHS: BAIZE

RAG, LIST AND HANDMADE RUGS

THE GAZEBO OF NEW YORK

▶ HIT-AND-MISS. Rag rugs. All cotton rag weft; all linen warp. 27½", 36", 48", 54", 72", 94" and 132" wide, any length. Multicolor. Reversible. Stock items; nonstandard widths and colors by special order.

HANDWOVEN

▶ HIT-AND-MISS. Rag rugs and stair runners. All cotton rag weft; strong polyester warp. Sizes to 10' wide, any length. Multicolor; and custom colors. Reversible. Special order.

HERITAGE RUGS

▶ HIT-AND-MISS. Handwoven rag rugs. All wool. Sizes to 15' wide seamless, 35' long. Multicolor. Special order.

IMPORT SPECIALISTS

▶ SPRINGFIELD TWILL PLAID. Cotton twill rugs. 2' x 3', 44" x 72" and 6' x 9'. Similar to document in Smithsonian Institution collection. No. F 1044 (green and rust plaid). Reversible. Stock items.

PEERLESS IMPORTED RUGS

▶ COLONIAL. Hit-and-miss pattern woven mat and area rag rugs. All cotton. 2' x 3½', 2½' x 4½', 3½' x 5½', 5½' x 8½' and 8' x 10'. No. 1117 (multicolor). Reversible. Stock items.

HIT-AND-MISS. Rag rug. Handwoven. Multicolor.

RASTETTER WOOLEN MILL

▶ HIT-AND-MISS. Handwoven rag rugs. All cotton or all wool; linen warps available. Sizes including 9' x 12' seamless; other custom sizes seamed together in the traditional manner. Multicolor. Stock items and custom made (e.g., will prepare rugs from cut-and-sewn carpet rags).

STARK CARPET CORPORATION

▶ HIT-AND-MISS. Rag rugs. All cotton. Custom sizes. Multicolor and monochromatic. Special order.

WEAVERS UNLIMITED

▶ HIT-AND-MISS. Rag rugs. All cotton. 2½' x 4', 2½' x 5', 2½' x 6', 3' x 4', 3' x 5', 3' x 6', 63" x 60", 63" x 72" and 63" x 84". Room-size rugs available using strips 24", 30", 36" or 63" wide. Multicolor or stripes. Special order.
▶ STENCILLED PATTERNS. Pineapples, flowers and custom designs applied to rag rugs above.

HIT-AND-MISS and VENETIAN. Rag rugs and Venetian carpet. Rastetter Woolen Mill. Multicolor.

THOS. K. WOODARD

Variety of traditional rag patterns based on 19th-century striped and patterned handwoven carpeting. Documents in Thos. K. Woodard collection. All cotton rag weft. All patterns available as runners 27" and 36" wide, to 24' long. Rugs 4' and 6' wide, to 24' long. Large sizes, 12' x 18' and 18' x 24', constructed from narrower widths sewn together in the traditional manner. Seamless 9' x 12' room-size rugs also available. Stock items.
Striped and plaid patterns include:
▶ ESSEX. No. 3 (blue, burgundy and tan plaid).
▶ JEFFERSON STRIPES. No. 22-A (rose, mustard, blue, green and beige); No. 22-B (blue, green, lavender and beige).
▶ LANCASTER. No. 23 (multicolor stripe on blue check); No. 23-B (multicolor stripe on burgundy).
▶ PENNSYLVANIA BARS. No. 1-A-6 (natural stripes on blue); No. 1-E-1 (slate blue on neutral); No. 21 (natural on red).
▶ PENNSYLVANIA STRIPES. No. 2-A-1 (multicolor stripes on neutral).

▶ READING. No. 19 (red stripes on natural); No. 19-D (natural on blue); No. 24 (natural on red).

▶ RITTENHOUSE SQUARE. No. 130-A (blue and white check); No. 130-BT (green and white); No. 130-CT (red and white).

▶ ROXBURY. No. 7 (red, black, tan, blue, green and yellow mix).

▶ SHAKER. No. 130 (teal, tan and brown plaid).

▶ WAINSCOTT. No. 11 (blue and tan plaid).

BRAIDED RUGS

BRAID AID

▶ DO-IT-YOURSELF. Braided-rug supplies. Wools, wool strips, cutters and braid folders. Stock items.

COUNTRY BRAID HOUSE

▶ BRAIDED RUGS. Hit-and-miss and planned pattern styles. All wool. Traditional materials and handlaced construction; medium- or heavy-weight braids. Reversible. Special order.

THE GAZEBO OF NEW YORK

▶ BRAIDED RUGS. Hit-and-miss and banded pattern styles. Traditional oval and round shapes. Braids handlaced together with linen thread. Multicolor or monochromatic. Special order.

PEERLESS IMPORTED RUGS

▶ PATTERN-BRAIDED YARN RUGS. No. 1725 (tan); No. 1825 (brick). Stock items.

PERSNICKETY

▶ BRAIDED RUGS. Patterned hit-and-miss. Adaptation of 19th-century handbraided rugs. Wool-acrylic blend. Oval, 27" x 84". Most suitable colors: No. 51685 (rust); No. 51687 (tan); No. 51688 (multicolor). Stock items.

RASTETTER WOOLEN MILL

▶ BRAIDED RUGS. Hit-and-miss and banded pattern braids. Interbraided with flax thread to connect the braids. All wool blanket remnants. Various sizes. Stock items and special order.

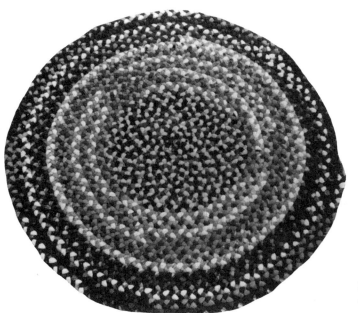

BRAIDED RUG. Rastetter Woolen Mill.

SCHUMACHER

▶ OLD COLONY WOOL 'O'. Braided-rug adaptation. Colonial hit-and-miss. Braided yarn wrapped around an inner core. Suitable where documentation is not required. All wool. Stock item and special order.

STARK CARPET CORPORATION

▶ HIT-AND-MISS. Rag weft and cotton warp rugs. All cotton. Various sizes. Special order.

STURBRIDGE YANKEE WORKSHOP

▶ BRAIDED STAIR TREADS. Adaptation of handbraided stair treads. Suitable where documentation is not required. Wool-acrylic blend. 8″ x 28″. Most suitable colors: No. 1-15-2368 (brown); No. 1-15-2369 (tan). Available individually or in sets of 13. Stock items.

THE CRAFTSMAN STUDIO

▶ DO-IT-YOURSELF. Hooked rugs and hearth and door mats. Also available are Joan Moshimer's *Craftsman Hooked Rug Patterns* (including hundreds of patterns for documented and adapted rugs and hearth and door mats), fabrics, dyes and equipment. Stock items.

HOOKED RUGS

HOOKED HEARTH RUGS. The Craftsman Studio. Various colors.

THE GAZEBO OF NEW YORK

▶ FOLK ART PATTERN HOOKED RUGS. Patterns based on quilt and antique hooked-rug patterns. All wool. Custom patterns and colors.

HEIRLOOM RUGS

▶ DO-IT-YOURSELF. Traditional hooked-rug patterns, materials and equipment. Stock items.

PEERLESS IMPORTED RUGS

▶ RICHMOND GEOMETRIC BLOCK. Hooked-rug adaptation. Geometric block with alternating floral and star motifs. Mid- to late 19th century. All wool yarn. No. 1360 (light-colored ground with multicolor and black). Stock item.

▶ RICHMOND NEW ENGLAND FLORAL. Hooked-rug adaptation. Floral and scroll pattern. Based on typical mid- and late 19th-century and early 20th-century Colonial Revival hearth-rug patterns. Suitable where documentation is not required. All wool yarn. 2' x 4', 3' x 5', 4' x 6', 6' x 9', 8' x 10' and 9' x 12'. No. 1361 (ivory); No. 1362 (blue); No. 1363 (rose). Stock items.

PERSNICKETY

▶ GARDEN HOOKED RUG. Hearth-rug adaptation.

Mid-19th century. All wool pile. 22″ x 42″. No. 51696 (cream, soft pinks and soft greens). Stock item.

THE RUGGING ROOM

▶ CUSTOM HOOKED RUGS. Traditional and custom patterns hooked to order.
▶ DO-IT-YOURSELF. Hooked-rug patterns and supplies. Stock items.

EVELYN WOOD

▶ TRADITIONAL HOOKED RUGS. Variety of traditional patterns including primitive, animal, Oriental and floral. Wool, cotton and mixed rag strips. Custom dyeing. Custom made and special order.

CASA QUINTAO

Also provides custom cross-stitch embroidery rugs in mid-19th-century designs and adaptations.
▶ HEXAGONS WITH FLOWERS. Cross-stitch embroidery. Hexagonal pattern with floral clusters and border. 1840–75. All wool on cotton canvas. No. 5032 (black and multicolor). Special order.
▶ MULTICOLORED FLOWERS. Cross-stitch embroidery. Floral block pattern with borders. 1840–75. All wool on cotton canvas. No. 1385 (white and multicolor). Special order.
▶ REPEATED FLORAL CLUSTERS. Cross-stitch embroidery. Floral clusters with decorative banding between motifs and a narrow border. Similar to patterns popular in the 1840s and 1850s. All wool on cotton canvas. No. 87 (black with red, olive and cream). Special order.
▶ TRELLIS PATTERN. Cross-stitch embroidery. Decorative trellis with plain center. Adaptation of an 1860s pattern. All wool on cotton canvas. No. 10.020 (cream, olive, gold and dark red brown). Special order.

CRAIGIE STOCKWELL CARPETS

Provides handtufted and handknotted duplications and adaptations of antique needlepoint rugs.
▶ VICTORIAN FLORAL. Hearth-rug adaptation. 1840–70. Document a tapestry velvet or needlepoint. All wool

NEEDLEPOINT AND EMBROIDERED RUGS

VICTORIAN FLORAL and VICTORIAN ROSE. Needlepoint rugs. Craigie Stockwell Carpets. Black or coffee with multicolor.

CHINESE NEEDLEPOINT VICTORIAN RUG. No. 2. Patterson, Flynn and Martin. Black and pastel colors.

pile. 4′ x 6′. Handtufted. Black with multicolor. Special order.

▶ VICTORIAN ROSE. Adaptation. Rose pattern duplicating design by de Robert Holmes. 8′ x 8′. Pale coffee with multicolor. Special order.

PATTERSON, FLYNN AND MARTIN

Also custom duplicates antique needlepoint rugs.

▶ CHINESE NEEDLEPOINT VICTORIAN RUG. Cross-stitch embroidery adaptation of mid-19th-century hearth rugs. Multicolor floral motif with floral border. 1860–75. Wool on cotton canvas. No. 1 (black, rose or cream grounds with pastel flowers). Special order.

▶ CHINESE NEEDLEPOINT VICTORIAN RUG. Cross-stitch embroidery adaptation of 19th-century hearth rug. Clusters of flowers on solid background; leaf and floral border with secondary border. Wool on cotton canvas. No. 2 (black and pastel colors). Special order.

STARK CARPET CORPORATION

Produces custom reproductions of original needlepoint rugs and adapts patterns from period rugs.

U.S. AXMINSTER

▶ FLORAL SQUARES. Axminster adaptation of mid-19th-century needlepoint carpets. 1840–75. All nylon pile. 12′ wide, 36″ x 36″ set-match repeat, 189 pitch/ 7 rpi. No. PLM-II-43 (black and multicolor). Stock item.

COLONIAL WILLIAMSBURG FOUNDATION

▶ FOLK ART FAVORITES NO. 1. Reproduction Venetian carpeting. Document is Deborah Goldsmith's 1832 portrait of the Talcott family. All cotton. "Abigail": No. 148627 (3′ x 5′); No. 152363 (6′ x 9′); No. 101014 (7′ x 10′). Green and yellow. "Betsey": No. 148619 (3′ x 5′); No. 149708 (6′ x 9′); No. 10918 (7′ x 10′). Red and blue. Stock items.

▶ FOLK ART FAVORITES NO. 2. Reproduction checked rug with fringed edges. Document a 19th-century sample in the Abby Aldrich Rockefeller Folk Art Center. No.

FLATWOVEN CARPETS: INGRAIN, JERGA AND VENETIAN

MAPLE LEAF. Ingrain carpet. Family Heir-Loom Weavers. Cream, red, brown and olive green.

SMITHSONIAN INSTI-TUTION. Ingrain car-pet. Scalamandre. Red, dark red, olive and brown.

116624 (4' x 6'); No. 104940 (6' x 9'); No. 105932 (9' x 12'). Gray and cream. Stock items (small sizes) and special order (largest size).

FAMILY HEIR-LOOM WEAVERS

▶ GEOMETRIC AND FLORAL. Ingrain reproduction. Foliate medallion surrounded by geometric banding. 1825–50. Document in a private collection. All worsted wool. 36" wide, 42" repeat. Document colors: red, brown and shades of olive green. Traditional two-ply construction. Made for the National Park Service. Special order.

▶ MAPLE LEAF. Ingrain. Alternating floral cartouche design with finely patterned ground. 1825–50. Document in a private collection. All worsted wool. 36" wide, 52" repeat. Traditional two-ply construction. Cream, red, brown and shades of olive green; and custom colors. Installed at National Park Service sites. Special order.

K. V. T. (PENNSYLVANIA WOVEN) CARPET MILLS

▶ QUATREFOIL IN DIAMOND BANDING. Brussels adaptation of ingrain. 1800–50. 80% wool, 20% nylon. 27" wide. No. 9858-A-5416 (cream, black and green). Special order.

SCALAMANDRE

Also duplicates historic patterns.

▶ METROPOLITAN MUSEUM. Ingrain reproduction. Alternating bordered squares and diamonds with rosette centers. 1830–50. Document at the Metropolitan Museum of Art, New York City. 90% wool, 10% nylon. 36" wide, 40" repeat. No. 97223-1 (olive, moss, red and cream). Made for the Metropolitan Museum of Art. Installed at the Richard Owens House, New Harmony, Ind. Special order.

▶ SMITHSONIAN INSTITUTION. Ingrain reproduction. Alternating rosette and medallion pattern. 1850–75. Document at the Smithsonian Institution, Washington, D.C. All wool. 36" wide, approximately 41½" repeat. No. 97358-1 (red, dark red, olive and brown). Made for the Smithsonian Institution. Installed at the Stonewall Jackson House, Lexington, Va. Special order.

▶ VENETIAN STRIPE. Documented warp-face striped carpet. Wool. 36″ wide. No. 994621. Made for the Ironmaster's House, Hopewell Village National Historic Site, Elverson, Pa. Special order.

SUNFLOWER STUDIO

▶ JERGA. Durable woven twill carpet with 2″ checks. Spanish colonial Southwest, 18th and 19th centuries. Similar to fabrics in the Museum of International Folk Art, Santa Fe, N.M. All wool. 24″ wide. 26 oz. Natural sheep brown and cream white; and custom colors. Special order.

▶ VENETIAN. Warp-face striped carpet. 19th century. Based on paintings of the period. 55% worsted wool, 45% linen. 30″ wide. Custom striped patterns and colors.

THOS. K. WOODARD

▶ THE TALCOTT COLLECTION. Reproduction Venetian rugs and stair runners. Document is Deborah Goldsmith's 1832 portrait of the Talcott family. All cotton. 27″ wide, 3′ x 5′, 9′ x 12′ and 6′ wide, any length. "Abigail Talcott": No. 28-A (green, blue, yellow, tan, rust and black). "Betsey Talcott": No. 28-B (brick red, blue, tan, green and black). "Charles Talcott": No. 28-C (gray, blue, tan, pink and black). Stock items.

PILE CARPETS: REPEAT PATTERNS

BLOOMSBURG CARPET INDUSTRIES

▶ CHESTNUT LEAF. Brussels. Overall leaf pattern with chestnut flowers. Mid-19th century. All wool. 27″ wide. No. W 888/3R (grape, green, tan, purples and red). Installed at the White House of the Confederacy, Richmond, Va. Special order.

▶ DERBYSHIRE. Brussels. Rococo scroll pattern. 1840–60. All wool. 27″ wide, 20″ x 21″ repeat. No. 41 B 356 1R (shades of gold on blue). Special order.

▶ DIAMOND WITH QUATREFOIL. Axminster. Gothic pattern. 80% wool, 20% nylon. 27″ wide. No. A 75 7 (red, black, orange, lavendar and gray). Special order.

▶ GOTHIC QUATREFOIL. Axminster. Gothic quatrefoil pattern on spotted ground. 1840–70. 80% wool, 20% nylon. 27″ wide, 12″ x 6″ drop-match repeat. No. A 29

1, 4 (green, white and black). Special order.

▶ HAZEL PARK. Brussels. Border of blocks of alternating colors with rose wreath center and rose bouquet. Mid-19th century. All wool. 27″ wide, 49″ x 24½″ drop-match repeat. No. 82 B 197/B (black or yellow ground with red and greens). Special order.

▶ INTERLOCKING LAUREL WREATHS AND FLOWERS. Wilton. 1840–75. All wool. 27″ wide, 51″ x 25½″ drop-match repeat. No. W 586 5C (shades of gray brown and dark brown). Special order.

▶ LARGE-SCALE FLORAL. Wilton. Overall large-scale repeat floral. Mid-19th century. 80% wool, 20% nylon. 27″ wide, 51″ drop-match repeat. No. W 890/4C (red with forest green, olive, light green and cranberry). Special order.

▶ RIBBON AND FLORAL. Wilton. Mid-19th century. 80% wool, 20% nylon. 27″ wide. No. W 1146/3R (grape with shades of rose, red and green). Installed at the White House of the Confederacy, Richmond, Va. Special order.

▶ SMALL DIAMOND. Axminster adaptation. 1860–70. Similar to c. 1870 wallpaper patterns. 80% wool, 20% nylon. 27″ wide. No. A 88 7. Special order.

▶ SMALL DIAMOND AND GOTHIC QUATREFOIL. Wilton. 80% wool, 20% nylon. 27″ wide. No. W 999 6R (red, blue and pink beige). Special order.

▶ STAR AND DIAMOND. Axminster adaptation of Brussels and ingrain. 1860–75. 80% wool, 20% nylon. 27″ wide, 6″ x 6″ set-match repeat. No. A 56 4 (shades of green and dark gold). Special order.

▶ WILTON. Wilton adaptation of ingrain. 1825–50. Alternating squares and diamonds. 80% wool, 20% nylon. 27″ wide, 13″ set-match repeat. WB 422 3C (red, burgundy, cream and black); and custom colors. Special order.

BRINTONS LIMITED

▶ CHAYTOR BROADLOOM. Axminster adaptation. Square with medallion center. 1830–60. 80% wool, 20% nylon. 39¼″ or 13′ 1½″ wide, 19¾″ set-match repeat. No. 2/2060. Special order.

▶ FLOORCLOTH ADAPTATION. Zenith Contract

Axminster adaptation. 1840–75. 80% wool, 20% nylon. 27″ wide, 12″ x 13½″ repeat. No. 3/8705. Special order.

▶ ORIENTAL ADAPTATION. Zenith Contract Axminster. 1850–70. Suitable where documentation is not required. 80% wool, 20% nylon. 27″ wide, 41″ set-match repeat, 189 pitch/9 rpi. No. 1/8149 (crimson, royal blue, light blue and green). Special order.

▶ SCATTERED FLORAL. Zenith Contract Axminster. 1850–75. 80% wool, 20% nylon. 27″ wide, 24″ x 27″ repeat. No. 7/6279 (brick, brown, tobacco, greens and black). Special order.

▶ SCROLL PATTERN. Wilton. c. 1840–75. 80% wool, 20% nylon. 27″ wide, 36″ repeat. No. 0825 (gray taupe on burgundy ground). Special order.

J. R. BURROWS AND COMPANY

▶ ARCHITECTURAL GOTHIC. Brussels or Wilton. Large-scale Gothic architectural motif. English, 1848. Document a point paper in manufacturer's collection. 80% wool, 20% nylon. 27″ wide, approximately 29″ repeat. Cream, yellow gold, brown and black with green accent. Special order.

▶ FLOWER SPRIGS. Brussels or Wilton. Small-scale pattern of flower sprigs on a moss-patterned ground. English, 1861. Document a point paper in manufacturer's collection. 80% worsted wool, 20% nylon. 27″ wide, 14½″ repeat. No. 87/1248 (gray, white, forest green and Kelly green). Special order.

▶ GEOMETRIC. Brussels. Linear geometric pattern of squares and Gothic rosettes. English, late 1860s. Document a point paper by Owen Mayloft in manufacturer's collection. All wool. 27″ wide, 25½″ repeat. No. 87/3382 (greens, red, gold and white). Special order.

▶ HEXAGONS AND SQUARES. Brussels or Wilton adaptation of printed floorcloth. Alternating hexagons and squares with central geometric rosette patterns in alternating colors. English, late 1860s. Document a point paper in manufacturer's collection. 80% wool, 20% nylon. 27″ wide, approximately 12″ drop-match repeat. No. 87/3386 (red, white, green, light blue on light brown and tan). Special order.

MEDALLION. Brussels carpet. J. R. Burrows and Company. Red, gold and brown.

▶ MEDALLION. Brussels. Medallion pattern alternating with floral or leaf centers and decorative banding. English, 1853. Document a point paper drawn for Watson and Company in manufacturer's collection. 80% worsted wool, 20% nylon. 27″ wide. No. 87/2859 (shades of red, gold and brown). Special order.

▶ MEDALLION WITH FLOWERS. Brussels or Wilton. Large medallion inset with flowers and surrounded with banding and leaves. English, 1856. Document a point paper in manufacturer's collection. 80% worsted wool, 20% nylon. 27″ wide, approximately 46″ drop-match repeat. No. 87/2892 (cream, yellow gold and deep blue). Special order.

▶ OCTAGON GEOMETRIC. Brussels. Geometric octagonal pattern. English, 1860s. Document a point paper in manufacturer's collection. 80% worsted wool, 20% nylon. 27″ wide, 27″ repeat. No. 87/3493 (gray, white, red and blue). Border available. Special order.

▶ PASSION FLOWER WITH LEAVES. Narrow-gauge Brussels or Wilton. English, 1870s. Document a point paper in manufacturer's collection. 80% worsted wool,

145

20% nylon. 27" wide, No. 19/6838 (maroon with light olive, yellow gold and cream). Special order.

▶ ROSETTES AND QUATREFOIL TRELLIS. Brussels or Wilton. Alternating octagonal rosettes on a ground diapered with a quatrefoil trellis. English, 1829; use continued into 1840–75. Document a point paper in manufacturer's collection. 80% worsted wool, 20% nylon pile. 27" wide, 25" repeat. No. 87/0644 (red, white, yellow gold, black and pink). Special order.

▶ STRIPES AND DIAMONDS. Brussels or Wilton. Interlaced banded pattern with stripes and diamond motifs. English, late 1860s. Document a point paper in manufacturer's collection. 80% worsted wool, 20% nylon. 27" wide, 25½" set-match repeat. No. 87/3385 (gray blue, golds, red, white and tobacco). Special order.

▶ TURKEY FLORAL. Brussels or Wilton adaptation of handknotted Axminster or Oriental carpet. Alternating stylized geometric flowers and small four-petal flowers in the Turkish style; border includes clusters of geometric flowers and pattern bands. English, 1825; use continued into the 1840s–50s but was not as popular as floral and tapestry carpets. Document a point paper in manufacturer's collection. 80% worsted wool, 20% nylon. 27" wide. No. 87/1405 (red, white, blue, green and black). ¾ (27" wide) and ⁴⁄₄ (36" wide) runners available. Special order.

COLEFAX AND FOWLER

▶ DALKEITH. Brussels. Gothic-style quatrefoil on a spotted ground. 1860s. Documents in manufacturer's collection. 80% wool, 20% nylon. 27" wide, 6¾" repeat. Brown mauve, black and gray. Special order.

▶ MEDALLION. Brussels adaptation. Gothic-cross pattern. English, late 1830s on. Based on patterns found in English country houses. 80% wool, 20% nylon. 27" wide, 6" repeat. Dark brick red, dark brown and tan. Border available. Special order.

▶ ROSES AND RIBBONS. Brussels. Ribbon and leaf trellis with scattered roses. Based on earlier period patterns. Document in manufacturer's collection. 80% wool, 20% nylon. 27" wide, 29½" repeat. Dark brown, cocoa and white. Special order.

▶ TATTON PARK. Brussels adaptation. English, 1840–

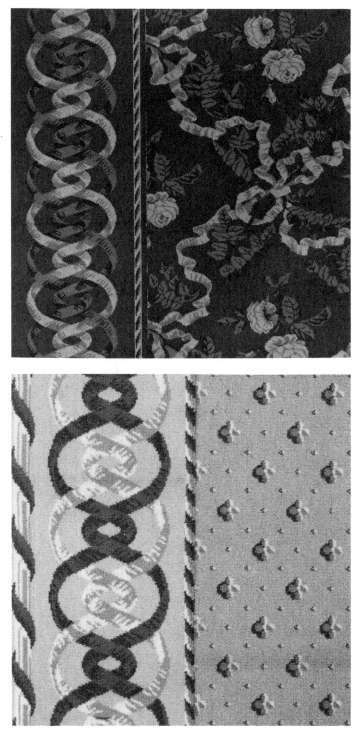

ROSES AND RIBBONS. Brussels carpet. Colefax and Fowler. Dark brown, cocoa and white.

TATTON PARK. Brussels carpet. Colefax and Fowler. Light beige, light and dark gray brown and cream.

75. Based on English carpets in manufacturer's collection. 80% wool, 20% nylon. 27" wide, 5" repeat. Light beige, light and dark gray brown and cream. Special order.

CRAIGIE STOCKWELL CARPETS

Also provides custom reproductions. All patterns are researched, designed and colored to order and hand-tufted or handknotted by Craigie Stockwell or its associated company, Stockwell Riley Hooley.

K. V. T. (PENNSYLVANIA WOVEN) CARPET MILLS

Also custom weaves Brussels and Wilton carpeting from historic documents in limited quantities.

▶ WILTON. Octagonal design with patterned center and rosette in square at corners. 1830–50. Suitable where documentation is not required. 80% wool, 20% nylon. 27" wide, approximately 13½" x 13½" repeat. No. 6329-A-6053 (red, dark green and brick on black); and custom colors. Special order.

LACEY-CHAMPION CARPETS

Produces custom handtufted carpets and duplications of period patterns.

LANGHORNE CARPET COMPANY

Also provides custom work, duplicating and adapting historic documents.

▶ HENRY FORD MUSEUM. Brussels adaptation of tapestry carpet. Urn with flowers. 1835–50. Document at the Henry Ford Museum, Greenfield Village, Mich. 80% wool, 20% nylon. 27" wide, 54" repeat, 85" drop-match repeat. No. 6031 (beige ground with red, purple, taupe, light and dark olive and brick). Special order.

▶ HONOLULU HOUSE. Wilton reproduction. Squared floral cluster. 1875–85. Document at the Honolulu House, Marshall, Mich. 80% wool, 20% nylon. 27" wide, 25" set-match repeat. No. 6025 (dark green with rust, gold, yellow and blue). Border No. 6026. Made for the Honolulu House. Available only through Susan's Interiors. Special order.

▶ JAMES LORAH HOUSE. Brussels adaptation of tapes-

HENRY FORD MUSEUM. Brussels adaptation of tapestry carpet. Langhorne Carpet Company. Beige with red, purple, taupe, light and dark olive and brick.

try carpet. Banded pattern with scroll alternating with flowers. 1840–70. Document at the James Lorah House, Doylestown, Pa. 80% wool, 20% nylon. 27″ wide, 29¼″ repeat. No. 5189 (rose, olive, tans, brick red and blue). Made for the Lorah House. Special order.

▶ JAMES LORAH HOUSE PARLOR. Brussels or Wilton adaptation of tapestry carpet. Large-scale leaf and floral pattern with cartouches and wreaths. 1830–50. Document at the James Lorah House, Doylestown, Pa. 80% wool, 20% nylon. 27″ wide, 62″ drop-match repeat. Burgundy, cream, rose and green. Made for the Lorah House. Special order.

▶ MARTIN VAN BUREN HOUSE. Brussels reproduction. Patterned stripes and diamonds. 1840–75. Document at Lindenwald (Martin Van Buren House), Kinderhook, N.Y. All worsted wool pile. 27″ wide, 18″ x 9″ drop-match repeat. No. 6050 (red, olive, blue and pale rose beige). Border No. 6051: 11″ wide, 8¾″ repeat. Made for the Van Buren House. Special order.

▶ OLD MERCHANT'S HOUSE. Brussels or Wilton reproduction. Large-scale cartouche and medallion pattern. 1830–50. Document at the Old Merchant's House, New York City. 80% wool, 20% nylon. 27″ wide, 55½″ drop-match repeat. No. 5294 (golds, red, black, blue and lavender). Border available: 13½″. Made for the Old Merchant's House. Special order.

▶ VICTORIAN TAPESTRY. Wilton adaptation of tapestry velvet carpet. Large-scale floral. 1840–70. Document in manufacturer's collection. 80% wool, 20% nylon. 27″ wide, 72″ drop-match repeat. Orange, shades of green, red, maroon, brown, tan and blue. Special order.

MILLIKEN CONTRACT CARPETING

▶ VICTORIAN ROSE. Tufted carpet with printed design. Mid-19th century. Based on period carpets. All nylon pile. 12′ wide, 24″ x 36″ set-match repeat. Most suitable color: No. 401 (green). Stock item.

PATTERSON, FLYNN AND MARTIN

▶ CARTOUCHE. Brussels reproduction. Alternating cartouche and leaf field. c. 1840–70. Document at Lorenzo, Cazenovia, N.Y. 80% wool, 20% nylon. 27″

JAMES LORAH HOUSE. Brussels adaptation of tapestry carpet. Langhorne Carpet Company. Rose, olive, tans, brick red and blue.

MARTIN VAN BUREN HOUSE. Brussels carpet. Langhorne Carpet Company. Red, olive, blue and rose beige.

wide, 31″ repeat. No. 1812/7381 (dark brown ground with white, tan, maroon and dark red). Special order.

▶ CROISSILONS DIRECTOIRE. Wilton. Diamond trellis pattern with flowers at crossings. 1840–50. All wool pile. 27″ wide. Rust and brick red. French Collection. Border available. Special order.

▶ DALKEITH. Brussels. Gothic-style quatrefoil on a spotted ground. 1860s. Documents in manufacturer's collection. 80% wool, 20% nylon. 27″ wide, 6³⁄4″ repeat. Brown mauve, black and gray. Special order.

left
VICTORIAN TAPES-
TRY. Wilton adaptation
of tapestry velvet car-
pet. Langhorne Carpet
Company. Orange,
green, red, maroon,
brown, tan and blue.

below left
FLORAL WITH
ROCOCO LEAVES.
Wilton carpet. Patter-
son, Flynn and Martin.
Brown, orange, reds
and black on cream.

▶ FLORAL WITH ROCOCO LEAVES. Wilton. Alternating floral clusters and rococo leaves. 1850–70. 80%
wool, 20% nylon. 27″ wide, approximately 32″ drop-
match repeat. No. 1817/7386 (brown, orange, reds and
black on cream). Special order.
▶ GOTHIC CROSS. Brussels. Gothic crosses with field
of small Gothic crosses. c. 1860. 80% wool, 20% nylon.
27″ wide, 9″ x 9″ set-match repeat. No. 1834/7394 (red
with black, yellow and gold). Special order.
▶ GOTHIC DIAMONDS. Brussels. Gothic-inspired dia-

CARTOUCHE. Brussels
carpet. Patterson, Flynn
and Martin. Dark
brown with white, tan,
maroon and dark red.

above left
GOTHIC CROSS. Brussels carpet. Patterson, Flynn and Martin. Red with black, yellow and gold.

above right
GOTHIC DIAMONDS. Brussels carpet. Patterson, Flynn and Martin. Cream, blue and black.

right
LEAF AND RIBBON TRELLIS. Brussels carpet. Patterson, Flynn and Martin. Dark red brown with honey and cream.

152

mond pattern. 1840s. 80% wool, 20% nylon. 27" wide, 9" x 7" set-match repeat. No. 1832/7393 (cream and blue on black). Special order.

▶ GOTHIC ROSETTE. Brussels. Interlaced band and Gothic-inspired rosette and band motif. 1860s–70s. Pattern and scale correspond to visual documentation of the period. 80% wool, 20% nylon. 27" wide, 30" repeat. No. 1813/7382 (brown, gray, yellow and tan). Border available. Special order.

▶ GROUP 159. Wilton. Large-scale adaptation of Oriental carpet. 1860s. All wool. 27" wide, 54" set-match repeat. No. 1456 (dark blue, beige, tobacco, red and blue green). Special order.

▶ GROUP 174. Wilton. Large-scale Oriental-style pattern. 1860s. All wool. 27" wide, approximately 72" x 54" drop-match repeat. No. 2694 (red, white tan, green, blue and dark blue). Special order.

▶ LEAF AND RIBBON TRELLIS. Brussels. Diagonal pattern of leaf and ribbon trellis with interspersed roses. 1840–75. Similar to documented patterns of the period. 80% wool, 20% nylon. 27" wide, 29¼" repeat. No. 1818/7369 (dark red brown with honey and cream). Special order.

GOTHIC ROSETTE. Brussels carpet. Patterson, Flynn and Martin. Brown, gray, yellow and tan.

▶ MEDALLION. Brussels. Gothic-cross pattern. English, late 1830s on. Based on patterns found in English country houses. 80% wool, 20% nylon. 27" wide, 6" repeat. Dark brick red, dark brown and tan. Border available. Special order.

▶ MELROSE DINING ROOM. Wilton or Brussels adaptation. Cross pattern with feathered central medallion and formal block and leaf motif. Natchez, Miss., c. 1845. Based on mid-19th-century furniture designs. 80% wool, 20% nylon. 27" wide. Cream gold and black. Special order.

▶ MELROSE DRAWING ROOM. Brussels or Wilton adaptation. Large-scale floral and scroll pattern. Natchez, Miss., c. 1845. Based on a mid-19th-century tapestry or Wilton carpet. 80% wool, 20% nylon. 27" wide, large-scale repeat. Cream ground with rust brown, reds and greens. Special order.

▶ OLD MERCHANT'S HOUSE. Brussels or Wilton reproduction. Large-scale cartouche and medallion pat-

153

MELROSE DRAWING ROOM. Brussels or Wilton carpet. Patterson, Flynn and Martin. Cream with rust brown, reds and greens.

TROPICAL LEAF AND FERN. Wilton or Brussels carpet. Patterson, Flynn and Martin. Black with yellow, orange and dark red.

tern. 1830–50. Document at the Old Merchant's House, New York City. All wool. 27″ wide, 55″ repeat. No. 5293 (golds, red, black, blue and lavender). Border No. 5294. Made for the Old Merchant's House. Special order.

▶ PERSIAN 1505. Moquette. c. 1855. All wool. 27″ wide. No. 159/18 (dark blue, red, tobacco, pale blue green, cream and olive green). Special order.

▶ TIRELLES LES GRENADES. Wilton. c. 1855. 80% wool, 20% nylon. 27″ wide. No. 1447. Special order.

▶ TROPICAL LEAF AND FERN. Wilton or Brussels reproduction. Large-scale pattern of tropical foliage and ferns. 1870–80. Document at the Bishop Museum, Honolulu. 80% wool, 20% nylon. 27″ wide, approximately 54″ repeat. No. 1811/7380 (black with yellow, orange and dark red). Made for Iolani Palace, Honolulu. Special order.

▶ WADSWORTH HOUSE. Wilton. Large-scale pattern of naturalistic floral clusters with leaf, scroll and cartouche surrounds. 1830–60. Suitable where documentation is not required. 80% wool, 20% nylon. 27″ wide.

Beige ground with dark brown, honey, rose, pink and blue. Installed at San Francisco Plantation, Reserve, La. Special order.

▶ WATTEAU. Brussels or Wilton. Large-scale floral cartouche pattern. 1835–50. Suitable where documentation is not required. 80% wool, 20% nylon. 27″ wide, approximately 54″ repeat. Beige with pale lavender, gray, tan, rose, deep rose and blue. Installed at San Francisco Plantation, Reserve, La. Special order.

ROSECORE CARPETS

Some available Wilton and Brussels carpets are suitable where documentation is not required. Custom work also is provided, including development of patterns and duplication of carpeting from historic materials in the company's collection.

SAXONY CARPET COMPANY

Also custom duplicates and adapts period patterns.

▶ AUTUMN LEAVES. Brussels. Overall leaf pattern. 1860s–70s. 80% fine worsted wool, 20% nylon. 27″ wide, 11½″ repeat. No. 629 A (shades of brown, cream, rust and blue). Border available: 18″ wide. Special order.

▶ DARBY. Brussels. Modified quatrefoil on diaper pattern ground. Mid- to late 19th century. 80% wool, 20% nylon. 27″ wide, 5¹¹/₁₆″ x 5¹¹/₁₆″ set-match repeat. Red, blue and gold on dark green. Special order.

▶ DIAMONDS. Brussels. Stripe, diamond and medallion pattern. Mid-19th century. 80% wool, 20% nylon. 12′ wide, 4⅔′ x 4″ repeat. No. 510 (forest green, dark red, gold and cream on dark blue green). Special order.

▶ FLORAL SQUARES. Axminster adaptation of needlepoint rug. Mid-19th century. All nylon pile. 12′ wide. No. 154 (black with rose, blue, greens and golds). Stock item.

▶ OLD MERCHANT'S HOUSE. Brussels or Wilton reproduction. Large-scale cartouche and medallion pattern. 1830–50. Document at the Old Merchant's House, New York City. All wool. 27″ wide, 55½″ drop-match repeat. No. A 490 (golds, red, black, blue and lavender). Made for the Old Merchant's House. Special order.

▶ SHADED GOTHIC CROSS. Brussels. Large Gothic

crosses with small crosses forming background pattern. 1840s. 80% wool, 20% nylon. 27" wide, 14" set-match repeat. V&A No. 7394 (custom color No. 5: brick with tan, light yellow, dark brown and rose). Special order.

▶ TORINO. Wilton. Alternating clusters of flowers and roses. Mid-19th century. 80% wool, 20% nylon. 27" or 54" wide, approximately 18" repeat. Red ground with shades of gold and olive green. Stair runner and border available. Special order.

SCALAMANDRE

Also duplicates historic patterns.

▶ BRIGHTON. Wilton. Large-scale rococo leaf pattern. English, 1840–75. 80% wool, 20% nylon. 27" wide, 54" drop-match repeat. 4 custom colors. Installed in the Hamill House dining room, Georgetown, Colo. Special order.

▶ CAMPBELL-WHITTLESEY. Brussels adaptation. Medallion-style pattern. 1835–50. Document at the Campbell-Whittlesey House, Rochester, N.Y. All wool. Handtufted. Document colors: red, maroon, cream, tan, rust, yellow and blue. Made for the Campbell-Whittlesey House. Special order.

▶ CANTERBURY. Brussels reproduction. Gothic cross with scattered Gothic-cross diapering. English, mid-19th century. Document at the Victoria and Albert Museum, London. All wool. 27" wide. 5 custom colors. Special order.

▶ HADDOW HOUSE. Brussels. Linear diamond with rosettes at the crossings. English, mid-19th century. Document at Haddow House, Aberdeenshire, England. All wool. 27" wide, 8½" set-match repeat. 3 custom colors. Special order.

▶ HAMPTON COURT. Brussels. Interlocking Gothic rosette and trellis pattern. English, mid-19th century. Document at the Victoria and Albert Museum, London. All wool. 27" wide, 27" set-match repeat. 5 colors. Installed at the Mamie Eisenhower Birthplace, Boone, Iowa, and the Hirshfeld House, Austin Tex. Special order.

▶ HILL-STEAD DRAWING ROOM. Wilton. Geometric-style adaptation of an Oriental rug. c. 1870–75. 80%

wool, 20% nylon. 27″ wide, 46″ repeat. Rust, brown, brown gold and olive. Made for the Hill-Stead House, Farmington, Conn. Special order.

▶ IOLANI. Wilton reproduction. Large-scale pattern of tropical foliage and ferns. 1870–80. Document at the Bishop Museum, Honolulu. 80% wool, 20% nylon. 27″ wide, 49″ repeat. 5 shades of red. Border available: 41″ repeat. Made for Iolani Palace, Honolulu. Special order.

▶ LORENZO. Brussels reproduction. Alternating cartouche and leaf field. c. 1840–70. Document at Lorenzo, Cazenovia, N.Y. All wool pile. 27″ wide, 31″ repeat. Dark and medium brown, tan, red and yellow tan. Border available: 14″ repeat. Special order.

▶ LYON. Wilton. Laurel medallions with patterned ground. French, c. 1840. 80% wool, 20% nylon. 27″ wide, 18″ drop-match repeat. Maroon ground with cranberry red, yellow, ochre and dark red. Made for the Judge Flanagan Residence, Peoria, Ill., and The Georgian (MacCracken-Huffman House), Lancaster, Ohio. Special order.

▶ PEEL. Wilton. Overall rococo leaf motif. English, 1850–75. 80% wool, 20% nylon. 27″ wide, 36″ drop-match repeat. 2 custom colors. Special order.

▶ SAN FRANCISCO PLANTATION. Brussels reproduction. Gothic diamond pattern. 1851. Document in the

SAN FRANCISCO PLANTATION. Brussels reproduction. Scalamandre. Green beige, red, honey and pink.

157

SHELTON. Brussels carpet. Scalamandre. Custom colors.

Victoria and Albert Museum, London. All wool. 27″ wide, 25″ repeat. Green beige, red, honey and pink. Made for San Francisco Plantation, Reserve, La. Installed at Sunnyside (Washington Irving House), Tarrytown, N.Y. Special order.

▶ SHELTON. Brussels. c. 1846–60. Similar to ingrain patterns of the period. All wool. 27″ wide, 26″ set-match repeat. 3 custom colors. Made for the Elmira Shelton House, Richmond, Va. Special order.

▶ SNOWDEN. Wilton. Pattern of rosettes surrounded by rococo foliage. English, 1850–70. 80% wool, 20% nylon. 27″ wide, 27″ set-match repeat. Red with gold, yellow and olive brown. Special order.

▶ TURNER. Wilton. Overall leaf pattern with interspersed florals. English, 1860–80. 80% wool, 20% nylon. 27″ wide. Custom colors. Installed at the Mamie Eisenhower Birthplace, Boone, Iowa. Special order.

▶ WALTER SCOTT. Wilton. Large-scale floral clusters and rococo-style leaves. English, c. 1840–50. Document at Abbotsford (Walter Scott home), Melrose, Scotland. 80% wool, 20% nylon. 27″ wide, 37″ drop-match repeat. 16 custom colors. Special order.

SNOWDEN. Wilton carpet. Scalamandre. Red with gold, yellow and olive brown.

TURNER. Wilton carpet. Scalamandre. Custom colors.

▶ WATERFORD. Brussels. Interlocking diamond pattern with floral center. 1840s. 80% wool, 20% nylon. 27″ wide, 25″ repeat. Teal blue with dark blue, olive green and peach. Special order.

▶ WICKFIELD. Brussels reproduction. Diagonal pattern of Gothic crosses. Suitable also as an ingrain adaptation. English, mid-19th century. All wool. Document at the Victoria and Albert Museum, London. 27″ wide, 6″ set-match repeat. 4 custom colors. Special order.

▶ WINDEMERE. Documented Wilton reproduction. Rococo rosettes intertwined with leaves on a moss-patterned ground. 1835–60. 80% wool, 20% nylon. 27″ wide, 46″ drop-match repeat. Browns and golds. Special order.

SCHUMACHER

▶ BELLE GROVE SAVONNERIE. Handtufted rug. Based on architectural details at Belle Grove, Middletown, Va. Mid-19th century. All wool. Custom colors. Design approved by the National Trust for Historic Preservation. Special order.

STARK CARPET CORPORATION

Duplicates and adapts carpets from historic documents in custom colors.

▶ LAYCOCK. Wilton or Brussels reproduction. Rose bunches tied with ribbons. English, c. 1840. Document at Lacock Abbey, Wiltshire, England. All wool pile. 27″ wide, 48″ repeat. No. 9385 (red, shades of tan, beige and green brown). Border No. 8369: 12″ wide. Special order.

▶ MARTIN VAN BUREN HOUSE. Brussels reproduction. Patterned stripes and diamonds. 1840–75. Document at Lindenwald (Martin Van Buren House), Kinderhook, N.Y. All worsted wool. 27″ wide, 18″ x 9″ drop-match repeat. Blue, olive, red, pale rose and beige. Border available: 11″ wide, 8¾″ repeat. Made for the Van Buren House. Special order.

U.S. AXMINSTER

▶ 18TH-CENTURY GARDEN. Palladium II Contract Axminster. Floral pattern. 1840–75; also suitable for the early 20th century. All nylon. 12' wide, 36" x 18" drop-match repeat, 189 pitch/7 rpi. No. PLM-II-54 (green and multicolor). Stock item.

▶ ROCKET WALK. Axminster adaptation of Brussels, Wilton or floorcloth. Diamond pattern with corner motifs. c. 1840. 80% wool, 20% nylon. 36" and 12' wide, 6" x 3" drop-match repeat, 189 pitch/8, 9 or 10 rpi. No. 26 (brick red and dark green). Design Inspiration Collection. Special order.

▶ ROYAL DAMASK. Axminster adaptation of ingrain. 1840–70. 80% wool, 20% nylon. 36" and 12' wide, 17¾" x 18" set-match repeat, 189 pitch/8, 9 or 10 rpi. No. 62 (red, apricot, light yellow, tan, light and dark coral). Design Inspiration Collection. Special order.

V'SOSKE

Provides handtufted duplications of historic patterns and develops custom adaptations.

KARASTAN BIGELOW

ORIENTAL RUGS

▶ FERAGHAN. Wilton reproduction. Classic Herati pattern. All worsted wool. Document at Penshurst Place, Kent, England. No. 0570-0528 (dark blue, medium blue, red and light yellow). Stately Homes Collection. Stock item.

▶ FERAGHAN FLORAL. Wilton reproduction. Rows of stylized flowers centered on a dark ground, with a geometric and floral border. Document at Knebworth House, Hertfordshire, England. All worsted wool. No. 0570-0531 (cream, reds, light and dark blue and light green). Stately Homes Collection. Stock item.

▶ MIR SERABEND. Wilton reproduction. Overall design of alternating rows of leaf designs with multiple geometric-pattern borders. Document at Chatsworth, Derbyshire, England. All worsted wool. No. 0570-0529 (red with cream, light red and shades of blue). Stately Homes Collection. Stock item.

1875 TO 1900:
THE LATE VICTORIAN INTERIOR

The last decades of the 19th century witnessed the consolidation of America as western territories became states bound together by transcontinental rail lines to form a national market. Farm produce and manufactured goods could now be shipped to distant points. Urban residents could examine a startling array of goods in those new phenomena, department stores, while their rural counterparts were enticed by mail-order catalogs from Montgomery Ward and Sears, Roebuck. Railroads made possible the homogenization of the American home; they swept aside regional differences by permitting rural as well as urban households to purchase manufactured goods from a few industrial centers. Americans celebrated their success with two national fairs, the 1876 Centennial Exhibition held in Philadelphia and the 1893 World's Columbian Exposition in Chicago. Like department stores and mail-order catalogs, these fairs celebrated material abundance and encouraged the consumer ethic at the same time—introducing millions of Americans to the latest fashions.

An important English design critic, Charles Locke Eastlake (1836–1906), emerged in this period. His book *Hints on Household Taste in Furniture, Upholstery & Other Details* (1868) had been reprinted in America in 1872 and found immediate success. According to Harriet Spofford, an American writer on household design and a disciple of Eastlake, his book met "a great want" in America and "not a young marrying couple who read English were to be found without *Hints on Household Taste* in their hands." Eastlake deplored the ornate, highly decorated furniture

ENCAUSTIC TILES. Tile flooring. H and R Johnson Tiles.

associated with the Rococo Revival style and favored simple pieces without veneers or excessive ornamentation. The popularity of his book spread his ideas to design reformers throughout America. At the Centennial Exhibition, one furniture manufacturer from New York City and another from Cincinnati exhibited suites designed in Eastlake's rectilinear, sparsely decorated style, which was vaguely termed Gothic. Visitors to the fair were also introduced to the designs of Christopher Dresser, Walter Crane and William Morris. American critics and consumers felt the tug of the reform philosophy stressing good, simple design.

But Eastlake and his fellow critics were not the only influence at work in 1876. The celebration of the national centennial and the sense of relief that the country had survived the Civil War promoted an interest in the colonial past. The kitchen of the exhibition's New England log house interested visitors with its walk-in fireplace, spinning wheel, candlesticks, cradle and costumed guides. The simplicity of the cabin—in sharp contrast to their Victorian homes—seemed to fit the philosophy of the reform movement espoused by Eastlake. In addition, it was a far more American style than Eastlake's Gothic. Clarence Cook in *The House Beautiful* (1881) found it "proof that our taste is getting a root in a healthier and more native soil." He concluded, "All this resuscitation of 'old furniture' and revival of old simplicity . . . is in reality much more sensible than it seems to be to those who look upon it as only another phase of the 'centennial' mania." Whether Americans decorated in the Eastlake or Colonial Revival style, they were encouraged to follow a reform philosophy of simplicity.

WOOD FLOORS. Nowhere is this philosophy more apparent than in the era's preference for floor coverings. For the first time wood floors became a popular choice rather than one prompted by rude necessity. Eastlake praised highly polished hardwood floors and illustrated several parquet patterns in *Hints on Household Taste*. American critics followed this lead. Clarence Cook told readers, "The advantage of a hard-wood floor, or of a common floor covered with wood-carpeting, is so great on the score of health and labor-saving, that it would seem as

PLATE XIV.

PARQUETRY FIELDS.

NEW YORK. **WOOD-MOSAIC CO.** ROCHESTER, N.Y.

Elaborate parquet flooring offered by a manufacturer in the late 19th century. (The Athenaeum of Philadelphia)

if only the prejudice that comes from old associations could long keep up the fashion of carpets."

American sawmills produced designs to suit every taste and budget. Hardwood parquet squares ranging in thickness from ⅜ to 1⅛ inches were illustrated in catalogs available in stores throughout the country. The thicker parquet was tongue-and-grooved for installation, while thinner ones were simply glued and face-nailed in place.

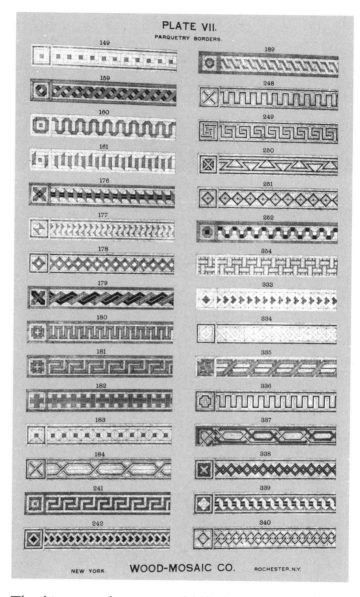

Decorative parquet borders available in the late 19th century. (The Athenaeum of Philadelphia)

The thinner product was useful if a homeowner wished to update the appearance of an earlier house constructed with softwood floors. However, it often results in problems for modern owners of old houses because sanding the floors too vigorously can cause the nails to appear. The same problem can occur with wood carpeting, an inexpensive product composed of ¼-inch thick wood strips glued to a heavy muslin backing, which was also

Patterned tiles available from Maw and Company about 1900. (The Athenaeum of Philadelphia)

Encaustic and geometric cut tile floor in the Pennsylvania Academy of the Fine Arts (1876, Frank Furness), Philadelphia. (H and R Johnson Tiles)

popular. It cost from $1 to $2 a yard, making it competitively priced with better ingrains as well as tapestry carpets. Critics recommended wood carpeting for all rooms in the house including kitchens, where its tight joints and close-grained hardwoods were easier to clean than softwood floors. For those who could not afford the costly parquet, floorcloths and linoleum with parquet patterns were affordable alternatives in the late 19th century.

Tile flooring sold by Maw and Company at the turn of the century. (The Athenaeum of Philadelphia)

TILE FLOORS. Tiles remained popular for vestibules and entry halls, and Americans could choose from both imported and domestic wares. Traditional encaustic patterns were joined by other types of design. One imitated mosaic tiles found at archeological sites such as Herculaneum and Pompeii. Small six- and eight-sided tiles were used for entries and bathrooms, where they were sometimes laid with borders. Art tiles with monochromatic transfer prints or clear colored glazes were produced for fireplace hearths and wainscoting in vestibules and bathrooms, with designs taken from both colonial America and the Aesthetic movement of the 1870s and 1880s.

FLOORCLOTHS. Now known as oilcloths, floorcloths continued in use to a lesser extent during the last quarter of the 19th century and even included a printed felt paper similar to a heavy-weight cardboard—a sort of "poor man's" floorcloth. Eastlake advocated traditionally made oilcloths for halls and passages printed with simple geometric patterns worked in two colors or two values of the same color. He condemned realistic shading or attempts to imitate marble or parquet. American critics and architects agreed. Robert W. Shoppell told readers of *Modern Houses, Beautiful Homes* (1887), "What are wanted are designs peculiar to floor-cloth itself, and not a pretentious imitation of something costlier."

KAMPTULICON AND LINOLEUM FLOORS. Consumers could also choose kamptulicon or linoleum. Kamptulicon, made from India rubber and granulated cork, had been invented by Elijah Galloway in 1844. It was a durable and resilient floor covering but expensive, which limited its popularity. Linoleum, invented in 1863 by another Englishman, Frederick Walton, was far less costly. While early samples were imported, Walton obtained an American patent and in 1875 began producing linoleum in New York as the American Linoleum Manufacturing Company, a subsidiary of his English firm. American imitators quickly followed. Ella Rodman Church, author of *How to Furnish a Home* (1882), praised linoleum as warmer, more durable and less expensive than oilcloth. By the end of the 19th century, linoleum was the popular choice. The Sears, Roebuck catalog for 1897 described it as "very much like oil cloth except that there is ground cork in its composition, which makes it much heavier, more durable; also, very much softer to walk on." Linoleum generally came in three- or six-foot widths, and catalogs illustrated designs imitating tiles, wood and even ingrain carpeting.

MATTING. Matting remained the least expensive floor covering through the end of the century. It was popular for summer use and often was the only floor covering in vacation cottages. Critics continued to praise it for bedrooms, where few houses had fine hardwood floors and where, before the electric vacuum cleaner, they opposed using carpeting for reasons of hygiene. Plain matting was highly recommended for most rooms, and some checked patterns, woven from dyed grasses, were deemed appropriate for halls and passages. While Chinese and Japanese matting came in patterns printed in colors, writers on interior decoration warned that these colors did not penetrate the grass fibers thoroughly and soon looked worn.

ORIENTAL RUGS. Ironically, just at the time most carpet mills had been mechanized and were able to produce affordable goods, critics following Eastlake's lead began to condemn wall-to-wall carpeting. Eastlake favored true Orientals because they illustrated the weaver's skill rather than the machine's regularity. Clarence Cook praised their durability, noting that "even if it strain our purse a little . . . a good rug will last a lifetime." Rugs were easier to clean than wall-to-wall carpeting because they could be taken up and beaten. According to the reform philosophy, Oriental carpets were appropriate for either Aesthetic or Colonial Revival interiors for, as Ella Rodman Church explained, they had "a sort of old-time and Eastern look." Critics recommended using one large rug in a room rather than several smaller ones, which gave a "patchy" look to the floor. However, a rug should not be so large that its design was obscured by pieces of furniture placed on it—advice that is suggested by interior designers today. Both geometric Turkish carpets and floral Persian patterns were found in late 19th-century homes.

BRUSSELS, WILTON AND INGRAIN CARPETS. American carpet manufacturers responded to the growing taste for rugs by weaving "Chlidema squares," ingrain "art squares" and Wilton and Axminster power-loomed imitations of Oriental carpets. Chlidema squares of Brussels or Wilton carpeting with borders woven as part of the carpet rather than as separate pieces were introduced to England and America in 1882. In 1884 the Hartford Carpet Company was one of the first to produce ingrain art squares, which, like Chlidema squares, were woven in one piece complete with borders. Art squares were naturally less expensive because they were ingrain carpets. In 1887 the Lowell Manufacturing Company marketed "Daghestan rugs" woven on Wilton looms to imitate Oriental carpets.

AXMINSTER CARPETS. Of all the early rugs, however, Axminsters most successfully captured the market. These late 19th-century versions should not be confused with the handknotted ones that originated in the 18th century and that a few British mills continued to produce. Following earlier precedents in power looms for weaving ingrain, Brussels and Wilton carpeting, the carpet industry developed various mechanized looms for Axminsters. By 1876 Halcyon Skinner, an employee of Alexander Smith and Sons Carpet Company of Yonkers, N.Y., perfected a "Royal Axminster" loom that operated on the spool principle still employed in the industry. Within two years, Tomkinsons of Kidderminster had imported Skinner's looms and begun weaving machined Axminsters in England. These developments were followed in 1892 by the "gripper Axminster" perfected by Brintons of Kidderminster, which marketed its product as "Imperial Axminster." (See "Changing Technologies" in the introduction for explanations of these terms.) Machine-woven Axminster carpets were a luxurious product favored by critics and more prosperous homeowners by the end of the 19th century and, together with tapestry carpets, which appealed to less-affluent households, they captured the American market, replacing ingrain, Brussels and Wilton carpeting in popularity.

While any power-loomed carpet could be designed to imitate the abstract patterns of handknotted Oriental carpets, Axminsters and tapestry carpets could employ more colors than ingrains, Brussels or Wiltons, and, consequently, their designs tended toward naturalistic

patterns with bright colors and realistic trompe l'oeil effects. Eastlake warned readers of *Hints on Household Taste,* "A carpet, of which the pattern is shaded in imitation of natural objects, becomes an absurdity when we remember that if it were really what it pretends to be, no one would walk on it with comfort." The American editor of Eastlake's 1872 edition echoed these sentiments: "How can a peaceful citizen, clad in a dressing gown, and with a long pipe in his mouth, be expected to walk over such a dangerous wilderness, which would be better suited to an inhabitant of the tropics?" Harriet Spofford labeled such patterns an "abomination to the eye." With so many critics condemning these designs, the obvious

Art gallery and family parlor of the Camron-Stanford House, Oakland, Calif., restored to its appearance about 1880. The carpeting was reproduced in England. (Helga Photo Studio for *The Magazine Antiques*)

171

conclusion is that many homeowners favored them.

Eastlake and other critics realized that not every household could afford an Oriental carpet and fine, hardwood floors. For homeowners who preferred wall-to-wall carpeting, critics recommended simple diaper patterns worked in only a few colors or various shades of one color. Eastlake illustrated two carpet patterns in his book; both were far more abstract than the designs William Morris was creating at the same time. Spofford added that small arabesques, mossy "mottlings," interwoven shapes neither distinctly floral nor leafy and Indian patterns were also acceptable.

Photographs of the 1880s and 1890s suggest that many homeowners followed the critics' advice, using rugs with Oriental patterns or carpeting with small, rather indistinct, patterns. Photographs also prove that some households used both techniques, placing small Oriental rugs on top of wall-to-wall carpeting. Another compromise was machine-made carpeting with coordinated borders laid wall to wall. This technique, often mistakenly attributed to all 19th-century carpeting in America, was most popular only at the end of the Victorian era.

One final point is carpet color. Authorities on design generally agreed that the floor should be the darkest color in the room because, in Spofford's words, a darker floor would "secure a thoroughly pictorial effect to the eye as a whole, and a comfortable one to the senses." However, color schemes might employ distinct, often contrasting hues or different values of a single color. Eastlake favored distinct hues and recommended that the "prevailing tint of a carpet should contrast rather than repeat that of the wall-paper," such as dark olive green carpeting with russet or Indian red wallpaper. Spofford, however, preferred schemes employing a single color so that the carpet was of the darkest value to "present the main body tint from which the rest of the room works up in lighter shades." Spofford's preference for using a single color throughout a room is one of the earliest descriptions of a monochromatic color scheme, which, although well known today, became popular only at the end of the 19th century.

HARRIS-TARKETT

▶ CANTERBURY. Solid hardwood flooring. Four equal squares with alternating diagonal center slats. Angelique teak, red oak, white oak and black walnut. Unfinished surface; paper faced. ⁵⁄₁₆″ thick, 13¼″ square. Stock item.

▶ CHAUCER. Solid hardwood flooring. Four alternating squares on the diagonal framed by pickets. Angelique teak, red oak, white oak and black walnut. Unfinished surface; paper faced. ⁵⁄₁₆″ thick, 13⁷⁄₁₆″ square. Stock item.

▶ HADDON HALL. Solid hardwood flooring. Four equal squares. Angelique teak, red oak, white oak, black walnut and ash. Unfinished surface; paper faced. ⁵⁄₁₆″ thick, 14¼″ square. Stock item.

▶ HERRINGBONE. Solid hardwood flooring. Angelique teak, red oak, white oak, black walnut and ash. Unfinished surface; paper faced. ⁵⁄₁₆″ thick, 14¼″ wide, 18⅛″ long, 4¾″ slat length; and ⁵⁄₁₆″ thick, 16¼″ wide, 18⅛″ long, 5½″ slat length. Stock items.

▶ MONTICELLO. Solid hardwood flooring. Four alternating squares with pickets. Angelique teak, red oak, white oak and black walnut. Unfinished surface; paper faced. ⁵⁄₁₆″ thick, 13¼″ square. Stock item.

▶ SAXONY. Solid hardwood flooring. Four squares on the diagonal and eight half-squares. Angelique teak, red oak, white oak and black walnut. Unfinished surface; paper faced. ⁵⁄₁₆″ thick, 19″ square. Stock item.

▶ STANDARD. Solid hardwood flooring. Sixteen alternating squares. Angelique teak, red oak, white oak, black walnut, ash and maple. Unfinished surface; paper faced. ⁵⁄₁₆″ thick, 19″ wide, 19″ long. Stock item.

KENTUCKY WOOD FLOORS

Custom parquet borders and floor patterns also duplicated and designed.

▶ CUSTOM BORDER. Parquet flooring. Elaborate interlaced border suitable for parlors. Mixed-species hardwoods. Unfinished surface. ⁵⁄₁₆″ thick, 12″ wide, 22″ long. Special order.

▶ FEATURE STRIP. Parquet border. Light and dark banded strip used as a decorative border in rooms and

WOOD FLOORING

FEATURE STRIP. Greek-key parquet border. Kentucky Wood Floors.

halls. Plain oak, quartered oak, ash, walnut and cherry. ³/4″ thick, random widths and lengths. Stock item.

▶ HERRINGBONE I. Parquet flooring. Red oak, tropical walnut and cherry. Unfinished surface; paper faced. ⁵/16″ thick, 14″ wide, 17″ long. Packaged 25 square feet per carton. Stock item.

▶ HERRINGBONE II. Parquet flooring. Plain oak, quartered oak, ash, walnut and cherry. Unfinished surface. ³/4″ thick, 2¼″ wide, 6³/4″–18″ long. Individual pieces bundled as ordered. Stock item.

▶ SIMPLICITY. Parquet flooring. Four-strip alternating vertical-horizontal pattern. Red oak, tropical walnut and cherry. Prefinished surface. ⁵/16″ thick, 9″ wide, 9″ long. Stock item.

▶ STRIP. Parquet flooring. Plain oak, quartered oak and maple. Unfinished surface; square edge. ³/4″ thick, 2½″ wide, random lengths. Stock item.

JANOS P. SPITZER FLOORING COMPANY

Parquet floor borders (after 1870) in mixed-species hardwoods available as stock items and custom made.

TILE FLOORING

AMERICAN OLEAN TILE COMPANY

▶ 1″ HEX. Porcelain ceramic hexagonal mosaic tiles. 1880s–1930s. Used for bathrooms, foyers, stores and restaurants. ¼″ thick, 1″ wide. Overall patterns and bordered designs prearranged on 1′ x 2′ sheets for installation. Unglazed. Black, white and various colors. Stock items.

▶ 1″ x 1″ SQUARE. Porcelain ceramic tile. 1880s–1920s. Used for bathrooms, stores, foyers and restaurants. ¼″ thick, 1″ square. Overall patterns and bordered designs prearranged on 1′ x 2′ sheets for installation. Slip-resistant surface. Black, white and various colors. Stock items.

▶ 2″ x 2″ HEX. Porcelain ceramic hexagonal mosaic tile. 1880s–1920s. Used for bathrooms, stores, foyers and restaurants. ½″ thick, 2″ wide. Overall patterns and bordered designs prearranged on 1′ x 2′ sheets for installation. Black, white and various colors. Stock items.

▶ 2″ x 2″ SQUARE. Porcelain ceramic tile. 1880s–1920s. Used for bathrooms, stores, foyers and restaurants. ¼″ thick, 2″ square. Overall patterns and bordered designs prearranged on 1′ x 2′ sheets for installation. Slip-resistant surface. Black, white and various colors. Stock items.

DESIGNS IN TILE

Also reproduces and adapts historic patterns; develops encaustic, cut and geometric tile designs; and provdes restoration and installation.

▶ GLAZED TILES. Square and rectangular tiles for hearth and fireplace surrounds. Various sizes. Period colors. Custom made.

▶ HEXAGONAL GEOMETRIC TILES. Porcelain ceramic tiles. Suitable for bathrooms, kitchens and foyers. 1″ square. Unglazed. Brick, white, black and green. Special order.

▶ 2″ x 2″ SQUARE GEOMETRIC TILES. Porcelain tiles. Late 19th century. Suitable for bathrooms and stores. 2″ square. Unglazed. White and black. Special order.

▶ VICTORIAN TRANSFER TILES. Ceramic tiles in the Anglo-Japanese style. Assorted patterns suitable for late 19th-century hearth borders. Corner blocks: No. AJ1 (6″ x 6″). Repeating borders: No. AJ2 (6″ x 6″) and No. AJ4 (3″ x 6″). Quadrat motif: No. AJ3 (6″ x 6″). Matte and glazed. Sepia and cream. Special order.

H AND R JOHNSON TILES

Restores, replaces and duplicates geometric cut tiles used for solariums, foyers, halls and public spaces, 1850–1920; available in period colors. Also provides patterned two-color decorative encaustic tiles for use with its geometric tiles, suitable for solariums, foyers, halls and public spaces of the period 1850–1900. Custom made and special order.

L'ESPERANCE TILEWORKS

Duplicates, restores and identifies encaustic, decorative, mosaic, geometric and Victorian fireplace tiles.

▶ DECORATIVE PATTERNS. Floral, geometric and pictorial tiles with border sections and corners. 3″ x 3″, 3″ x 6″, 4″ x 4″ and 6″ x 6″. Custom made and special order.

above left and right
ENCAUSTIC TILES.
Tile flooring. H and R
Johnson Tiles.

right
GEOMETRIC TILES.
Tile flooring. H and R
Johnson Tiles.

GEOMETRIC TILES.
Tile flooring. H and R
Johnson Tiles.

ENCAUSTIC TILES.
Tile flooring. H and R
Johnson Tiles.

above left
FIREPLACE TILES.
Unglazed terra cotta.
L'Esperance Tileworks.

above right
ART TILES. Moravian
Pottery and Tile
Works.

▶ VICTORIAN HEARTH AND FIREPLACE TILES. Glazed ceramic tiles. 1″ x 6″, 1½″ x 1½″, 1½″ x 6″, 2″ x 2″ and corresponding triangular tiles. Period colors to match original tiles. Special order.

MORAVIAN POTTERY AND TILE WORKS

Also provides various patterned borders with high-relief and incised designs.

▶ ART TILES. Handcrafted Arts and Crafts–style tiles based on originals developed by Henry Chapman Mercer before the opening of the Moravian Pottery and Tile Works c. 1915. 1885–1930. Special order.

▶ QUARRY TILES: HEXAGONS. Ceramic tiles. Glazed, unglazed and smoked, unglazed. No. 29 (2¾″); No. 26 (3¼″); No. 540 (4″). Special order.

▶ QUARRY TILES: RECTANGLES. Ceramic tiles. Glazed, unglazed and smoked, unglazed. "Border Bar": No. 545 (1″ x 6″). "Brickpoint": No. 543 (2″ x 3″). "Quarry": No. 542 (2″ x 4″). Special order.

▶ QUARRY TILES: SQUARES. Ceramic tiles. Glazed,

unglazed and smoked unglazed. "Cluny Quarry": No. 185 (2" x 2"). "English Quarry": No. 72 (4" x 4"). "French Quarry": No. 19 (2¾" x 2¾"). "L Quarry": No. 544 (4" notched). Special order.

▶ QUARRY TILES: TRIANGLES. Ceramic tiles. Glazed, unglazed and smoked unglazed. "Cluny Triangle": No. 541 (2"). "English Triangle": No. 175 (4"). "French Triangle": No. 177 (3").

TERRA DESIGNS

Also duplicates and adapts period tiles.

▶ CUSTOM HANDCRAFTED CERAMIC TILES. Ceramic pictorial mosaic inserts for floors or walls. c. 1890–1900. Installed in New York City subway station mosaics. Period colors. Custom made and special order.

ARMSTRONG WORLD INDUSTRIES

Contact local suppliers. No custom work provided.

▶ CAMBRAY LINCOLN PARK. Vinyl adaptation of printed felt paper or floorcloth parquet rug border. Late 19th century. Suitable for residential use, not for heavy traffic areas. 6' and 12' wide, 18" repeat. No. 68401 (oak); No. 68402 (pecan). Stock items.

▶ CONSTANZA IMPERIAL ACOTONE. Vinyl adaptation of printed floorcloths. Late 19th century. Suitable where documentation is not required; for residential use, not for heavy traffic areas. 6', 9' and 12' wide, 9" repeat. Rotogravure structure. No-wax surface. No. 65714 (rust). Stock item.

▶ ROYELLE PAINTED INSET. Vinyl adaptation of

RESILIENT FLOORING

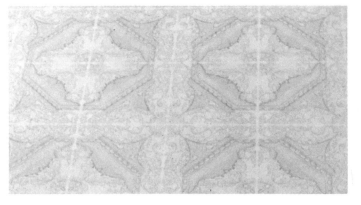

CONSTANZA IMPERIAL ACOTONE. Vinyl adaptation of printed floorcloths. Armstrong World Industries. Rust.

printed floorcloths. Late 19th century. Suitable where documentation is not required; for residential use, not for heavy traffic areas. 6', 9' and 12' wide, 18" repeat. Rotogravure structure. No-wax surface. No. 61230 (almond); No. 61232 (blue); No. 61233 (peach). Stock items.

MANNINGTON MILLS

▶ DECORA DIAMOND. Vinyl adaptation of printed floorcloths. Diamond pattern. Late 19th century. 6' and 12' wide. No. 7229 (brown and cream). Stock item.

▶ DECORA OCTAGON. Vinyl adaptation of printed floorcloths and felt paper. Octagonal pattern. Late 19th to early 20th century. Suitable where documentation is not required. 6' and 12' wide. No. 7135 (green); No. 7139 (brown). Stock items.

MATTING

STARK CARPET CORPORATION

▶ CHINESE SEA GRASS MATTING. Basket-weave pattern of sea grass cords with braided bast fiber warp. Texture, scale and sheen similar to coarse 19th-century straw mattings. 13'2" wide. Natural grass shades of pale gold, pale green and honey brown. Stock item.

ERNEST TREGANOWAN

▶ TATAMI GRASS MATTING. Japanese matting resembling Indian matting. Late 19th to early 20th century. (Coarse Chinese straw mattings, 36"–54", are no longer commercially made.) Period installation requires tacks or narrow U-shaped staples; fabric tape bindings must be removed before wall-to-wall installation, and ends must be turned under. 36" wide. No. 180 (natural greenish grass). Stock item.

RAG, LIST AND HANDMADE RUGS

THE GAZEBO OF NEW YORK

▶ HIT-AND-MISS. Rag rugs. All cotton rag weft; all linen warp. 27½", 36", 48", 54", 72", 94" and 132" wide, any length. Multicolor. Reversible. Stock items; nonstandard widths and colors by special order.

HANDWOVEN

▶ HIT-AND-MISS. Rag rugs and stair runners. All cotton rag weft; strong polyester warp. Sizes to 10' wide, any length. Multicolor; and custom colors. Reversible. Special order.

HERITAGE RUGS

▶ HIT-AND-MISS. Handwoven rag rugs. All wool and all cotton. Sizes to 15' wide seamless, 35' long. Multicolor. Special order.

PEERLESS IMPORTED RUGS

▶ COLONIAL. Hit-and-miss pattern woven rag rugs. All cotton. 2' x 3½', 2½' x 4½', 3½' x 5½', 5½' x 8½' and 8' x 10'. No. 1117 (multicolor). Reversible. Stock items.

RASTETTER WOOLEN MILL

▶ HIT-AND-MISS. Handwoven rag rugs. All cotton or all wool; linen warps available. Sizes including 9' x 12' seamless; other custom sizes seamed together in the traditional manner. Multicolor. Stock items and custom made (e.g., will prepare rugs from cut-and-sewn carpet rags).

STARK CARPET CORPORATION

▶ HIT-AND-MISS. Rag rugs. All cotton. Custom sizes. Multicolor and monochromatic. Special order.

WEAVERS UNLIMITED

▶ HIT-AND-MISS. Rag carpets. All cotton. 2½' x 4', 2½' x 5', 2½' x 6', 3' x 4', 3' x 5', 3' x 6', 63" x 60", 63" x 72" and 63" x 84". Room-size rugs available using handsewn strips 24", 30", 36" or 63" wide. Multicolor or stripes. Special order.
▶ STENCILLED PATTERNS. Pineapples, flowers and custom designs applied to rag carpets above. Custom made and special order.

THOS. K. WOODARD

Variety of traditional rag patterns based on 19th-century striped and patterned handwoven carpeting. Documents in Thos. K. Woodard collection. Cotton rag weft. All patterns available as runners 27" and 36" wide, to 24' long. Rugs 4' and 6' wide, to 25' long. Large sizes, 12' x

PENNSYLVANIA BARS. Rag rug. Thos. K. Woodard. Solid stripes on neutral.

18' and 18' x 24' constructed from narrower widths sewn together in the traditional manner. Seamless 9' x 12' room-size rugs also available. Stock items.
Striped and plaid patterns include:

▶ AMISH. Subtle mix of blue, green, purple, pink and lavender.

▶ ESSEX. Blue, burgundy and tan plaid.

▶ JEFFERSON STRIPES. Blue, green, lavender and beige.

▶ LANCASTER. Multicolor stripe on burgundy or blue check.

▶ PENNSYLVANIA BARS. Solid stripes on a neutral ground.

▶ PENNSYLVANIA STRIPES. Multicolor stripes on a neutral ground.

▶ READING. Natural stripes on a blue ground.

▶ RITTENHOUSE SQUARE. Blue and white check.

▶ ROXBURY. Red, black, tan, blue, green and yellow mix.

▶ SHAKER. Teal, tan and brown plaid.

▶ WAINSCOTT. Blue and tan plaid.

BRAID-AID

▶ DO-IT-YOURSELF. Braided-rug supplies to braid your own rug. Wools, wool strips, cutters and braid folders. Stock items.

COUNTRY BRAID HOUSE

▶ BRAIDED RUGS. Hit-and-miss and planned pattern styles. Traditional materials and handlaced constructions; medium- or heavy-weight braids. All wool. Reversible. Special order.

THE GAZEBO OF NEW YORK

▶ BRAIDED RUGS. Hit-and-miss and banded pattern styles. Traditional oval and round shapes. Braids handlaced together with linen thread. Special order.

PEERLESS IMPORTED RUGS

▶ PATTERN-BRAIDED YARN RUGS. No. 1725 (tan); No. 1825 (brick). Stock items.

PERSNICKETY

▶ BRAIDED RUGS. Patterned hit-and-miss. Adaptation of 19th-century handbraided rugs. Wool-acrylic blend. Oval, 27″ x 84″. Most suitable colors: No. 51685 (rust); No. 51687 (tan); No. 51688 (multicolor). Stock items.

RASTETTER WOOLEN MILL

▶ BRAIDED RUGS. Hit-and-miss and banded pattern braids. Interbraided with flax thread to connect the braids. All wool blanket remnants. Various sizes. Stock items and special order.

SCHUMACHER

▶ OLD COLONY WOOL 'O'. Braided-rug adaptation. Colonial hit-and-miss. Braided yarn wrapped around an inner core. Suitable where documentation is not required. All wool. Stock item and special order.

STARK CARPET CORPORATION

▶ HIT-AND-MISS. Rag weft and cotton warp rugs. All cotton. Various sizes. Special order.

BRAIDED RUGS

STURBRIDGE YANKEE WORKSHOP

▶ BRAIDED STAIR TREADS. Adaptation of handbraided stair treads. Suitable where documentation is not required. Wool-acrylic blend. 8″ x 28″. Most suitable colors: No. 1-15-2368 (brown); No. 1-15-2369 (tan). Available individually or in sets of 13. Stock items.

HOOKED RUGS

THE CRAFTSMAN STUDIO

▶ DO-IT-YOURSELF. Hooked rugs and hearth and door mats. Also available are Joan Moshimer's *Craftsman Hooked Rug Patterns* (including hundreds of patterns for documented and adapted rugs and hearth and door mats), fabrics, dyes and equipment. Stock items.

THE GAZEBO OF NEW YORK

▶ FOLK ART PATTERN HOOKED RUGS. Patterns based on quilt and antique hooked rug patterns. All wool. Custom patterns, sizes and colors.

HEIRLOOM RUGS

▶ DO-IT-YOURSELF. Traditional hooked-rug patterns, materials and equipment. Stock items.

PEERLESS IMPORTED RUGS

▶ RICHMOND GEOMETRIC BLOCK. Hooked-rug adaptation. Geometric block with alternating floral and star motifs. Mid- to late 19th century. All wool yarn. No.

DECATUR VINE. Needlepoint rug. Schumacher. Navy or cream.

1360 (light-colored ground with multicolor and black). Stock items.

▶ RICHMOND NEW ENGLAND FLORAL. Hooked-rug adaptation. Floral and scroll pattern. Based on typical mid- and late 19th-century and early 20th-century Colonial Revival hearth-rug patterns. Suitable where documentation is not required. All wool yarn. 2' x 4', 3' x 5', 4' x 6', 6' x 9', 8' x 10' and 9' x 12'. No. 1361 (ivory); No. 1362 (blue); No. 1363 (rose). Stock items.

PERSNICKETY

▶ GARDEN HOOKED RUG. Hearth-rug adaptation. Mid-19th century. All wool. 22" x 42". No. 51696 (cream, soft pinks and soft greens). Stock item.

THE RUGGING ROOM

▶ CUSTOM HOOKED RUGS. Traditional and custom patterns hooked to order.

▶ DO-IT-YOURSELF. Hooked-rug patterns and supplies. Stock items.

EVELYN WOOD

▶ TRADITIONAL HOOKED RUGS. Variety of patterns including primitive, animal, Oriental and floral. Wool, cotton or mixed rag strips. Custom dyeing. Custom made and special order.

CASA QUINTAO

Provides stock and custom cross-stitch embroidered rugs in mid-19th-century designs and adaptations.

CRAIGIE STOCKWELL CARPETS

Provides handtufted and handknotted duplications and adaptations of antique needlepoint rugs.

PATTERSON, FLYNN AND MARTIN

Duplicates antique needlepoint rugs.

SCHUMACHER

▶ DECATUR VINE. Handmade Brazilian needlepoint rug. Muticolored floral motif. Design adapted from dinner service at Decatur House, Washington, D.C. All

NEEDLEPOINT AND EMBROIDERED RUGS

wool. 6' x 9', 9' x 12', 10' x 14' and 12' x 18'. Navy or cream ground. Design approved by the National Trust for Historic Preservation. Stock items and special order.

STARK CARPET CORPORATION

Produces custom reproductions of original needlepoint rugs and adapts patterns from period rugs.

U.S. AXMINSTER

▶ FLORAL SQUARES. Axminster adaptation of mid-19th-century needlepoint carpets. 1840–75. All nylon pile. 12' wide, 36" x 36" set-match repeat, 189 pitch/7 rpi. No. PLM-II-43 (black and multicolor). Stock item.

FLATWOVEN CARPETS: INGRAIN AND VENETIAN

FAMILY HEIR-LOOM WEAVERS

▶ DAMASK INGRAIN STAIR RUNNER. Bordered ingrain for stairs and halls. c. 1870. All wool. Special order.

SCALAMANDRE

Also duplicates historic patterns.
▶ VENETIAN STRIPE. Documented warp-face striped carpet. All wool. 36" wide. No. 994621. Made for the Ironmaster's House, Hopewell Village National Historic Site, Elverson, Pa. Special order.

SUNFLOWER STUDIO

▶ VENETIAN. Warp-face striped carpet. 19th century. Based on paintings of the period. 1800–1920. 55% worsted wool, 45% linen. 30" x 22". Custom striped patterns and colors.

THOS. K. WOODARD

▶ THE TALCOTT COLLECTION. Reproduction Venetian rugs and stair runners. Document is Deborah Goldsmith's 1832 portrait of the Talcott family. All cotton. 27" wide, 3' x 5', 9' x 12' and 6' wide, any length. "Abigail Talcott": No. 28-A (green, blue, yellow, tan, rust and black). "Betsey Talcott": No. 28-B (brick red, blue, tan, green and black). "Charles Talcott": No. 28-C (gray, blue, tan, pink and black). Stock items.

BLOOMSBURG CARPET INDUSTRIES

▶ INTERLOCKING LAUREL WREATHS AND FLOWERS. Wilton. 1840–75. All wool. 27″ wide, 51″ x 25½″ drop-match repeat. No. W 586 5C (shades of gray brown and dark brown). Special order.

▶ MOSS. Axminster. Overall moss pattern. 1870s. Similar to period patterns. 80% wool, 20% nylon. 27″ wide, 19″ x 27″ set-match repeat. No. A 180 6 (red, gray and black on tan). Special order.

▶ ORIENTAL RUG. Wilton adaptation of Oriental rug. Geometric pattern. 1875–1900. 80% wool, 20% nylon. 27″ wide, 36″ set-match repeat. No. W 621 3C (red with green, tan, blue, burgundy and brown). Special order.

▶ SACRAMENTO. Documented reproduction. Large-scale pattern reflecting revival of early 19th-century patterns. 1875–85. All wool. 27″ wide, 56″ repeat. No. W 582 4C (red or green with black). Made for the California State Capitol, Sacramento. Restrictions may apply on use of pattern. Special order.

▶ STAR AND DIAMOND. Axminster adaptation of Brussels and ingrain. 1860–75. 80% wool, 20% nylon. 27″ wide, 6″ x 6″ set-match repeat. No. A 56 4 (shades of green and dark gold). Special order.

▶ WILLIAM MORRIS-STYLE FLORAL. Axminster. Art Nouveau stylized floral motif inspired by William Morris. c. 1880–1900. 80% wool, 20% nylon. 27″ wide. No. A 10 8 (reds and shades of brown and tan). Special order.

BRINTONS LIMITED

▶ ART NOUVEAU. Zenith Axminster. Art Nouveau–inspired pattern. c. 1895 to early 1900s. 80% wool, 20% nylon. 27″ wide, 27″ drop-match repeat. No. 5/2539 (red, brown, black and cream). Stock item.

▶ BRONZE IOLANTHE. New Tradition Axminster adaptation. Traditional paisley motif. 1870–80. 80% wool, 20% nylon. 27″ wide, 18″ repeat. No. 8/8896 (dark brown, bronze and tan). Stock item.

▶ FIN DE SIÈCLE. Axminster. Overall small-scale floral pattern inspired by Tiffany glass. Late 19th century. 80% wool, 20% nylon. 27″ wide, 19″ repeat. New Tradition

PILE CARPETS: REPEAT PATTERNS

top
ORIENTAL RUG. Wilton carpet. Bloomsburg Carpet Industries. Red, green, tan, blue, burgundy and brown.

bottom
WILLIAM MORRIS-STYLE FLORAL. Axminster carpet. Bloomsburg Carpet Industries. Reds, brown and tan.

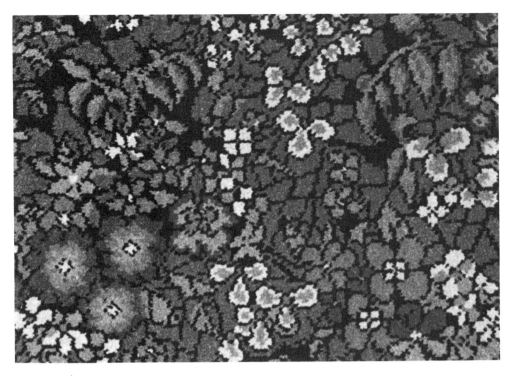

FIN DE SIÈCLE. Axminster carpet. Brintons Limited. Olive, red, gold and rust; blue, cream, olive and black.

MIDNIGHT BLUE BUXTON. Axminster carpet. Brintons Limited. Navy, olive, gold and cream.

SCATTERED FLORAL. Axminster carpet. Brintons Limited. Brick, brown, tobacco, greens and black.

No. 1/8846 (olive, red, gold and rust); No. 3/8846 (blue, cream, olive and black). Stock items.

▶ FLOORCLOTH ADAPTATION. Zenith Contract Axminster adaptation. 1840–75. 80% wool, 20% nylon. 27″ wide, 12″ x 13½″ repeat. No. 3/8705. Special order.

▶ FLORA DORA. Zenith Axminster. 1880–90. Also available in Super Zenith and Zenith Jr. grades. 80% wool, 20% nylon. 27″ wide, 4″ set-match repeat, 7 pitch/ 8 rpi. New Tradition No. 6/8826 (gold); No. 9/8826 (coral). Stock items.

▶ MIDNIGHT BLUE BUXTON. Axminster. Floral and medallion Oriental adaptation. 1880–90. 80% wool, 20% nylon. 27″ wide, 9″ repeat. New Tradition No. 3/8840 (navy, olive, gold and cream). Stock item.

▶ ORIENTAL ADAPTATION. Zenith Contract Axminster adaptation of Oriental pattern. 1850–70. 80% wool, 20% nylon. 27″ wide, 27″ set-match repeat. No. 7/8736 (reds and blues). Stock item.

▶ SCATTERED FLORAL. Zenith Contract Axminster. 1850–75. 80% wool, 20% nylon. 27″ wide, 24″ x 27″ repeat. No. 7/6279 (brick, brown, tobacco, greens and black). Special order.

▶ SCROLL PATTERN. Wilton. c. 1840–75. 80% wool, 20% nylon. 27″ wide, 36″ repeat. No. 0825 (gray taupe on burgundy ground). Special order.

J. R. BURROWS AND COMPANY

▶ ANGLO-JAPANESE. Brussels or Wilton. Irregular frames enclosing stylized floral figures. 1878. Document a point paper in manufacturer's collection. 80% worsted wool, 20% nylon. 27″ wide, 23″ repeat. No. 12/6840 (gray green, yellow gold and black with red and blue). 2/4 border available. Special order.

▶ BANDED PATTERN WITH PALMETTES. Brussels or Wilton adaptation of ingrain. Banded pattern with stylized palmettes and flowers. 1889. Document a point paper in manufacturer's collection. 80% worsted wool, 20% nylon. 27″ wide, 17″ repeat. No. 87/5178 (green, gold, red and burgundy). 2/4 border available. Special order.

▶ FLORAL WITH ROCOCO LEAVES. Brussels or Wilton.

Floral pattern with rococo-style leaves. 1890. Document a point paper in manufacturer's collection. 80% worsted wool, 20% nylon. No. 87/5287 (olive brown, burgundy, green, tan, red and tobacco). 2/4 border available. Special order.

▶ FOLIATE AND FLORAL. Brussels or Wilton. 1876. Document a point paper by M. Barclay in manufacturer's collection. 80% worsted wool, 20% nylon. 27″ wide. No. 39/6792 (olive brown, olive green, black and shades of red orange, pale yellow and gold). 2/4 foliate border available. Special order.

▶ GEOMETRIC. Brussels. Linear geometric pattern of squares and Gothic rosettes. English, late 1860s. Document a point paper by Owen Mayloft in manufacturer's collection. All wool. 27″ wide, 25½″ repeat. No. 87/3382 (dark and light green, red, gold and white). Special order.

▶ HEXAGONS AND SQUARES. Brussels or Wilton adaptation of printed floorcloth. Alternating hexagons and squares with central geometric rosette patterns in alternating colors. English, late 1860s. Document a point paper in manufacturer's collection. 80% wool, 20% nylon. 27″ wide, approximately 12″ drop-match repeat. No. 87/3386 (red, white, green, light blue on light brown and tan). Special order.

ANGLO-JAPANESE. Brussels or Wilton carpet. J. R. Burrows and Company. Gray green, yellow gold, black, red and blue.

▶ IVY LEAVES. Brussels or Wilton. Overall ivy leaf pattern. 1891. Document a point paper in manufacturer's collection. 80% worsted wool, 20% nylon. 27″ wide. No. 21/6645 (shades of brick, maroon, blue gray, sea green, tan and cream). 2/4 border and runner available. Special order.

▶ LILY AND TULIP. Brussels or Wilton. Stylized banded floral motif by William Morris. 1870s. 80% worsted wool, 20% nylon. 27″ wide, 10″ repeat. No. 04/7899 (rose, cream, blue, green and dark blue). Runner available. Special order.

▶ ORIENTAL ADAPTATION. Narrow-gauge Brussels or Wilton. 1876. Document a point paper by R. Campbell in manufacturer's collection. 80% worsted wool, 20% nylon. 27″ wide. No. 21/6796 (red, yellow, tan, black and blue). 2/4 border available. Special order.

▶ PASSION FLOWER WITH LEAVES. Narrow-gauge Brussels or Wilton. English, 1870s. Document a point paper in manufacturer's collection. 80% worsted wool, 20% nylon. 27″ wide. No. 19/6838 (maroon with light olive, yellow gold and cream). Special order.

▶ PEACOCK FEATHER. Brussels or Wilton. Overall large-scale peacock feather pattern with feathers and "eyes" incorporated into the border. English, 1877. Document a point paper in manufacturer's collection. 80% worsted wool, 20% nylon. 27″ wide. No. 87/4153 (shades of gold and peacock blue on black). 2/4 border available. Special order.

▶ RED AND BLACK WITH STARBURST DIAPER. Brussels or Wilton. Figured and starburst diaper ground with geometric pattern borders. English, c. 1870. 80% worsted wool, 20% nylon. 27″ wide, 13″ repeat. No. 11/6888 (red and black with yellow and blue). 4/4 runner available. Special order.

▶ ROSETTES AND QUATREFOIL TRELLIS. Brussels or Wilton. Alternating octagonal rosettes on a ground diapered with a quatrefoil trellis. English, 1829; 1840–75. Document a point paper in manufacturer's collection. 80% worsted wool, 20% nylon pile. 27″ wide, 25″ repeat. No. 87/0644 (red, white, yellow gold, black and pink). Special order.

▶ STRIPES AND DIAMONDS. Brussels or Wilton.

IVY LEAVES. Brussels or Wilton carpet. J. R. Burrows and Company. Brick, maroon, blue gray, sea green, tan and cream.

LILY AND TULIP. Brussels or Wilton carpet. J. R. Burrows and Company. Rose, cream, blue, green and dark blue.

TROPICAL LEAVES AND FLOWERS. Brussels or Wilton carpet. J. R. Burrows and Company. Gray green, bright green, red, orange, blue and yellow.

Interlaced banded pattern with stripes and diamond motifs. English, late 1860s. Document a point paper in manufacturer's collection. 80% worsted wool, 20% nylon. 27" wide, 25½" set-match repeat. No. 87/3385 (gray blue, golds, red, white and tobacco). Special order.

▶ TROPICAL LEAVES AND FLOWERS. Brussels or Wilton. English, 1875. Document a point paper by Benjamin Parks in manufacturer's collection. 80% worsted wool, 20% nylon. 27" wide, 43" drop-match repeat. No. 26/6791 (gray green, bright green, red, orange, blue and yellow accents). ²⁄4 border available. Special order.

CARPETS OF WORTH

▶ KHYBER. Berkeley Axminster adaptation of Persian rug. Classic garden design incorporating prayer niches. Turkish, 1870s–80s. Style found around Kayseri, capital of Cappacdocia, in central Anatolia. 80% wool, 20% nylon. 27" wide, 27" reapeat. No. 9/9016 (tobacco, tan, beige, cream, reds and blues). Special order.

▶ TURKEY STYLE. Olympus Axminster adaptation of Oriental carpet. 1875–1900. 80% wool, 20% nylon. 27" wide. No. 2/6050 (red, dark blue, dark green and olive). Special order.

▶ VICTORIANA. Axminster. Fractured diamond pattern with banding and stylized leaf in center of diamonds. 1875–1900. 80% wool, 20% nylon. 27″ wide. No. 3/6115 (black, tan, apricot, gray brown and rust). Special order.

COLEFAX AND FOWLER

▶ PERSIAN LEAVES. Brussels adaptation. Overall Persian-style pattern popular during the period. 1870–80. 80% wool, 20% nylon. 27″ wide, 29½″ repeat. Maroon, apricot, olive brown, gray blue and medium red. Border available. Special order.

▶ ROSE SPRIG. Brussels adaptation. Sprigs of rose buds and leaves. Late 19th century. Based on documented English examples. 80% wool, 20% nylon. 27″ wide. Off-white, pink, dark rose, olive and brown. Special order.

▶ TATTON PARK. Brussels adaptation. English, 1840–75. Based on English carpets in manufacturer's collection. 80% wool, 20% nylon. 27″ wide, 5″ repeat. Light beige, light and dark gray brown and cream. Special order.

CRAIGIE STOCKWELL CARPETS

Provides custom reproductions. All patterns are reasearched, designed and colored to order and hand-tufted or handknotted by Craigie Stockwell or its associated company, Stockwell Riley Hooley.

K. V. T. (PENNSYLVANIA WOVEN) CARPET MILLS

Custom weaves Brussels and Wilton carpeting from historic documents in limited quantities.

LACEY-CHAMPION CARPETS

Produces custom handtufted carpets and duplications of period patterns.

LANGHORNE CARPET COMPANY

Also duplicates and adapts patterns from historic documents.

▶ FLORAL LATE VICTORIAN. Brussels adaptation. Flo-

above left
FLORAL LATE VICTO-
RIAN. Brussels carpet.
Langhorne Carpet
Company. Rust, old
gold, off-white and tan.

above right
HONOLULU HOUSE.
Wilton carpet.
Langhorne Carpet
Company. Dark green,
rust, gold, yellow and
blue.

ral pattern with clusters of small flowers. 1875–1900. All wool. 27″ wide. No. 4317 (rust, old gold, off-white and tan). Special order.

▶ HONOLULU HOUSE. Wilton reproduction. Squared floral cluster. 1875–85. Document at the Honolulu House, Marshall, Mich. 80% wool, 20% nylon. 27″ wide, 25″ set-match repeat. No. 6025 (dark green with rust, gold, yellow and blue). Border No. 6026. Made for the Honolulu House. Available only through Susan's Interiors. Special order.

MILLIKEN CONTRACT CARPETING

▶ VICTORIAN ROSE. Tufted carpet with printed design. All nylon pile. 12′ wide, 24″ x 36″ set-match repeat. Most suitable color: No. 401 (green). Stock item.

EDWARD MOLINA DESIGNS

▶ LATTICE ROSE. Axminster. Asymmetrical Japonaise-style pattern. 1880s. 80% wool, 20% nylon. 27″ wide, 189 pitch/9 rpi. No. 528/16 (beige, tan, brown gold and shades of brick). Special order.

MELROSE OFFICE. Wilton carpet. Patterson, Flynn and Martin. Yellow, tan, rose, black and off-white.

PATTERSON, FLYNN AND MARTIN

▶ GOTHIC ROSETTE. Brussels adaptation. Interlaced band and Gothic-inspired rosette and band motif. 1860s–70s. Pattern and scale correspond to visual documentation of the period. 80% wool, 20% nylon. 27″ wide, 30″ repeat. No. 1813/7382 (brown, gray, yellow and tan). Border available. Special order.

▶ LEAF AND RIBBON TRELLIS. Brussels adaptation. Diagonal pattern of leaf and ribbon trellis with interspersed roses. 1840–75. Similar to documented patterns of the period. 80% wool, 20% nylon. 27″ wide, 29¼″ repeat. No. 1818/7369 (dark red brown with honey and cream). Special order.

▶ MEDALLION. Brussels. Gothic-cross pattern. English, late 1830s on. Based on patterns found in English country houses. 80% wool, 20% nylon. 27″ wide, 6″ repeat. Dark brick red, dark brown and tan; beige gray, cream and olive. Border available. Special order.

▶ MELROSE OFFICE. Wilton adaptation. Alternating crosses with floral center of stepped blocks. 1870s. Pattern and colors similar to hooked-rug patterns popular at the time. 80% wool, 20% nylon. 27" wide, 18" x 15" set-match repeat. Yellow, tan, rose, black and off-white. Made for Melrose, Natchez, Miss. Special order.

▶ OAK LEAVES. Brussels adaptation of ingrain. Overall pattern of leaves. 80% wool, 20% nylon. 27" wide, 9" x 11" repeat. Light blue, gray, rose tans, shades of brick and cream. Border available. Stock item.

▶ PERSIAN LEAVES. Brussels adaptation. Persian floral and leaf pattern. 80% wool, 20% nylon. 27" wide, 29⅛" repeat. Maroon, medium red, apricot, gray blue and olive brown. Border available. Special order.

▶ ROSE SPRIG. Brussels. Light-colored ground with sprigs of rose buds and leaves. Late 19th century. 80% wool, 20% nylon. 27" wide, 14½" repeat. Pink, dark rose, olive and brown. Special order.

ROSECORE CARPETS

Some available Wilton and Brussels carpets are suitable where documentation is not required. Custom work also is provided, including development of patterns and duplication of carpeting from historic materials in the company's collection.

SAXONY CARPET COMPANY

Also custom duplicates and adapts period patterns.

▶ AUTUMN LEAVES. Brussels. Leaf pattern. 1860s–70s. 80% fine worsted wool, 20% nylon. 27" wide, 11½" repeat. No. 629 A (8 colors). Border available: 18". Special order.

▶ DARBY. Brussels. Modified quatrefoil on diaper-pattern ground. Mid- to late 19th century. 80% wool, 20% nylon. 27" wide, 5¹¹/₁₆" x 5¹¹/₁₆" set-match repeat. Red, blue and gold on dark green. Special order.

▶ LEAVES. Wilton. Overall small leaf pattern. 1870s–80s. All wool or 80% wool, 20% nylon. 27" wide. No. 7631/81072 (beige tan, light brick and gold on cream). Special order.

▶ ZODIAC. Wilton adaptation of floorcloth or ingrain. 1890–1920. 80% wool, 20% nylon. 27" wide, 6½" x 6¾" repeat. No. 45–4/8338 (dark olive green, light olive, brick and cream). Special order.

SCALAMANDRE

Also duplicates historic patterns.

▶ BRIGHTON. Wilton. Large-scale rococo leaf pattern. English, 1840–75. 80% wool, 20% nylon. 27″ wide, 54″ drop-match repeat. 4 custom colors. Installed in the Hamill House dining room, Georgetown, Colo. Special order.

▶ HAMPTON. Brussels or Wilton reproduction. Overall pattern of rococo-inspired stylized leaf and floral motifs. 1875–1900. 80% wool, 20% nylon. 27″ wide, 21″ drop-match repeat. Installed at the Mamie Eisenhower Birthplace, Boone, Iowa, and the Hirshfeld House, Austin, Tex. Special order.

▶ HAMPTON COURT. Brussels reproduction. Interlocking Gothic rosette and trellis pattern. English, mid-19th century. Document in the Victoria and Albert Museum, London. All wool. 27″ wide, 27″ set-match repeat. 5 colors. Special order.

▶ HILL-STEAD DRAWING ROOM. Wilton adaptation of an Oriental rug. Geometric pattern. c. 1870–75. 80% wool, 20% nylon. 27″ wide, 46″ repeat. Rust, brown, brown gold and olive. Made for the Hill-Stead House, Farmington, Conn. Special order.

▶ HILL-STEAD LIBRARY. Wilton. Gothic-inspired overall diamond pattern with rosettes at the crossings and quatrefoil diamond centers. 1890s. 80% wool, 20% nylon. 27″ wide. Made for the Hill-Stead House, Farmington, Conn. Special order.

HILL-STEAD DRAWING ROOM. Wilton carpet. Scalamandre. Rust, brown, brown gold and olive.

THE OAKS. Brussels carpet. Scalamandre. Purple brown, sage green, medium red, beige and medium blue.

▶ THE OAKS. Brussels. Banded pattern of small squares surrounded by stylized leaves and tiny flowers. 1875–1900. Based on a carpet in the Booker T. Washington House dining room, Tuskegee, Ala. 80% wool, 20% nylon. 27″ wide, 19″ repeat. Purple brown, sage green, medium red, beige and medium blue. Special order.

▶ PEEL. Documented Wilton reproduction. Overall rococo leaf motif. English, 1850–75. 80% wool, 20% nylon. 27″ wide, 36″ drop-match repeat. 2 custom colors. Special order.

▶ SOMERSET. Wilton. Diagonal trellis banding with stylized, alternating octagonal rosette motifs in the centers. 1875–1900. 80% wool, 20% nylon. 27″ wide, 27″ set-match repeat. 5 colors. Installed at the Hamill House, Georgetown, Colo. Special order.

▶ TURNER. Wilton. Overall leaf pattern with interspersed florals. English, 1860–80. 80% wool, 20% nylon. 27″ wide. Custom colors. Installed at the Mamie Eisenhower Birthplace, Boone, Iowa. Special order.

▶ WILLIAM MORRIS FLORAL. Wilton. Overall stylized lily, tulip and leaf pattern in the banded style typical of

William Morris. 1880–1910. All wool. 27″ wide, 11″ repeat. Dark blue, lavender, cream, olive green and lavender rose. Special order.

STARK CARPET CORPORATION

Duplicates and adapts carpets from historic documents in custom colors.

CHARLES R. STOCK/V'SOSKE

▶ CHIRVAN PANEL. Axminster. Pattern typical of Near Eastern rugs copied domestically. 1875–1920s. Usually installed wall to wall without borders or as an unbordered rug. All wool. 36″ (cut from 12′ goods) and 12′ wide. No. 106/80210 (red); No. 377/80210 (green). Stock items.

▶ ROYAL TURKEY RED. Axminster. Stylized geometric Oriental pattern. Late 19th to early 20th century. Usually installed wall to wall without borders or as an unbordered rug. All wool pile. 36″ (cut from 12′ goods) and 12′ wide. No. 18/80217 (red ground). Stock item.

TOMKINSONS CARPETS

▶ ANJOU ROSE. Contract Axminster adaptation. Persian flower garden pattern. 1875–1900. 80% wool, 20% nylon. 36″ and 12′ wide. No. 19/2065. Special order.

▶ PERSIAN FLORAL. Contract Axminster. Small patterned Persian floral design. 1875–1930. Similar to domestic reproductions of late 19th-century Oriental carpets. Usually installed wall to wall without borders. 80% wool, 20% nylon. 36″ and 12′ wide. No. 20/677 (red ground). Special order.

U.S. AXMINSTER

▶ DIAMOND DRIVE. New Directions Contract Axminster. Small-figured motif in a subtle diamond pattern. 1875–1900. 80% wool, 20% nylon. 12′ wide, 4⅔″ x 6″ set-match repeat, 189 pitch/9 rpi. No. NWD-09 (blues, corals and maroon). Stock item.

▶ 18TH-CENTURY GARDEN. Palladium II Contract Axminster. Floral pattern. 1840–1900; early 20th century. All nylon. 12′ wide, 36″ x 18″ drop-match repeat, 189 pitch/7 rpi. No. PLM-II-54 (green and multicolor). Stock item.

▶ MOROCCAN RED. Palladium II Contract Axminster adaptation of Oriental rug. Geometric pattern. 1875–1900. All nylon pile. 12' wide, 36" x 18" drop-match repeat, 189 pitch/7 rpi. No. PLM-II-53 (beiges, blues and red). Stock item.

▶ ORIENTAL CLASSIQUE. Palladium II Contract Axminster. Oriental-style overall pattern. 1875–1900. All nylon. 12' wide, 36" x 36" set-match repeat, 189 pitch/7 rpi. No. PLM-II-40 (rusts, beiges, blues and dark brown). Stock item.

▶ ORNAMENTAL WILTON. Contract Axminster adaptation of ingrain. 1880s–90s. All nylon or 80% wool, 20% nylon. 12' wide, 9¾" x 18" set-match repeat, 189 pitch/8, 9 or 10 rpi. No. 21 (3-color pattern; 500 colors available, including light and dark maroon with cranberry and red, maroon and red orange). Design Inspiration Collection. Stock item.

▶ PLANTATION. Axminster. Diamond pattern with flowers and meander. 1870s. All nylon or 80% wool, 20% nylon. 12' wide, 9" x 9" set-match repeat, 189 pitch/8, 9 or 10 rpi. No. 63 (6-color pattern; 150 colors available, including rust, salmon, teal blue and lavender browns). Design Inspiration Collection. Stock item.

ORIENTAL RUGS

COURISTAN

▶ ALL-OVER KERMAN. Wilton adaptation. Overall small floral and medallion pattern, with borders. 1875–

ALL-OVER KERMAN. Wilton carpet. Couristan. Regal red, blues and ivory; ivory, reds and blues.

1920. All worsted wool. 27″ x 60″ to 11′6″ x 18′. Handknotted fringed ends. Roll runners: 27″ wide, any length. Finished runners: 2′3″ x 9′6″ and 2′3″ x 12′6″. Knotted fringed ends. No. 7205/427 (regal red with blues and ivory); No. 7205/428 (ivory with reds and blues). Stock items.

▶ BOKHARA. Wilton adaptation. Quartered oval octagons over entire field, with borders. 1875–1920. All worsted wool. 27″ x 60″ to 9′10″ x 14′4″. Handknotted fringed ends. Roll runners: 27″ wide, any length. Finished runners: 2′3″ x 12′6″. Handknotted ends. No. 7208/795 (Persian red, dark red and ivory). Stock items.

KARASTAN BIGELOW

▶ ANTIQUE BOKHARA. Wilton. Turkoman design with rows of small octagons. All worsted wool. No. 734 (brick red with dark blue, cream and brick). Stock item.

▶ FERAGHAN. Wilton reproduction. Classic Herati pattern. All worsted wool. Document at Penshurst Place, Kent, England. No. 0570-0528 (dark blue, medium blue, red and light yellow). Stately Homes Collection. Stock item.

▶ FERAGHAN FLORAL. Wilton reproduction. Rows of stylized flowers centered on a dark ground, with a geometric and floral border. Document at Knebworth House, Hertfordshire, England. All worsted wool. No. 0570-0531 (cream, reds, light and dark blue and light

FERAGHAN FLORAL. Wilton carpet. Karastan Bigelow. Cream, reds, light and dark blue and light green.

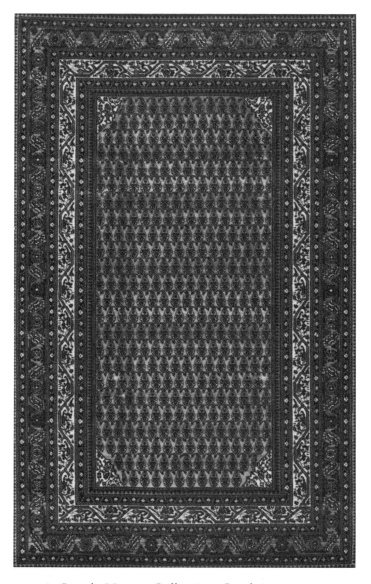

MIR SERABEND.
Wilton carpet. Kara-
stan Bigelow. Red,
cream, light red and
blue.

green). Stately Homes Collection. Stock item.

▶ MIR SERABEND. Wilton reproduction. Overall design of alternating rows of leaf designs with multiple geometric-pattern borders. Document at Chatsworth, Derbyshire, England. All worsted wool. No. 0570-0529 (red with cream, light red and shades of blue). Stately Homes Collection. Stock item.

KARASTAN BIGELOW
COLONIAL WILLIAMSBURG REPRODUCTIONS

▶ CARTER'S GROVE RUG. Adaptation of a Feraghan rug. Overall Herati pattern. Document from the entrance hall of Carter's Grove, James City County, Va. Skein-dyed wool pile. Williamsburg No. 133389 (4'3" x 5'9"); No. 133397 (5'8" x 8'11"); No. 133405 (8'3" x 11'7"). Karastan No. 554. Stock items (small sizes) and special order (largest size).

▶ CHURCH MEDALLION RUG. Version of "Turkish Church Rug" with cream background. Based on a 17th- or 18th-century Transylvanian prayer rug. All worsted wool pile. Williamsburg No. 133355 (3'10" x 5'3"); No. 133363 (5'7" x 8'8"); No. 133371 (8'2" x 11'9"). Karastan No. 555. Cream, dark blue, tobacco and red. Stock items (small sizes) and special order (largest size).

▶ TRANSYLVANIA CHURCH RUG. Adaptation of an antique "Turkey" carpet. Document at the Governor's Palace, Colonial Williamsburg, Va. All worsted wool. Williamsburg No. 10272 (5'2" x 4'1"). Karastan No. 550. Beige, red orange, gold and olive greens. Stock item.

▶ TURKISH BIRD RUG. Adaptation of a 17th-century antique. All worsted wool. Williamsburg No. 10629 (3'10" x 5'6"). Karastan No. 551. Red, light and dark blue, cream and tobacco. Stock item.

▶ TURKISH CHURCH RUG. Adaptation of a handknotted Transylvanian prayer rug. Balkans, 17th or 18th century. All worsted wool. Williamsburg No. 10777 (3'10" x 5'3"); No. 10801 (5'7" x 8'8"); No. 10272 (8'2" x 11'9"). Karastan No. 553. Red, blue, tan and cream. Stock items (smaller sizes) and special order (largest size).

▶ USHAK RUG. Adaptation of an antique rug. Document at the Brush-Everard House, Colonial Williamsburg, Va. All worsted wool. Williamsburg No. 10678 (4'3" x 5'9"); No. 10744 (5'8" x 8'11"); No. 10710 (8'3" x 11'7"). Karastan No. 552. Red orange with gold and patterned blue border. Stock items (small sizes) and special order (largest size).

1900 TO 1930:
THE MODERN INTERIOR

The stock market crash of October 1929 heralded the start of a worldwide economic depression whose political undercurrents would inexorably lead to World War II. In the seemingly halcyon decades preceding those events, America, barely touched by the horrors of World War I, reveled in the successes of its industrial economy. The outpouring of goods and services for the American home was one manifestation. The efficient and bright light of the tungsten-filament bulb developed in 1909 was rapidly adopted in urban houses throughout the country; rural residents would have to wait until 1935. Other inventions dependent on electricity, including the vacuum cleaner, quickly followed. According to the catalog of the R. Armstrong Manufacturing Company of Cincinnati, the vacuum cleaner abolished the "toil, dust and confusion of sweeping day [and] spring and fall house cleaning." Hailing its product as the "new servant in the home, one that you don't have to *pay,* one that you don't have to *feed,*" the company indirectly noted the increasing lack of hired help in American houses.

The floor plans of new houses differed from those of their predecessors. The quintessential Victorian house had been highly compartmentalized, with spaces created to serve special functions such as the entry hall, parlor, sitting room, library, possibly even a lady's boudoir and a man's smoking room. The modern house compressed these activities into fewer rooms and adopted a more open plan. In the ubiquitous bungalow, for example, the front door might open directly into the living room, which served as parlor, sitting room and occasionally library.

INTERLOCKING GEO-METRIC. Axminster carpet. Brintons Limited.

The dining room opened directly off the living room, sometimes divided by doors with glass panels, but often only a simple archway separated the spaces. Even houses whose exteriors appeared traditional, such as those in the Colonial Revival style, contained open plans that tested the householder's decorating ingenuity.

WOOD FLOORS. When rooms flowed together, the floors had to be treated in a uniform manner. One solution was hardwood flooring, such as oak, chestnut, maple or birch, laid in uniform, narrow boards tongue-and-grooved together. In a nod to the Colonial Revival, some wood floors were composed of wider boards laid with what appeared to be wood pegs, occasionally in a contrasting wood. As explained in the first chapter, this type of floor had no historical basis but apparently arose from a misinterpretation of the colonial "doweled" floor. (Floors of this type are still manufactured but they are suitable only for Colonial Revival interiors, not for other early 20th-century buildings.) A still more expensive solution was parquet in simple patterns such as herringbone. The ornate borders favored by Victorian critics and homeowners were not recommended for modern houses.

The preferred treatment for these hardwood floors was stain followed by varnish and wax. Contemporary critics suggested that the floor should always be the darkest element in the room to create a foundation for the rest of the decoration. "A light yellow taffy-colored floor violates this principle," warned Ross Crane in *Interior Decoration* (1928). He explained, "The raw wood of a natural oak finished floor is out of key with dark toned, richly colored rugs and contrasts disagreeably with the mellow tones of walnut and mahogany furniture."

PAINTED FLOORS. Not all floors were hardwood, of course. To economize, softwood floors were often laid in less public rooms, such as bedrooms or kitchens, or throughout the rooms of modest houses built in the early 20th century. Although softwood floors were occasionally treated with stain and varnish, paint was a popular finish. Often it was applied only around the perimeter of the room, with a rug placed in the center. The 1900 trade catalog of Heath and Milligan Manufacturing Company of Chicago, paint producers, assured readers, "No room can be made more artistic at less expense than to paint the floor border of one color and the baseboards of the same fundamental color in another shade [which should] match the draperies and rug . . . ." Critics reminded householders that a darker color on the floor would give a sense of stability to the room.

LINOLEUM FLOORS. Linoleum, floorcloths and tiles also were used as floor coverings. Linoleum was sold in printed or inlaid patterns. The former was produced using large wooden blocks, much like oilcloth. Inlaid linoleum, also called "mosaic," was produced by two methods. One involved cutting pieces of plain-colored linoleum into various shapes, arranging them on a burlap ground and then bonding them together under the pressure of a heavy, heated plate. A second method employed granules of linoleum that were stencilled in patterns onto burlap and then set by heat. Inlaid linoleum was about twice the price of the printed variety, and its patterns were less varied; however, it was far more durable because the colors permeated the material and the design was lost only when the entire surface had worn away. Consequently, critics such as William A. Vollmer praised "linoleum of a good inlaid pattern [that], while more expensive than oilcloth, proves the best and most economical length of service."

Design critics also recommended small geometric or simple mosaic patterns for printed linoleum and generally condemned patterns imitating the large, scrolling, naturalistic designs found in carpet patterns. Ross Crane suggested marble or tile patterns for linoleum in sun rooms, breakfast rooms, living rooms, halls and vestibules; plain colors or muted two-toned designs for living rooms, dining rooms and libraries; and "quaint small figured designs in a variety of colors" for bedrooms. In addition to these spaces, linoleum was favored for bathrooms, kitchens, pantries, maids' rooms and nurseries.

MATTING. Grass matting declined in popularity during the early decades of the 20th century. One of the reasons may have been price. According to the 1906 catalog of H. Pray and Sons of Boston, a six-by-nine-foot "wire grass rug" cost more than a printed linoleum carpet of the same size and was less durable. Furthermore, modern houses with handsome hardwood floors had no need for matting,

209

and electrical devices, such as fans and vacuum cleaners, eliminated the seasonal changes that had previously dictated its use. Matting, however, was used on porches and in solariums. New forms included printed Japanese grass matting.

TILE FLOORS. Tiles remained popular. In bathrooms, critics recommended small, white, unglazed tiles in round, octagonal or hexagonal shapes for floors and larger, white, rectangular, glazed tiles for bathroom walls. By the 1920s homeowners could also chose square tiles in a variety of colors for use in bathrooms and on kitchen walls.

Quarry tile, brick, bluestone and slate were recommended for entrance halls, small studies, libraries, dining rooms and even living rooms depending on the architectural style of the house and its construction. These floors were heavy and best laid on a slab or over reinforced joists. (Bathroom floors were small enough not to require such underpinning.) Tile floors were more expensive than wood, although they required little upkeep or renewal.

AREA RUGS. Area rugs were used atop hardwood, tile and stone floors. Critics praised "the prevalent taste for bare floors," citing health, beauty and economy. Theodore M. Dillaway wrote in *Decoration of the School and Home* (1914), "The day of tacked-down carpets has about gone by, except in old houses when the condition of the floors will not permit them to be exposed. Even when carpeting is bought by the yard it is now usually made up into rug form with a border." Critics also derided the late 19th-century fashion of strewing several small rugs "artistically" about a room and insisted they be laid straight, so their borders were parallel with the walls. "Rugs scattered about at assorted angles," warned Harold D. Eberlein in *Book of Decoration* (1931), "are just as indefensible as pieces of furniture stuck across corners or tipped about irresponsibly, as though the whole room were just about to be turned out for a thorough cleaning."

The style of the house and its furnishings determined the choice of carpet. A bungalow finished in the Craftsman style would look well with Navajo rugs or blankets, which no less an authority than Candace Wheeler (once part of Tiffany's Associated Artists) praised for their thickness, durability, softness and excellence of color and design. Vollmer even illustrated a California bungalow furnished with 18th-century pieces—"old heirlooms of furniture from the Eastern ancestors of the family"—in which "the Navajo rugs seem to add a tone of vigor that is not found in the rag rugs generally used in this connection." Through its railroad facilities, the Fred Harvey Company did much to popularize the taste for Southwest Indian crafts during the first decades of the 20th century. Patterns included stripes and geometrics in red, cream, brown, black and dark blue.

RAG RUGS. Design authorities described two types of rag rugs—woven and braided—and recommended them for bedrooms, bathrooms, children's rooms or, in hot climates, throughout the house. Woven rag rugs were square or rectangular. Traditionally the weft of rag rugs was strips of old cloth that formed random patterns in the carpets. By the 20th century Wheeler noted an improvement, which was to use "*new* rags, carefully selected as to colour both of rags and warp." She pronounced these rugs "surprisingly good [and] very durable." The traditional random patterns lost favor; the newer types favored a few colors and were woven in stripes or even patterns. Critics advised braided rag rugs for interiors furnished in the colonial style. In *The New Interior* (1916), Hazel H. Adler explained, "Braided rugs are made from strips of rag dyed the required colors, braided and sewn together row after row." These carpets were usually oval or circular. Adler noted, "The center area is usually in a solid color which is worked out into deeper shades of the same and of black." Both woven and braided rag rugs came in a variety of sizes, from mats and area rugs to room size.

HOOKED RUGS. "Pulled" or hooked rugs, popular in the mid-19th century, enjoyed a revival because they were associated with colonial interiors. Most writers credited New England with producing the best. Wheeler thought the early rugs, made by drawing finely cut rags through a layer of strong, loosely woven cloth like burlap, were durable but ugly. She and other critics praised the modern products made with carefully dyed cloth or wool yarn. Wheeler particularly liked designs imitating Oriental carpets. Most critics derided the "baskets of flowers which were so popular in the old rugs of this class." Hooked chair seats were also popular in Colonial Revival interiors.

INGRAIN CARPETS. Ingrain carpeting began its slide into obscurity during the first decades of the 20th century. Looms continued to produce it in 36-inch widths, and companies introduced large, seamless ingrain rugs known as art squares that cost between $2 and $5. However, by 1919, R. S. Brinton noted in *Carpets* that ingrain production, once widespread in Scotland, England and America, was "more or less obsolete at the present time, having given way before other types." Eberlein described ingrain as "old-fashioned" in 1931 but still praised its range of colors and patterns, its durability and—during the Depression—its cheap price. Patterns included rococo designs of leaves and flowers in the muted shades of the late 19th century. (Few suitable reproductions, adaptations or alternatives are currently manufactured for this period.)

AXMINSTER CARPETS. The best rug remained the handknotted Oriental, which was suited to both Craftsman and Colonial Revival interiors. These carpets were expensive; however, critics had other suggestions for households with modest budgets. One was machine-made Axminsters woven on chenille, spool and gripper looms. Brinton attributed their popularity to "the taste of carpet users all over the world [which] has tended in recent times more and more in the direction of seamless carpets." Chenille Axminsters, in particular, challenged Brussels, Wilton, tapestry and even woven Axminsters because they were seamless, could use nearly a limitless number of colors in their designs and, with a luxurious appearance using a minimum of wool, were relatively inexpensive. Many of the patterns imitated handknotted Chinese carpets. Their designs were copied in Axminster as well as Wilton construction, and sometimes were sculpted. Blue, green or multicolored Chinese symbols appeared on solid cream, blue, gold and other grounds.

TAPESTRY CARPETS. Tapestry carpets did not fare so well. Critics continued to condemn their floral patterns and realistic shading, and middle-class homeowners began to heed their advice. Increasingly, tapestry carpets and their often garishly colored patterns were relegated to mail-order sales, where their cheap price was a major factor in their favor. The Depression particularly affected farmers and the working class—the major purchasers of tapestry carpets—and did what the critics' complaints could not: tapestry carpets generally ceased to be woven in the 1930s.

BRUSSELS AND WILTON CARPETS. Design authorities favored rugs or carpets in overall figured designs that had more the effect of texture than pattern. Wilton and Brussels looms, with their limitations on color, were particularly suited for weaving patterns employing only two or three colors or shades of a single color, which the critics praised. Some companies used these looms to weave carpets in a "moresque" effect, achieved by twisting two or three colors of thread together to form a multicolored yarn for the face pile.

However, by the 1920s Brussels carpeting rapidly lost whatever small percentage it had held of the market. Fashion favored cut-pile over level-loop carpets, and consumers followed the lead. Price was another factor. For homeowners with modest budgets, tapestry carpets cost less than Brussels, while those who could afford Brussels often preferred Axminsters, which cost about the same and offered more designs and a more luxurious appearance. By 1930 Brussels looms ceased production.

Wiltons, however, were able to make the transition when critics began to praise single-colored carpets or rugs of a single color bordered with a darker shade of the same color. By 1928 the Bigelow Hartford Carpet Company had perfected a Wilton loom 18 feet wide, which helped avoid seeming. These low-cut pile carpets were sold as velvets and met with some early reluctance from both consumers and other manufacturers. Consumers objected to the fact that single-colored velvet carpets showed footprints, while manufacturers found them both exacting to produce and lacking in artistic challenge. They were installed first as rugs, later wall to wall. The soft or muted colors included beige, gray, greens, maroon and other shades, all enhanced by subtle color shifts when the pile was brushed or stepped on. Despite the early objections, plain-colored rugs and carpeting won gradual acceptance in American homes and remain popular choices today. Patterned carpets were increasingly relegated to commercial interiors such as hotels, restaurants and—the newest form of entertainment—movie theaters.

WOOD FLOORING

AGED WOODS

▶ ANTIQUE CYPRESS. Flooring planks. ½", ⅝" and ¾" thick, 2"–11" wide, 2'–12' random lengths. Special order.

▶ ANTIQUE DISTRESSED AMERICAN CHESTNUT. Flooring planks. ⅝" thick, 3"–7" wide; ¾" thick, 3"–10" wide; 1" thick, 3"–10" wide; 2'–12' random lengths. Special order.

▶ ANTIQUE DISTRESSED OAK. Flooring planks. ⅝" and ¾" thick, 3"–10" wide; 6/4" thick, 3"–12" wide; 2'–12' random lengths. Special order.

▶ ANTIQUE FIR. Flooring planks. ⅝" thick, 3"–12" wide; ¾" and 6/5" thick, 3"–15" wide; 2'–12' random lengths. Special order.

▶ ANTIQUE MILLED AMERICAN CHESTNUT. Flooring planks. ⅝", ¾" and 6/5" thick, 3"–7" wide; 2'–12' random lengths. Special order.

▶ ANTIQUE MILLED OAK. Flooring planks. ⅝" and ¾" thick, 3"–10" wide; 6/4" thick, 3"–12" wide; 2'–12' random lengths. Special order.

▶ ANTIQUE POPLAR. Flooring planks. ⅝" thick, 3"–12" wide; ¾" thick, 3"–15" wide; 6/4" thick, 3"–15" wide; 2'–12' random lengths. Special order.

▶ ANTIQUE WHITE PINE. Flooring planks. ⅝" thick, 3"–12" wide; ¾" thick, 3"–15" wide; 6/4" thick, 3"–15" wide; 2'–12' random lengths. Special order.

▶ ANTIQUE YELLOW HEART PINE. Flooring planks. ⅝" thick, 3"–12" wide; ¾" thick, 3"–12" wide; 6/4" thick, 3"–12" wide; 2'–12' random lengths. Special order.

CARLISLE RESTORATION LUMBER

▶ SHIPLAP PINE BOARDS. 8"–12" wide, 8"–12' long. Special order.

▶ WIDE OAK BOARDS. 8"–12" wide, 8'–16' long. Special order.

▶ WIDE PINE BOARDS. ⅞″ and 1″ thick, 14″–21″ wide, 8′–16′ long. Special order.

CASTLE BURLINGAME

Booklets on antique flooring selection, installation and finishing available ($5 each postpaid).

▶ ANTIQUE VIRGIN EASTERN WHITE PINE (KINGS PLANKS). Pumpkin pine with pit-sawn markings, double-tongue and double-groove edges. Random widths. Special order.

▶ ANTIQUE VIRGIN SOUTHERN LONGLEAF YELLOW HEART PINE. Georgia pine with natural edges for later shiplap, butt joint or tongue-and-groove finish. ⅞″ thick, random widths to 16″, random lengths. Special order.

HARRIS-TARKETT

▶ CANTERBURY. Solid hardwood flooring. Four equal squares with alternating diagonal center slats. Angelique teak, red oak, white oak and black walnut. Unfinished surface; paper faced. 5/16″ thick, 13¼″ square. Stock item.

▶ CHAUCER. Solid hardwood flooring. Four alternating squares on the diagonal framed by pickets. Angelique teak, red oak, white oak and black walnut. Unfinished surface; paper faced. 5/16″ thick, 13⁷/16″ square. Stock item.

▶ HADDON HALL. Solid hardwood flooring. Four equal squares. Angelique teak, red oak, white oak, black walnut and ash. Unfinished surface; paper faced. 5/16″ thick, 14¼″ square. Stock item.

▶ HERRINGBONE. Solid hardwood flooring. Angelique teak, red oak, white oak, black walnut and ash. Unfinished surface; paper faced. 5/16″ thick, 14¼″ wide, 18⅛″ long, 4¾″ slat length; and 5/16″ thick, 16¼″ wide, 18⅛″ long, 5½″ slat length. Stock items.

▶ MONTICELLO. Solid hardwood flooring. Four alternating squares with pickets. Angelique teak, red oak, white oak and black walnut. Unfinished surface; paper faced. 5/16″ thick, 13¼″ square. Stock item.

▶ SAXONY. Solid hardwood flooring. Four squares on the diagonal and eight half squares. Angelique teak, red oak, white oak and black walnut. Unfinished surface;

paper faced. $5/16''$ thick, 19" square. Stock items.

▶ STANDARD. Solid hardwood flooring. Sixteen alternating squares. Angelique teak, red oak, white oak, black walnut, ash and maple. Unfinished surface; paper faced. $5/16''$ thick, 19" square. Stock item.

THE JOINERY COMPANY

▶ ANTIQUE SOUTHERN LONGLEAF YELLOW HEART PINE. Flooring, millwork, cabinetry, furniture and timber frames. Remilled and handcrafted from structures 100–200 years old. Quarter-sawn, edge-grain and original surfaces. Prime grade and antique original grade. $7/16''$ thick, to 20" wide, 16' long. Installed at King's Arms Tavern, Colonial Williamsburg, Va. Special order.

KENTUCKY WOOD FLOORS

Custom parquet borders and floor patterns also duplicated and designed.

▶ CUSTOM BORDER. Parquet. Elaborate interlaced border suitable for parlors. Mixed-species hardwood. Unfinished surface. $5/16''$ thick, 12" wide, 22" long. Special order.

▶ FEATURE STRIP. Parquet border. Light and dark banded strip used as a decorative border in rooms and halls. Plain oak, quartered oak, ash, walnut and cherry. $3/4''$ thick, random widths and lengths. Stock item.

▶ HERRINGBONE I. Parquet flooring. Red oak, tropical walnut and cherry. Unfinished surface; paper faced. $5/16''$ thick, 14" wide, 17" long. Packaged 25 square feet per carton. Stock item.

▶ HERRINGBONE II. Parquet flooring. Plain oak, quarterd oak, ash, walnut and cherry. Unfinished surface. $3/4''$ thick, $2 1/4''$ wide, $6 3/4''$–18" long. Individual pieces bundled as ordered. Stock item.

▶ SIMPLICITY. Parquet flooring. Four-strip alternating vertical-horizontal pattern. Red oak, tropical walnut and cherry. Prefinished surface. $5/16''$ thick, 9" square. Stock item.

▶ STRIP. Parquet flooring. Plain oak, quartered oak and maple. Unfinished surface; square edge. $3/4''$ thick, $2 1/2''$ wide, random lengths. Stock item.

ANTIQUE SOUTHERN LONGLEAF YELLOW HEART PINE. Wood flooring. Mountain Lumber Company.

MOUNTAIN LUMBER COMPANY

▶ ANTIQUE SOUTHERN LONGLEAF YELLOW HEART PINE. Flooring, period moldings, paneling and trim. Milled from timbers taken from pre-1900 structures; graded and kiln dried. Tongue-and-groove planks. 3"–6" and 6"–10" random widths and lengths. Prime grade free of most knots and imperfections; cabin grade with knots, nail holes and some hairline cracks. Installed at Monticello, Charlottesville, Va. Stock items.

JANOS P. SPITZER FLOORING COMPANY

Parquet floor borders in mixed-species hardwoods available both as stock items and custom made.

VINTAGE LUMBER AND CONSTRUCTION COMPANY

▶ NEW OAK, WALNUT, CHERRY, MAPLE, POPLAR AND WHITE PINE. Random-width wide flooring. 3/4" thick, 3"–8" wide, random lengths. Stock items.
▶ SOUTHERN LONGLEAF YELLOW HEART PINE. Random-width flooring. Remilled; kiln dried. Tongue-and-groove planks. 3"–10" wide, random lengths. Stock items.

▶ YELLOW AND WHITE PINE, CHESTNUT AND ANTIQUE OAK. Wide, random-width flooring. Tongue-and-groove planks. 4″–10″ wide. Stock items.

BRICK FLOORING

VICTOR CUSHWA AND SONS

▶ CALVERT COLONIAL PAVING BRICK. New brick. Suitable for Colonial Revival brick floors and hearth treatments. Formed in sand-coated wooden molds using Maryland shale clay. 4″ x 2¾″ x 8½″. No. 30-200 (rose, full range); No. 103-200 (medium red, full range). Installed at National Park Service sites. Stock items.

TILE FLOORING

AMERICAN OLEAN TILE COMPANY

▶ 1″ HEX. Porcelain ceramic hexagonal mosaic tiles. 1880s–1930s. Used for bathrooms, foyers, stores and restaurants. ¼″ thick, 1″ wide. Overall patterns and bordered designs prearranged on 1′ x 2′ sheets for installation. Unglazed. Black, white and various colors. Stock items.

▶ 1″ x 1″ SQUARE. Porcelain ceramic tiles. 1880s–1920s. Used for bathrooms, stores, foyers and restaurants. ¼″ thick, 1″ square. Overall patterns and bordered designs prearranged on 1′ x 2′ sheets for installation. Slip-resistant surface. Black, white and various colors. Stock items.

▶ 2″ x 2″ HEX. Porcelain ceramic hexagonal mosaic tiles. 1880s–1920s. Used for bathrooms, stores, foyers and restaurants. ½″ thick, 2″ wide. Overall patterns and bordered designs prearranged on 1′ x 2′ sheets for installation. Black, white and various colors. Stock items.

▶ 2″ x 2″ SQUARE. Porcelain ceramic tiles. 1880s–1920s. Used for bathrooms, stores, foyers and restaurants. ¼″ thick, 2″ square. Overall patterns and bordered designs prearranged on 1′ x 2′ sheets for installation. Slip-resistant surface. Black, white and various colors. Stock items.

DESIGNS IN TILE

Also reproduces and adapts historic patterns; develops encaustic, cut and geometric tile designs; and provides restoration and installation.

▶ EARTHENWARE AND UNGLAZED ENCAUSTIC TILES. Porcelain and ceramic tiles for hearth and fireplace surrounds. Late 19th to early 20th century. Period colors; custom color matching. Custom made and special order.

▶ GLAZED TILES. Square and rectangular tiles for hearth and fireplace surrounds. Various sizes. Period colors. Custom made.

▶ HEXAGONAL GEOMETRIC TILES. Porcelain ceramic tiles. Suitable for bathrooms, kitchens and foyers. 1″ square. Unglazed. Brick, white, black and green. Special order.

▶ PATTERNED MOSAIC BORDERS AND FIELDS. Porcelain ceramic tiles. 1880s to c. 1915. Suitable for baths, restaurants, foyers and other commercial installations. 1″ hexagon, 1″ square, 2″ square. Unglazed. White, black and other colors. Special order.

▶ 2″ x 2″ SQUARE GEOMETRIC TILES. Porcelain tiles. Late 19th century. Suitable for bathrooms and stores. 2″ square. Unglazed. White and black. Special order.

H AND R JOHNSON TILES

Restores, replaces and duplicates geometric cut tiles used for solariums, foyers, halls and public spaces, 1850–1920; available in period colors. Also provides patterned two-color decorative encaustic tiles for use with its geometric tiles, suitable for solariums, foyers, halls and public spaces of the period 1850–1900. Custom made and special order.

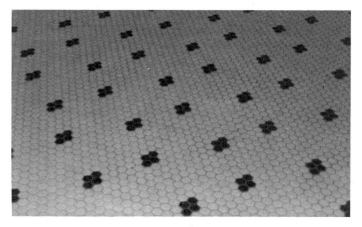

HEXAGONAL GEOMETRIC TILES. Tile flooring. Designs in Tile. Brick, white, black or green.

NOUVEAU. Tile flooring (reproduction at left, original at right). L'Esperance Tileworks. Green.

PATTERNED MOSAIC TILES. Tile flooring. Moravian Pottery and Tile Works.

L'ESPERANCE TILEWORKS

Duplicates, restores and identifies encaustic, decorative, mosaic, geometric and Victorian fireplace tiles.

▶ DECORATIVE PATTERNS. Floral, geometric and pictorial tiles with border sections and corners. 3" x 3", 3" x 6", 4" x 4" and 6" x 6". Custom made and special order.

▶ VICTORIAN HEARTH AND FIREPLACE TILES. Glazed ceramic tiles. 1" x 6", 1½" x 1½", 1½" x 6", 2" x 2" and corresponding triangular tiles. Period colors to match original tiles. Special order.

MORAVIAN POTTERY AND TILE WORKS

Also provides various patterned borders with high-relief and incised designs.

▶ ART TILES. Handcrafted Arts and Crafts–style tiles based on originals developed by Henry Chapman Mercer before the opening of the Moravian Pottery and Tile Works c. 1915. 1885–1930. Special order.

▶ MEDALLIONS. Patterned one-piece glazed tiles. Two or several colors and mosaics. Special order.

▶ PATTERNED MOSAIC TILES. Tile pieces cut and fitted to create pictoral designs. 1906. Documents at the Pennsylvania State Capitol, Harrisburg. Period colors. Custom made and special order.

▶ QUARRY TILES: HEXAGONS. Ceramic tiles. Glazed, unglazed and smoked, unglazed. No. 29 (2¾"); No. 26 (3¼"); No. 540 (4"). Special order.

▶ QUARRY TILES: RECTANGLES. Ceramic tiles.

QUARRY TILES. Unglazed tile flooring. Moravian Pottery and Tile Works.

Glazed, unglazed and smoked, unglazed. "Border Bar": No. 545 (1″ x 6″). "Brickpoint": No. 543 (2″ x 3″). "Quarry": No. 542 (2″ x 4″). Special order.
▶ QUARRY TILES: SQUARES. Ceramic tiles. Glazed, unglazed and smoked, unglazed. "Cluny Quarry": No. 185 (2″ x 2″). "English Quarry": No. 72 (4″ x 4″). "French Quarry": No. 19 (2¾″ x 2¾″). "L Quarry": No. 544 (4″ notched). Special order.
▶ QUARRY TILES: TRIANGLES. Ceramic tiles. Glazed, unglazed and smoked, unglazed. "Cluny Triangle": No. 541 (2″). "English Triangle": No. 175 (4″). "French Triangle": No. 177 (3″).

TERRA DESIGNS

Also duplicates and adapts period tiles.
▶ CUSTOM HANDCRAFTED CERAMIC TILES. Ceramic pictorial mosaic inserts for floors or walls. c. 1890–1900. Installed in New York City subway station mosaics. Period colors. Custom made and special order.

RESILIENT FLOORING

ARMSTRONG WORLD INDUSTRIES

Contact local suppliers. No custom work provided.
▶ CAMBRAY LINCOLN PARK. Vinyl adaptation of printed felt paper or floorcloth parquet rug border. Late 19th century. Suitable for residential use, not for heavy traffic areas. 6′ and 12′ wide, 18″ repeat. No. 68401 (oak); No. 68402 (pecan). Stock items.
▶ COLONIAL CLASSIC RED. Vinyl adaptation similar to the popular linoleum pattern No. 5352. 1932–74. 6′ wide, 18″ repeat. Suitable for light commercial use, not for heavy traffic areas. Mirabond XL no-wax surface; inlaid color structure. No. 89242 (red). Designer Solarian. Stock item.
▶ FEATURE TILES. Vinyl with matching feature strips. After 1920s. Used for bands, borders, inserts and spot accent colors. Suitable for heavy traffic areas; solid colors show more scratches and require more maintenance. ⅛″ thick, 1″ to 24″ long. Black, white, teal, blue gray, pewter, blue, red and orange. Excelon Tile. Stock items.
▶ CONSTANZA IMPERIAL ACOTONE. Vinyl adaptation of printed floorcloths. Late 19th century. Suitable where documentation is not required; for residential use, not

COLONIAL CLASSIC RED. Vinyl adaptation of linoleum. Armstrong World Industries. Red.

for heavy traffic areas. 6', 9' and 12' wide, 9" repeat. Rotogravure structure. No-wax surface. No. 65714 (rust). Stock item.

▶ IMPERIAL MODERN. Vinyl adaptation of granite linoleum patterns. Small-scale, mottled pattern. 1920s–30s. Used as a neutral base for rugs and a covering for all residential rooms. Suitable for heavy traffic areas. ⅛" thick, 12" square. No. 51851 (mellow sand); No. 51855 (medium cork). Stock items.

▶ IMPERIAL TEXTURE. Vinyl adaptation of granite linoleum patterns. Small-scale, mottled pattern. 1920s–30s. Suitable for heavy traffic areas. ⅛" thick, 12" square. No. 51844 (cathedral gold); No. 51847 (nutmeg); No. 51890 (desert tan). Stock items.

▶ ROYELLE PAINTED INSET. Vinyl adaptation of printed floorcloths. Late 19th century. Suitable where documentation is not required; for residential use, not for heavy traffic areas. 6', 9' and 12' wide, 18" repeat. Rotogravure structure. No-wax surface. No. 61230 (almond); No. 61232 (blue); No. 61233 (peach). Stock items.

▶ STANDARD HANDCUT INSETS. Vinyl insets available in many popular trademark, monogram and insignia designs. Black, white, teal, blue gray, pewter, blue, red and orange. Patterns include:
"Alphabet Characters." Modern, block and script letters

and numerals. One character per block. ⅛″ thick, 9″, 12″ and 18″ square. No. 50579 (2-color pattern). Stock item.

"Manhattan." Stemmed-glass pattern. ⅛″ thick, 18″, 27″ and 36″ square. No. 50599. (3-color pattern). Stock item.

"16-Point Compass." ⅛″ thick, 27″, 36″ and 63″ square. No. 50523 (4-color pattern). Stock item.

"Treble Clef." ⅛″ thick, 18″, 27″, 36″ and 63″ square. No. 50594 (3-color pattern). Stock item.

A-2-Z

▶ LINO RUGS. Vinyl and vinyl-composition adaptations of linoleum rugs. Indian blanket and quilt designs. 1920s–30s. Used in place of carpeting. 2½′ x 4′, 3′ x 5′, 4′ x 6′ and 3′ x 8′. Cut and pieced 3-color patterns

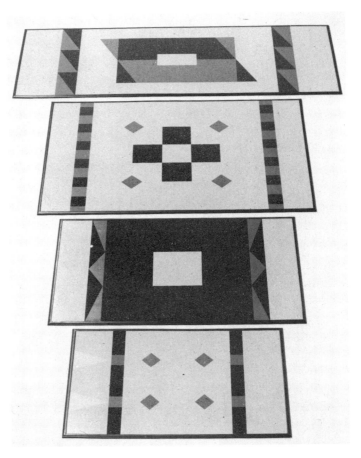

LINO RUGS. Vinyl adaptation of linoleum rugs. A–2–Z. Various colors.

mounted on a rigid panel and edged with vinyl trim strip. "Classic": Red, black and white. "Primary": Red, dark green and orange gold. "Secondary": Black, mottled tan, teal blue, dark green and orange gold. Custom made, special order and stock items.

BANGOR CORK COMPANY

▶ PLAIN BATTLESHIP LINOLEUM. Forbo linoleum. Early 20th century. 2 mm and 3.2 mm thick, 79″ wide. 8 solid colors suitable for period installations. Stock items.

CONGOLEUM CORPORATION

▶ FAIRFIELD TERRA COTTA. Vinyl adaptation of linoleum. Small, variable-size brick tile pattern. After 1932. 9′ and 12′ wide. No-wax finish. No. 8264 (shades of brick red). Stock item.

FAIRFIELD TERRA COTTA. Vinyl adaptation of linoleum. Congoleum Corporation. Brick red.

DLW FLOORING SYSTEMS

▶ JASPÉ. Linoleum reproduction. Striated, marblelike pattern. After 1918. Based on popular period designs. 2.5 mm thick, 6'6" wide. Period colors. Stock items.

▶ MARMORETTE. Documented linoleum reproduction. Marble pattern. After 1918. 2.5 mm thick, 6'6" wide. Most neutral colors suitable for period installations. Stock items.

▶ SUPER MOIRÉ. Linoleum reproduction. Coarse marble pattern. After 1918. 2.5 mm thick, 6'6" wide. Period colors. Stock items.

▶ UNI WALTON. Battleship linoleum. Solid colors through to the burlap base. After 1869. 2 mm, 2.5 mm and 3.2 mm thick, 6'6" wide. No. 37, No. 50, No. 58, No. 88 and No. 96 (neutral colors, including beiges and grays). Stock items.

KENTILE FLOORS

▶ BEAUX ARTS. Vinyl adaptation of linoleum. Tiles and coordinating feature strip. Late 1920s–30s. Tiles: 1/8" thick, 12" square. Feature strips: 1/8" and 3/32" thick, 1" wide, 24" long. No. 512 (regal brown); No. 514 (white); No. 533 (black). Stock items.

▶ KENTILE ASPHALT TILE. Asphalt tile. Striated, marbelized pattern through to bottom of tile. After 1918. Suitable for installation on, above and below grade. 1/8" thick, 9" sqaure. "Grand Antique": No. B-204. "Sarrancolin": No. B-254. "Veined Carnelian": No. C-206. "Greek Skyros": No. C-221. "Genoa Green": No. C-244. "Etruscan": No. C-277. Stock items.

MANNINGTON MILLS

▶ COUNTRY MANOR. Vinyl adaptation of linoleum. Random-size tile design. After 1932. 6', 9' and 12' wide, 18" repeat. No. 3159 (earth tones). Stock item.

▶ DECORA DIAMOND. Vinyl adaptation of printed floorcloths. Diamond pattern. Late 19th century. 6' and 12' wide. No. 7229 (brown and cream). Stock item.

▶ DECORA OCTAGON. Vinyl adaptation of printed floorcloths and felt paper. Octagonal pattern. Late 19th to early 20th century. Suitable where documentation is not required. 6' and 12' wide. No. 7135 (green); No. 7139 (brown). Stock items.

▶ DECORA TERRA COTTA. Vinyl adaptation of linoleum. Small, random-pattern terra cotta tile. After 1932. 6' and 12' wide. Embossed, no-wax surface. No. 7196 (shades of red). Stock item.

▶ PARK SOUTH. Vinyl tiles. Alternating squares of black and white. Suitable where marble or battleship linoleum tiles were used. 9" square. Embossed surface. No. 30061 (black and white). Stock items.

▶ RICHMOND HILL. Vinyl adaptation of printed floorcloths. Late 19th to early 20th century. 6' and 12' wide. No. 3109 (beige, brown and cream). Stock items.

▶ WHEATON HALL. Vinyl adaptation of narrow-width, random-match wood parquet flooring. No. 4157 (golden oak). Stock item.

PED PRODUCTS COMPANY

▶ LINOFLEX. Linoleum. Lightly marbleized pattern with minimal color variation. After 1918. 2.5 mm thick, 12" square. Forbo Nos. 3901 and 3908 (tans); No. 3903 (gray); No. 3905 (pumpkin); No. 3910 (black). Stock items.

▶ MARMOLEUM. Linoleum. Marbleized pattern in distinctly varied colors. After 1918. 2 mm, 2.5 mm and 3.2 mm thick, 79" wide, 32 meters long. Stock colors suitable except Forbo Nos. 3028, 3052 and 3059. Stock items.

TARKETT

▶ ARCHITECTURAL. Vinyl-tile adaptation of linoleum. Granite pattern. After 1918. 1/8" thick, 12" square. Commercial grade. No. 3565 (gray beige); No. 3577 (tan); No. 3581 (dark yellow beige); No. 5241 (gray). Stock items.

ARMSTRONG WORLD INDUSTRIES

MATTING

Contact local suppliers. No custom work provided.

▶ RUSTIC WEAVE WHEAT. Vinyl adaptation of straw matting squares stitched together. Early 20th century. Suitable where the visual effect of matting is required but the traditional covering is inappropriate because of wear or cleanliness; for residential use only, not for heavy traffic areas. 6' and 12' wide, 9" repeat. Rotogravure structure. Mirabond XL no-wax surface. No. 66720 (natural straw shades of gold). Sundial Solarian. Stock items.

IMPORT SPECIALISTS

▶ MAIZE CHECKERBOARD SQUARES. Braided corn husks worked into 2″ squares and stitched together to form mats and rugs. 20th century. 4′ x 6′, 6′ x 9′ and 9′ x 36′. No. CT 120 (pale cream). Stock items.

▶ MAIZE SQUARES. Braided corn husks worked into 12″ squares and stitched together to form mats and rugs. 20th century. 4′ x 6′, 6′ x 9′ and 9′ x 36′. No. CT 160 (pale cream). Stock items.

▶ RICE STRAW SQUARES. Braided rice straw worked into 12″ squares and stitched together to form mats and rugs. 4′ x 6′, 6′ x 9′ and 9′ x 12′. No. CK 213 (golden straw). Stock items.

▶ SEA GRASS DOORMATS. Braided sea grass worked into rectangles, half-rounds and ovals. 1″ thick. Rectangles: No. CT 201C (14″ x 24″); No. CT 201E (16″ x 27″); No. CT 201G (18″ x 20″); No. CT 201K (22″ x 36″); No. CT 201P (38″ x 60″). Half-rounds: No. CT 205E (16″ x 27″); No. CT 205G (18″ x 30″); No. CT 205K (22″ x 36″). Ovals: No. CT 230E (16″ x 27″). Natural grass shade of greenish gold. Stock items.

▶ SEA GRASS SQUARES. Braided sea grass worked into 12″ squares and stitched together to form mats and rugs. 4′ x 6′, 6′ x 9′ and 9′ x 36′. No. CK 218 (greenish gold). Stock items.

STARK CARPET CORPORATION

▶ CHINESE SEA GRASS MATTING. Basket-weave pattern of sea grass cords with braided bast fiber warp. Texture, scale and sheen similar to coarse 19th-century straw mattings. 13′2″ wide. Natural grass shades of pale gold, pale green and honey brown. Stock item.

ERNEST TREGANOWAN

▶ GRASS MATTING. Extremely fine matting resembling popular Japanese mattings. Late 18th century to 1920s. Cotton warp. 36″ wide, 40-yard rolls. Black fabric tape edges. No. 330 (variegated greenish gold). Stock item.

SEA GRASS DOORMAT: HALF-ROUND. Matting. Import Specialists. Greenish gold.

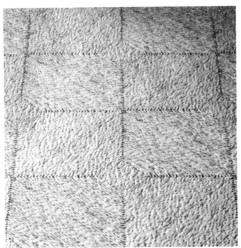

▶ TATAMI GRASS MATTING. Japanese matting resembling Indian matting. Late 19th to early 20th century. (Coarse Chinese straw mattings, 36″–54″, are no longer commercially made.) Printed with Anglo-Japonaise patterns during the early 20th century. Period installation requires tacks or narrow U-shaped staples; fabric tape bindings must be removed before wall-to-wall installation, and ends must be turned under. Fabric bindings in black or other colors are suitable in 20th-century installations where matting is used as a rug. 36″ wide. No. 180 (natural greenish grass). Stock item.

W. A. G. (WAVENY APPLE GROWERS)

▶ DOORMATS. Used as early as 1766 in Virginia. Suitable for Colonial Revival interiors. Half-round, oval and rectangular (see description below). Custom sizes and shapes.

▶ HANDMADE RUSH CARPETS. Nine-ply weave made of nine strands of two or more rushes of even thickness braided in strips 3″ wide and sewn together, forming carpets of various widths and lengths. Ends are bound with a fine rush binding. Suitable for Colonial Revival interiors. Custom sizes and shapes.

above left
RICE STRAW, MAIZE, SEA GRASS and MAIZE CHECKERBOARD SQUARES. Matting. Import Specialists. Gold; pale cream; greenish gold; pale cream.

above right
RUSTIC WEAVE WHEAT. Vinyl adaptation of matting. Armstrong World Industries. Gold.

RAG, LIST AND HANDMADE RUGS

THE GAZEBO OF NEW YORK

▶ HIT-AND-MISS. Rag rugs. Suitable for Colonial Revival interiors. All cotton weft; all linen warp. 27½″, 36″, 48″, 54″, 72″, 94″ and 132″ wide, any length. Multicolor. Reversible. Stock items; nonstandard widths and colors by special order.

HANDWOVEN

▶ HIT-AND-MISS. Rag rugs and stair runners. Suitable for Colonial Revival interiors. All cotton rag weft; strong polyester warp. Sizes to 10′ wide, any length. Custom colors. Multicolor. Reversible. Special order.

HERITAGE RUGS

▶ HIT-AND-MISS. Handwoven rag rugs. Suitable for Colonial Revival interiors. All wool. Sizes to 15′ seamless, 35′ long. Multicolor. Special order.

PEERLESS IMPORTED RUGS

▶ COLONIAL. Hit-and-miss pattern woven rag rugs. Suitable for Colonial Revival interiors. All cotton. 2′ x 3½′, 2½′ x 4½′, 3½′ x 5½′, 5½′ x 8½′ and 8′ x 10′. No. 1117 (multicolor). Reversible. Stock items.

RASTETTER WOOLEN MILL

▶ HIT-AND-MISS. Handwoven rag rugs. Suitable for Colonial Revival interiors. All cotton or all wool; linen warps available. Sizes including 9′ x 12′ seamless; other custom sizes seamed together in the traditional manner. Multicolor. Stock items and custom made (e.g., will prepare rugs from cut-and-sewn carpet rags).

STARK CARPET CORPORATION

▶ HIT-AND-MISS. Rag rugs. Suitable for Colonial Revival interiors. All cotton. Custom sizes. Multicolor and monochromatic. Special order.

WEAVERS UNLIMITED

▶ HIT-AND-MISS. Rag rugs. Suitable for Colonial Revival interiors. All cotton. 2½′ x 4′, 2½′ x 5′, 2½′ x 6′, 3′ x 4′, 3′ x 5′, 3′ x 6′, 63″ x 60″, 63″ x 72″ and 63″ x 84″. Room-size rugs available using handsewn strips 24″,

30", 36" or 63" wide. Multicolor or stripes. Special order.

▶ STENCILLED PATTERNS. Pineapples, flowers and custom designs applied to rag carpets above. Custom made and special order.

THOS. K. WOODARD

Variety of traditional rag patterns based on 19th-century striped and patterned handwoven carpeting. Documents in Thos. K. Woodard collection. Suitable for Colonial Revival interiors. Cotton rag weft. All patterns available as runners 27" and 36" wide, to 24' long. Rugs 4' and 6' wide, to 25' long. Large sizes, 12' x 18' and 18' x 24', constructed from narrower widths sewn together in the traditional manner. Seamless 9' x 12' room-size rugs also available. Stock items.

Striped and plaid patterns include:

▶ AMISH. Subtle mix of blue, green, purple, pink and lavender.

▶ ESSEX. Blue, burgundy and tan plaid.

▶ JEFFERSON STRIPES. Blue, green, lavender and beige.

▶ LANCASTER. Multicolor stripe on burgundy or blue check.

▶ PENNSYLVANIA BARS. Solid stripes on a neutral ground.

▶ PENNSYLVANIA STRIPES. Multicolor stripes on a neutral ground.

▶ READING. Natural stripes on a blue ground.

▶ RITTENHOUSE SQUARE. Blue and white check.

▶ ROXBURY. Red, black, tan, blue, green and yellow.

▶ SHAKER. Teal, tan and brown plaid.

▶ WAINSCOTT. Blue and tan plaid.

BRAID-AID

▶ DO-IT-YOURSELF. Braided-rug supplies to braid your own rug. Wools, wool strips, cutters and braid folders. Stock items.

COUNTRY BRAID HOUSE

▶ BRAIDED RUGS. Hit-and-miss and patterned. All wool. Traditional materials and handlaced construction; medium- or heavy-weight braids. Reversible. Special order.

ESSEX. Rag rug. Thos. K. Woodard. Blue, burgundy and tan.

WAINSCOTT. Rag rug. Thos. K. Woodard. Blue and tan.

BRAIDED RUGS

THE GAZEBO OF NEW YORK

▶ BRAIDED RUGS. Hit-and-miss and banded pattern styles. Traditional oval and round shapes. Braids handlaced together with linen thread. Special order.

PEERLESS IMPORTED RUGS

▶ PATTERN-BRAIDED YARN RUGS. No. 1725 (tan); No. 1825 (brick). Stock items.

PERSNICKETY

▶ BRAIDED RUGS. Patterned hit-and-miss. Adaptation of 19th-century handbraided rugs. Wool-acrylic blend. Oval, 27″ x 84″. Most suitable colors: No. 51685 (rust); No. 51687 (tan); No. 51688 (multicolor). Stock items.

RASTETTER WOOLEN MILL

▶ BRAIDED RUGS. Hit-and-miss and banded pattern braids. Interbraided with flax thread to connect the braids. All wool blanket remnants. Various sizes. Stock items and special order.

SCHUMACHER

▶ OLD COLONY WOOL 'O'. Braided-rug adaptation. Colonial hit-and-miss. Braided yarn wrapped around an inner core. Suitable where documentation is not required. All wool. Stock item and special order.

STARK CARPET CORPORATION

▶ HIT-AND-MISS. Rag weft and cotton warp rugs. All cotton. Various sizes. Special order.

STURBRIDGE YANKEE WORKSHOP

▶ BRAIDED STAIR TREADS. Adaptation of handbraided stair treads. Suitable where documentation is not required. Wool-acrylic blend. 8″ x 28″. Most suitable colors: No. 1-15-2368 (brown): No. 1-15-2369 (tan). Available individually or in sets of 13. Stock items.

HOOKED RUGS

COURISTAN

▶ BLACK COLONIAL FLORAL. Hooked-rug adaptation. Floral wreath and floral border pattern. 1920–30. Based on late 19th-century design. Suitable for Colonial Revival interiors. Pastel colors not suitable where documentation is required. All wool pile. 2' x 3'10", 2'6" x 4'6", 3'6" x 5'6", 5'6" x 8'6", 7'10" x 9'6" and 8'3" x 11'6". No. 30/320 (pastels and black). Jamestown Collection. Stock items.

▶ GEOMETRIC BLOCK. Hooked rug. Alternating blocks of floral clusters and octagonal star. 1920–30. Pattern similar to period hooked-rug and quilt designs. All wool pile. 2' x 3'10", 2'6" x 4'6", 3'6" x 5'6", 5'6" x 8'6", 7'10" x 9'6" and 8'3" x 11'6". Cream and multicolor. Jamestown Collection. Stock items.

GEOMETRIC BLOCK. Hooked rug. Couristan. Cream and multicolor.

BLACK COLONIAL FLORAL. Hooked rug. Couristan. Pastels and black.

THE CRAFTSMAN STUDIO

▶ DO-IT-YOURSELF. Hooked rugs and hearth and door mats. Also available are Joan Moshimer's *Craftsman Hooked Rug Patterns* (including hundreds of patterns for documented and adapted rugs and hearth and door mats), fabrics, dyes and equipment. Stock items.

THE GAZEBO OF NEW YORK

▶ FOLK ART PATTERN HOOKED RUGS. Patterns based on quilt and antique hooked-rug patterns. All wool. Custom patterns and colors.

HEIRLOOM RUGS

▶ DO-IT-YOURSELF. Traditional hooked-rug patterns, materials and equipment. Stock items.

PEERLESS IMPORTED RUGS

▶ RICHMOND GEOMETRIC BLOCK. Hooked-rug adaptation. Geometric block with alternating floral and star motifs. Mid- to late 19th century. All wool yarn. No. 1360 (light-colored ground with multicolor and black). Stock item.
▶ RICHMOND NEW ENGLAND FLORAL. Hooked-rug adaptation. Floral and scroll pattern. Based on typical mid- and late 19th-century and early 20th-century Colonial Revival hearth-rug patterns. Suitable where documentation is not required. All wool yarn. 2' x 4', 3' x 5', 4' x 6', 6' x 9', 8' x 10' and 9' x 12'. No. 1361 (ivory); No. 1362 (blue); No. 1363 (rose). Stock items.

PERSNICKETY

▶ GARDEN HOOKED RUG. Hearth-rug adaptation. Suitable for Colonial Revival interiors. All wool. 22" x 42". No. 51696 (cream, soft pinks and soft greens). Stock item.

THE RUGGING ROOM

▶ CUSTOM HOOKED RUGS. Traditional and custom patterns hooked to order.
▶ DO-IT-YOURSELF. Hooked-rug patterns and supplies. Stock items.

STURBRIDGE YANKEE WORKSHOP

▶ HOOKED RUGS. Adaptations of 19th-century oval and rectangular hooked rugs. 1920s–30s. 22″ x 42″, 30″ x 50″, 42″ x 66″, 5′6″ x 8′6″ and 8′3″ x 11′6″. Oval: Ivory with rose, greens and blues. Rectangular: Black or cream with rose, greens and blues. Stock items.

EVELYN WOOD

▶ TRADITIONAL HOOKED RUGS. Variety of patterns including primitive, animal, Oriental and floral. Wool, cotton or mixed rag strips. Custom dyeing. Custom made and special order.

SCALAMANDRE

Also duplicates historic patterns.
▶ VENETIAN STRIPE. Documented warp-face striped carpet. Suitable for Colonial Revival interiors. All wool. 36″ wide. No. 994621. Made for the Ironmaster's House, Hopewell Village National Historic Site, Elverson, Pa. Special order.

FLATWOVEN
CARPETS:
VENETIAN

SUNFLOWER STUDIO

▶ VENETIAN. Warp-face striped carpet. Based on visual materials of the period. 1800–1920. 55% worsted wool, 45% linen. 30″ x 22.1″. Custom striped patterns and colors.

THOS. K. WOODARD

▶ THE TALCOTT COLLECTION. Reproduction Venetian rugs and stair runners. Document is Deborah Goldsmith's 1832 portrait of the Talcott family. Suitable for Colonial Revival interiors. All cotton. 27″ wide, 3′ x 5′, 9′ x 12′ and 6′ wide, any length. "Abigail Talcott": No. 28-A (green, blue, yellow, tan, rust and black). "Betsey Talcott": No. 28-B (brick red, blue, tan, green and black). "Charles Talcott": No. 28-C (gray, blue, tan, pink and black). Stock items.

BLOOMSBURG CARPET INDUSTRIES

▶ ARROW MOTIF. Wilton reproduction. Stylized arrow motif. 1929. Document a Frank Lloyd Wright pattern used in the Arizona Biltmore Hotel, Phoenix. 80% wool,

PILE CARPETS:
REPEAT
PATTERNS

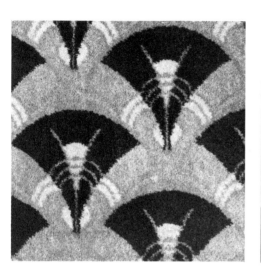

above left
ART DECO SWAG.
Axminster carpet.
Bloomsburg Carpet
Industries. Rose, gray
and maroon.

above right
ART DECO SHELL.
Axminster carpet.
Bloomsburg Carpet
Industries. Red, bur-
gundy and black.

right
HERRINGBONE.
Axminster carpet.
Bloomsburg Carpet
Industries. Grape,
cream and tan.

ART NOUVEAU.
Axminster carpet.
Brintons Limited.

20% nylon. 27″ x 27″ repeat. No. Wx599 (red, lime green and sand). Special order.

▶ ART DECO SHELL. Axminster. Stylized overlapping shell motif. 1920–30. No. A 146 3 (shades of red, burgundy and black). Special order.

▶ ART DECO SWAG. Axminster. Stylized swag and tassel motif. 1920–30. 80% wool, 20% nylon. 27″ wide, 18″ drop-match repeat. No. A 297 5 (rose, gray and maroon). Special order.

▶ HERRINGBONE. Axminster. Interrupted herringbone pattern. c. 1930. 80% wool, 20% nylon. 27″ wide, 24″ drop-match repeat. No. A 788 (grape, cream and tan). Special order.

▶ NAVAJO. Wilton. Overall Arts and Crafts–style geometric adaptation of a Navajo pattern. 1900–30. 80% wool, 20% nylon. 27″ wide. No. W 779 BC (black, white and shades of gray). Special order.

▶ ORIENTAL RUG. Wilton adaptation of an Oriental rug. Geometric pattern. 1875–1900. 80% wool, 20% nylon. 27″ wide, 36″ x 36″ set-match repeat. No. W 621 3C (red with green, tan, blue, burgundy and brown). Special order.

▶ WILLIAM MORRIS–STYLE FLORAL. Axminster. Art Nouveau stylized floral motif inspired by William Morris. c. 1880–1900. 80% wool, 20% nylon. 27″ wide. No. A 10 8 (reds and shades of brown and tan). Special order.

BRINTONS LIMITED

▶ ART NOUVEAU. Zenith Axminster. Art Nouveau–inspired pattern. c. 1895 to early 1900s. 80% wool, 20% nylon. 27″ wide, 27″ drop-match repeat. No. 5/2539. Stock item.

▶ INTERLOCKING GEOMETRIC. Zenith Axminster. Interlocking linear geometric Art Deco pattern. Late 1930s. Also available in Super Zenith and Zenith Jr. grades. 80% wool, 20% nylon. 27″ wide, 13½″ set-match repeat, 189 pitch/9 rpi. No. 5/8387. Stock item.

▶ ORIENTAL ADAPTATION. Zenith Contract Axminster adaptation of an Oriental pattern. Late 19th century. 80% wool, 20% nylon. 27″ wide, 27″ set-match repeat. No. 7/8736 (reds and blues). Stock items.

J. R. BURROWS AND COMPANY

Provides by special order reproductions of documented 20th-century Wiltons and Brussels from its collection of point papers. Patterns, color selection and loom preparation by special arrangement only.

CARPETS OF WORTH

▶ FANTASIA. Axminster. Art Deco–inspired diamond pattern with stylized fan motif. 1920s–30s. 80% wool, 20% nylon. 27″ wide, 9″ x 9″ drop-match repeat. No. 3/6039 (green, gray blue, cream and red). Stock item.

▶ POPPY. Axminster. Art Nouveau–type poppy pattern in the style of William Morris. c. 1900. 80% wool, 20% nylon. 27″ wide. No. 7/6119 (reds, lavender, blue black and blue). Stock item.

▶ VICTORIANA. Axminster. Fractured diamond pattern with banding and stylized leaf in center of diamonds. 1875–1900. 80% wool, 20% nylon. 27″ wide. No. 3/6115 (black, tan, apricot, gray brown and rust). Stock item.

CRAIGIE STOCKWELL CARPETS

Provides custom reproductions. All patterns are researched, designed and colored to order and hand-tufted or handknotted by Craigie Stockwell or its associated company, Stockwell Riley Hooley.

▶ ART NOUVEAU. Art Nouveau–style leaf and scroll pattern with sculpted pile. c. 1900. All wool pile. 6′ x 6′. Handtufted. Beige. Special order.

▶ WESTDEAN COLLEGE. Wilton. Footprint pattern. Document a carpet designed by Edward Jones to showcase the beautiful feet of his wife, ballerina Tilly Losch. Green with cream. Custom made.

ART NOUVEAU. Pile carpet. Craigie Stockwell Carpets. Beige.

K. V. T. (PENNSYLVANIA WOVEN) CARPET MILLS

Custom weaves Brussels and Wilton carpeting from historic documents in limited quantities.

LACEY-CHAMPION CARPETS

Produces custom handtufted carpets and duplications of period patterns.

LANGHORNE CARPET COMPANY

Also duplicates and adapts patterns from historic documents.

▶ FLORAL LATE VICTORIAN. Brussels adaptation. Floral pattern with clusters of small flowers. 1875–1900. All wool. 27″ wide. No. 4317 (rust, old gold, off-white and tan). Special order.

▶ L. V. RAILROAD RUG. Wilton. Geometric pattern. Early 20th century. Originally made as a gift or premium for favored customers on the Lehigh Valley Railroad. 24″ x 35″. No. 6021 (brown, black, purple, forest green, rose and tobacco). Distributed by Keystone Fabricating. Special order.

▶ PULLMAN CARPET. Wilton. Small medallion pattern. Early 20th century. Document is Pullman train carpeting, known as "semi-Oriental Jacquard," made originally by Mohawk and Karagheusian and woven through to the back to provide greater durability. All wool. 27″ wide, 3¾″ repeat. No. 5018 (beige with black, dark tan, red and olive). Special order.

EDWARD MOLINA DESIGNS

Provides custom work, developing patterns and colors and copying period patterns.

PATTERSON, FLYNN AND MARTIN

▶ KEARNEY MANSION DINING ROOM. Handwoven carpet adaptation. Dark ground with clusters of naturalistic flowers. 1900–50s. Based on popular early 20th-century floral patterns. All wool. Black with green, rose, yellow and blue. Made for the Kearney Mansion Museum, Fresno, Calif. Special order.

▶ KEARNEY MANSION HALL AND STAIR. Wilton adaptation. Small rococo overall foliate pattern. 1900–50s. 80% wool, 20% nylon. 27″ wide. Shades of green. Border available. Made for the Kearney Mansion Museum, Fresno, Calif. Special order.

▶ KEARNEY MANSION PARLOR. Handwoven carpet adaptation. Small clusters of flowers on foliate ground. 1900–50s. All wool. Black with rose, yellow, blue and green. Border available. Made for the Kearney Mansion Museum, Fresno, Calif. Special order.

L. V. RAILROAD RUG.
Wilton carpet.
Langhorne Carpet
Company. Brown,
black, purple, forest
green, rose and
tobacco.

PULLMAN CARPET.
Wilton carpet.
Langhorne Carpet
Company. Beige, black,
dark tan, red and olive.

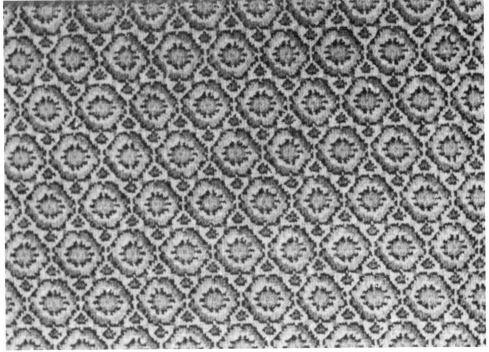

▶ ROSE SPRIG. Brussels. Light-colored ground with sprigs of rose buds and leaves. Late 19th century. 80% wool, 20% nylon. 27″ wide, 14½″ repeat. Pink, dark rose, olive and brown. Special order.

▶ VELVETS. Wilton. 1900–30s. All wool or 80% wool, 20% nylon. 27″ and 12′ wide. Variety of solid colors. Stock items and special order.

ROSECORE CARPETS

Some available Wilton and Brussels carpets are suitable where documentation is not required. Custom work also is provided, including development of patterns and duplication of carpeting from historic materials in the company's collection.

▶ VELVETS. Wilton. 1900–30s. All wool or 80% wool, 20% nylon. 27″ and 12′ wide. Variety of solid colors. Stock items and special order.

SAXONY CARPET COMPANY

Also custom duplicates and adapts period patterns.

▶ BEDE. Axminster. Art Deco–style geometric motif. 1920–30. 80% wool, 20% nylon. 27″ wide. No. X1775/ 3372 (blue, green, red, salmon, tan, gray and black). Special order.

▶ BOUQUET. Axminster. Rococo Revival–style floral. Early 20th century. All nylon. 12′ wide, 36″ x 36″ repeat. No. 163 (multicolor). Stock item.

▶ DIAGONAL BANDS. Wilton. Art Deco–style pattern with diagonal bands of geometric circles. 1920–30. 80% wool, 20% nylon. 27″ wide, 14″ x 14″ repeat. No. 853/ 666 (brick, gray blue, tangerine, medium blue and tan). Special order.

▶ FANTASY. Axminster adaptation of needlepoint or hooked rug. Realistic floral clusters separated by banding. Early 20th century. Muted colors compatible with Colonial Revival hooked rugs. All nylon pile. 12′ wide, 36″ x 36″ repeat. No. 158 (rose, beige, green and blue). Stock item.

▶ FIESTA. Wilton. Abstract geometric pattern. 1920– 30. 80% wool, 20% nylon. 27″ wide, 27″ x 13½″ repeat. No. 1792 (rose beige, cream, orange, rust and pale blue gray). Special order.

▶ HALF DAISY. Wilton. Art Deco–style half-daisy pattern. 1930s. 80% wool, 20% nylon. No. 7749/83407 (dark red orange, light gray and gray blue). Special order.

▶ LEON. Brussels. Small geometric pattern of overlapping circles. 1930s. 80% wool, 20% nylon. 27″ wide, approximately 8″ drop-match repeat. No. 1/3 (cream, brown and orange). Special order.

▶ NOUVELLE. Axminster. Art Nouveau pattern. 1900–20. All nylon. 12′ wide. No. 150 (melon, sea green, gray blue, brick and rose beige). Special order.

▶ ROCOCO FLORAL. Wilton. Overall Rococo Revival floral pattern. 1900–30. 80% wool, 20% nylon. 27″ wide, approximately 27″ repeat. No. DES 7504/80018 (shades of green). Special order.

▶ TRIANGLE. Wilton. Overlapping triangle pattern. 1920–30. 80% wool, 20% nylon. 27″ wide, 3″ repeat. No. 7849/85094 (cocoa, rose, black and teal blue). Special order.

▶ VELVETS. Wilton. 1900–30s. All wool or 80% wool, 20% nylon. 27″ and 12′ wide. Variety of solid colors. Stock items and special order.

▶ ZODIAC. Wilton adaptation of floorcloth or ingrain. 1890–1920. 80% wool, 20% nylon. 27″ wide, 6½″ x 6¾″ repeat. No. 45-4/8338 (dark olive green, light olive, brick and cream). Special order.

SCALAMANDRE

Also duplicates historic patterns.

▶ HAMPTON. Brussels or Wilton reproduction. Overall pattern of rococo-inspired stylized leaf and floral motifs. 1875–1900. 80% wool, 20% nylon. 27″ wide, 21″ drop-match repeat. Installed at the Mamie Eisenhower Birthplace, Boone, Iowa, and the Hirshfeld House, Austin, Tex. Special order.

▶ HILL-STEAD LIBRARY. Wilton. Gothic-inspired overall diamond pattern with rosettes at the crossings and quatrefoil diamond centers. 1890s. 80% wool, 20% nylon. 27″ wide. Made for the Hill-Stead House, Farmington, Conn. Special order.

▶ THE OAKS. Brussels. Banded pattern of small squares surrounded by stylized leaves and tiny flowers. 1875–

1900. Based on a carpet in the Booker T. Washington dining room, Tuskegee, Ala. 80% wool, 20% nylon. 27″ wide, 19″ repeat. Purple brown, sage green, medium red, beige and medium blue. Special order.

▶ VELVETS. Wilton. 1900–30s. All wool or 80% wool, 20% nylon. 27″ and 12′ wide. Variety of solid colors. Stock items and special order.

▶ WILLIAM MORRIS FLORAL. Wilton. Overall stylized lily, tulip and leaf pattern in the banded style typical of William Morris. 1880–1910. All wool. 27″ wide, 11″ repeat. Dark blue, lavender, cream, olive green and lavender rose. Special order.

SCHUMACHER

▶ BOGK HOUSE. Handmade pile adaptation. Geometric cross-shaped motif. 1916. Document a carpet by Frank Lloyd Wright for the Bogk House, Milwaukee, Wis. All wool. Any size (minimum 6′ x 9′). Peach, blue and green on sand. Design approved by the Frank Lloyd Wright Foundation. Special order.

▶ IMPERIAL ARROW. Handmade pile adaptation. Square motif filled with triangles and crossed by an

IMPERIAL ARROW. Pile carpet. Schumacher. Blue, brown, olive green and tan on sand.

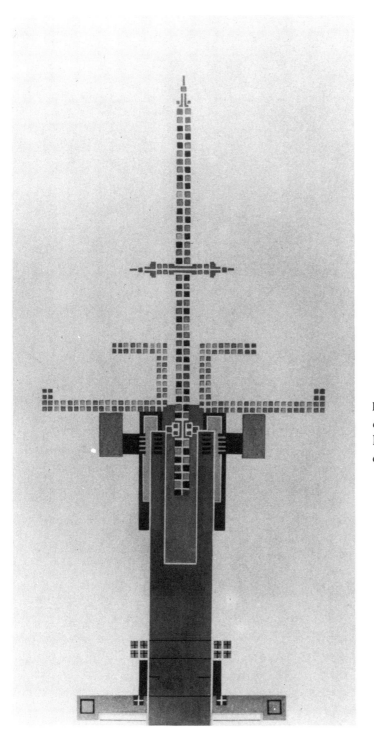

BOGK HOUSE. Pile carpet. Schumacher. Peach, blue and green on sand.

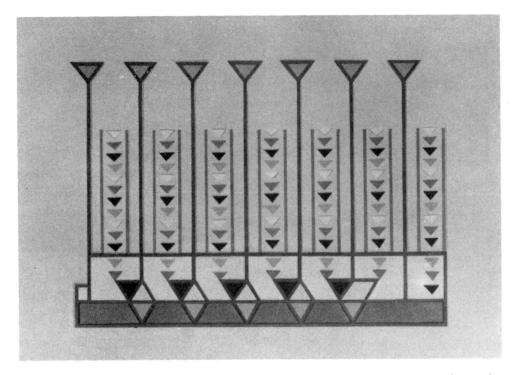

IMPERIAL PAPYRUS. Pile carpet. Schumacher. Azure blue, yellow, green and brown on beige.

arrow. 1915. Document a large square rug from the Imperial Hotel, Tokyo, designed by Frank Lloyd Wright; originally, the motif was repeated in all four corners. All wool. Any size (minimum 6' x 9'). Blue, brown, olive green and tan on sand. Design approved by the Frank Lloyd Wright Foundation. Special order.

▶ IMPERIAL PAPYRUS. Handmade pile adaptation. Stylized motif using triangles. 1915. Document a papyrus-flower border for a large rug in the Imperial Hotel, Tokyo, designed by Frank Lloyd Wright. All wool. Any size (minimum 6' x 9'). Azure blue, yellow, green and brown on beige. Design approved by the Frank Lloyd Wright Foundation. Special order.

▶ IMPERIAL TRIANGLE. Handmade pile adaptation. Geometric pattern of triangles and diagonals. 1915. Document a corner motif of a large square rug for the Imperial Hotel, Tokyo, designed by Frank Lloyd Wright; original has been modified to create an overall pattern. All wool. Any size (minimum 6' x 9'). Rust, tan and grays on pale mauve. Design approved by the Frank Lloyd Wright Foundation. Special order.

▶ VELVETS. Wilton. 1900–30s. All wool or 80% wool, 20% nylon. 27″ and 12′ wide. Variety of solid colors. Stock items and special order.

STARK CARPET CORPORATION

Provides by special order a variety of nondocumented Art Deco–style and overall floral Axminsters, Brussels and Wiltons from the early 20th century. Also duplicates and adapts carpets from historic documents.

▶ NAVARRE. Wilton. Small medallion pattern similar to that used for train carpeting. 1900–30s. All wool. 27″ wide, approximately 3″ repeat. No. 5018 (tan, red, olive and black). Special order.

▶ VELVETS. Wilton. All wool or 80% wool, 20% nylon. 27″ and 12′ wide. Variety of solid colors. Stock items and special order.

CHARLES R. STOCK/V'SOSKE

▶ CHIRVAN PANEL. Axminster. Pattern typical of Near Eastern rugs copied domestically. 1875–1920s. Usually installed wall to wall without borders or as an unbordered

IMPERIAL TRIANGLE. Pile carpet. Schumacher. Rust, tan and grays on pale mauve.

247

rug. All wool. 36″ wide (cut from 12′ goods), 12′ long. No. 106/80210 (red); No. 377/80210 (green). Stock items.

▶ ROYAL TURKEY RED. Axminster. Stylized geometric Oriental pattern. Late 19th to early 20th century. Usually installed wall to wall without borders or as an unbordered rug. All wool pile. 36″ wide (cut from 12′ goods), 12′ long. No. 18/80217 (red ground). Stock item.

TOMKINSONS CARPETS

▶ ANJOU ROSE. Contract Axminster adaptation. Persian flower garden pattern. 1875–1900; 1930s. 80% wool, 20% nylon. 36″ and 12′ wide. No. 19/2065. Special order.

▶ FLORAL CLUSTER. Contract Axminster. Rococo Revival pattern of naturalistic floral clusters. 1915–20s. 80% wool, 20% nylon. 3′, 12′ and 15′ wide. No. 12/2066 (pink beige, rose, yellow and sage green). Stock item.

▶ PERSIAN FLORAL. Contract Axminster. Small-pattern Persian floral design. 1875–1930. Similar to domestic reproductions of late 19th-century Oriental carpets. Usually installed wall to wall without borders. 80% wool, 20% nylon. 36″ and 12′ wide. No. 20/677 (red ground). Special order.

▶ ROCOCO FLORAL. Axminster. Rococo Revival floral pattern. 1915–20s. 80% wool, 20% nylon. 3′, 12′ and 15′ wide. No. 50/678 (browns, cream and shades of sage green). Stock item.

▶ ROCOCO REVIVAL. Axminster. 1920s. 80% wool, 20% nylon. 3′, 12′ and 15′ wide. No. 90/2100 (rose beige, gray brown, red brown and cream). Stock item.

Tompkinsons has adapted the following patterns for carpeting from documented designs by Charles F. A. Voysey, an English designer and disciple of William Morris who was active from about 1890 to 1910. Custom colors and different pile specifications are available and require a minimum order of 100 square meters.

▶ THE BULLRUSH. Axminster. Art Nouveau–inspired floral pattern. 1900–20. 80% wool, 20% nylon. 18″ set-match repeat. 7 pitch/8 rpi. No. 48/2095 (shades of brown, gray and brick). Special order.

▶ THE COLUMBINE. Axminster. Stylized floral pattern.

1900–20. 80% wool, 20% nylon. 26" set-match repeat, 7 pitch/8 rpi. No. 50/2098 (gray green, blue, lavender, red and black). Special order.

▶ THE COUNTRY GARDEN. Axminster. Floral and foliate pattern. 1900–20. 80% wool, 20% nylon. 27" set-match repeat, 7 pitch/8 rpi. No. 40/2097 (green, gold, pink, cocoa and black). Special order.

▶ THE DAISY. Axminster. Scattered daisy motifs with leaf ground. 1900–20. 80% wool, 20% nylon. 27" set-match repeat, 7 pitch/8 rpi. No. 20/2092 (red, coral and black). Special order.

▶ THE DOVE. Axminster. Rounded intertwined foliate pattern with birds. 1900–20. 80% wool, 20% nylon. 18¾" set-match repeat, 7 pitch/8 rpi. No. 70/2099 (green, blue green and blue with red and off-white). Special order.

▶ THE SILVER LEAF. Axminster. Stylized interlocking leaf pattern. 1900–20. 80% wool, 20% nylon. 7½" set-match repeat, 7 pitch/8 rpi. No. 80/2096 (gray, black, gray brown and red orange). Special order.

▶ THE TULIP. Axminster. Stylized leaf and tulip pattern. 1900–20. 80% wool, 20% nylon. 27" drop-match repeat, 7 pitch/8 rpi. No. 49/2094 (salmon, gray green and shades of brown). Special order.

▶ THE VINE. Axminster. Stylized leaf and tulip pattern. 1900–20. 80% wool, 20% nylon. 23" set-match repeat, 7 pitch/8 rpi. No. 90/2093 (green, black and shades of brick). Special order.

U.S. AXMINSTER

▶ ABSTRACT AVENUE. New Directions Contract Axminster. Art Deco adaptation of a fragmented quarter-circle in a square. 1920s–30s. 80% wool, 20% nylon. 12' wide, 12" x 6" drop-match repeat, 189 rpi. No. NWD-15 (blue green, black, lavender, rose and rusts); No. NWD-16 (grays and reds). Stock items.

▶ CLOSE KNIT. Contract Axminster. Art Deco-inspired, 3-color shaded diamond pattern. 1930s. 80% wool, 20% nylon. 12" x 12" set-match repeat, 189 pitch/8, 9 or 10 rpi. No. 73 (beige, blue gray and rose; black and shades of tan). Design Inspiration Collection. Stock items.

▶ DIGITAL DISPLAY. Contract Axminster. Art Deco–inspired, 5-color pattern of curves, bars and dots. 1920s–30s. 80% wool, 20% nylon. 12' wide, 9" x 18" set-match repeat, 189 pitch/8, 9 or 10 rpi. No. 93 (gray, brown maroon and shades of purple gray; mustard, brick, dark blue and gray; shades of blue, brown and gray rose). Design Inspiration Collection. Stock items.

▶ FANFARE. Axminster. Art Deco 5-color adaptation of log cabin pattern. 1920s–30s. 80% wool, 20% nylon. 12' wide, 4" x 9" repeat, 189 pitch/8, 9 or 10 rpi. No. 90 (gray with black, shades of blue and maroon; tan with shades of blue green; tan with pink, blue green and purple gray). Design Inspiration Collection. Stock items.

▶ JAZZ FLAVORS. Contract Axminster. Art Deco adaptation of repeated abstract pattern. 1920s–30s. 80% wool, 20% nylon. 12' wide, 189 pitch/8, 9 or 10 rpi. No. 61 (green, brick and pale yellow; red, gray green, gray and light yellows; and gray pink, shades of gray, brick and blue). Design Inspiration Collection. Stock items.

▶ MOROCCAN RED. Palladium II Contract Axminster adaptation of Oriental rug. Geometric pattern. 1875–1900; early 20th century. All nylon pile. 12' wide, 36" x 18" drop-match repeat, 189 pitch/7 rpi. No. PLM-II-53 (beiges, blues and red). Stock item.

▶ NOUVELLE FLEUR. Palladium II Contract Axminster. Art Nouveau–inspired floral pattern. c. 1900. All nylon pile. 12' wide, 20" x 12" drop-match repeat, 189 pitch/7 rpi. No. PLM-II-49 (shades of blue green, mauve, salmon, black and red). Stock item.

▶ ORIENTAL CLASSIQUE. Palladium II Contract Axminster. Oriental-style overall pattern. 1875–1900; first decade of 20th century. All nylon. 12' wide, 36" x 36" set-match repeat, 189 pitch/7 rpi. No. PLM-II-40 (rusts, beiges, blues and dark brown). Stock item.

▶ SEA BREEZE. Contract Axminster. Two-color pattern with overall vermicelli-like motif. 1920s–30s. 80% wool, 20% nylon. 12' wide, 12" x 12" drop-match repeat, 189 pitch/8, 9 or 10 rpi. No. 97 (gray and beige; dark rose and gray; dark blue green and dark beige). Design Inspiration Collection. Stock items.

▶ SUNBURST. Contract Axminster. Art Deco–inspired pattern with overlapping fishscale motif. 80% wool, 20%

nylon. 12' wide, 9" x 9" set-match repeat, 189 pitch/8, 9 or 10 rpi. No. 60 (melon, cream and beige; dark brown, cream and rose brown). Design Inspiration Collection. Stock items.

▶ TIFFANY. Contract Axminster. Art Nouveau–inspired floral diamond pattern. Early 20th century. 80% wool, 20% nylon. 12' wide, 26⁴⁄₅" x 12" repeat, 189 pitch/8, 9 or 10 rpi. No. 69 (gray, gray blue, gray green, shades of brick and pale yellow). Design Inspiration Collection. Stock item.

▶ TOY TOP. Contract Axminster. Five-color, diagonally striped squares alternating with speckled filling. 1920–30. 80% wool, 20% nylon. 12' wide, 6" x 12" set-match repeat, 189 pitch/8, 9 or 10 rpi. No. 20 (maroon, shades of brick, white and black). Design Inspiration Collection. Stock item.

▶ TRIPLE CROWN. Contract Axminster. Light- and dark-colored diagonally divided square with striped triangle overlay. 1920s–30s. 80% wool, 20% nylon. 12' wide, 3" x 3" set-match repeat, 189 pitch/8, 9 or 10 rpi. No. 87 (tan, rose, lavender brown; shades of gray blue). Design Inspiration Collection. Stock items.

V'SOSKE

Provides handtufted duplications of historic patterns and develops custom adaptations.

COURISTAN

ORIENTAL RUGS

▶ ALL-OVER KERMAN. Wilton adaptation. Overall small floral and medallion pattern, with borders. 1875–1920. All worsted wool. 27" x 60" to 11'6" x 18'. Handknotted fringed ends. Roll runners: 27" wide, any length. Finished runners: 2'3" x 9'6" and 2'3" x 12'6". Knotted fringed ends. No. 7205/427 (regal red with blues and ivory); No. 7205/428 (ivory with reds and blues). Stock items.

▶ BOKHARA. Wilton adaptation. Quartered oval octagons over entire field, with borders. 1875–1920. All worsted wool. 27" x 60" to 9'10" x 14'4". Handknotted fringed ends. Roll runners: 27" wide, any length. Finished runners: 2'3" x 12'6". Handknotted ends. No. 7208/795 (Persian red, dark red and ivory). Stock items.

▶ GREEN TRANQUILITY FLORAL. Chinese-style adaptation. Large floral corner motifs on opposite diagonal corners and small motifs on alternate opposites, with stylized border. 1920s. All wool. 3'10" x 6', 5'10" x 9', 8'3" x 12' and 9'10" x 14'. Handknotted with fringed ends. No. 7148/396 (green with shades of green, red orange, apricot and rose beige). Stock items.

▶ GREEN TRANQUILITY PEKING. Chinese-style adaptation. Central medallion, four corner motifs and ancient Chinese symbols in center, with double border. 1920s. All wool. 3'10" x 6', 5'10" x 9', 8'3" x 12' and 9'10" x 14'. Handknotted with fringed ends. No. 1673/396 (green, blues and shades of green, brick and apricot). Stock items.

▶ ISPAHAN. Wilton. Overall Oriental floral design. 1875–1920. Suitable as unbordered rug or for wall-to-wall installation. All worsted wool. 12' wide. No. 8486/2307 (red ground with cream, tan and blues); No. 8486/2268 (beige with rust brown, gray blue and navy). Stock items.

▶ ISPAHAN CHAMPAGNE. Wilton adaptation. Stylized foliate and vine pattern, with floral medallion border. 1880–1920. All worsted wool. 4'8" x 7'1", 6'7" x 10'4", 8'3" x 12' and 9'10" x 14'4". Handknotted fringed ends. No. 8477/1848 (pale gold with browns, red, blue and black). Installed at the First State Bank, St. Charles, Mo. Stock items.

▶ ROYAL SAROUK. Wilton adaptation. Central medallion pattern, with floral borders. 1900–30. All worsted wool pile. 4'8" x 7'1", 6'7" x 10'4", 8'3" x 12' and 9'10" x 14'4". Handknotted fringed ends. No. 8490/2483 (China red, burgundy, pale rose cream, brick and browns). Stock items.

▶ SANDALWOOD BEIGE FLORAL. Chinese-style adaptation. Large floral corner motif in diagonally opposite corners and small motif in other two, with stylized border. 1920s. All wool. 3'10" x 6', 5'10" x 9', 8'3" x 12' and 9'10" x 14'. Handknotted fringed ends. No. 7148/201 (pale yellow cream with greens, apricots and brown beiges). Stock items.

▶ SANDALWOOD BEIGE PEKING. Chinese-style adaptation. Central medallion surrounded by ancient Chinese

ISPAHAN CHAMPAGNE.
Wilton carpet. Couris-
tan. Pale gold, browns,
red, blue and black.

symbols and four corner motifs, with double border.
1920s. All wool. 3'10" x 6', 5'10" x 9', 8'3" x 12' and
9'10" x 14'. Handknotted. No. 1673/201 (cream with
blues and shades of apricot, gray lavender and brown
gold). Stock items.

KARASTAN BIGELOW

▶ ANTIQUE BOKHARA. Wilton. Turkoman design with
rows of small octagons. All worsted wool. No. 734
(brick red with dark blue, cream and brick). Stock item.
▶ FERAGHAN. Wilton reproduction. Classic Herati
pattern. Document at Penshurst Place, Kent, England.
All worsted wool. No. 0570-0528 (dark blue, medium
blue, red and light yellow). Stately Homes Collection.
Stock item.
▶ FERAGHAN FLORAL. Wilton reproduction. Rows of
stylized flowers centered on a dark ground, with a geometric and floral border. Document at Knebworth
House, Hertfordshire, England. All worsted wool. No.
0570-0531 (cream, reds, light and dark blue and light
green). Stately Homes Collection. Stock item.

▶ MIR SERABEND. Wilton reproduction. Overall design of alternating rows of leaf designs, with multiple geometric-pattern borders. Document at Chatsworth, Derbyshire, England. All worsted wool. No. 0570-0529 (red with cream, light red and shades of blue). Stately Homes Collection. Stock item.

KARASTAN BIGELOW
COLONIAL WILLIAMSBURG REPRODUCTIONS
▶ CARTER'S GROVE RUG. Adaptation of a Feraghan rug. Overall Herati pattern. Document from the entrance hall of Carter's Grove, James City County, Va. Skein-dyed wool. Williamsburg No. 133389 (4'3" x 5'9"); No. 133397 (5'8" x 8'11"); No. 133405 (8'3" x 11'7"). Karastan No. 554. Stock items (small sizes) and special order (largest size).
▶ CHURCH MEDALLION RUG. Version of "Turkish Church Rug" with cream ground. Based on a 17th- or 18th-century Transylvanian prayer rug. All worsted wool pile. Williamsburg No. 133355 (3'10" x 5'3"); No. 133363 (5'7" x 8'8"); No. 133371 (8'2" x 11'9"). Karastan No. 555. Cream, dark blue, tobacco and red. Stock items (small sizes) and special order (largest size).
▶ TRANSYLVANIA CHURCH RUG. Adaptation of an antique "Turkey" carpet. Document at the Governor's Palace, Colonial Williamsburg, Va. All worsted wool. Williamsburg No. 10272 (5'2" x 4'1"). Karastan No. 550. Beige, red orange, gold and olive greens. Stock item.
▶ TURKISH BIRD RUG. Adaptation of a 17th-century antique. All worsted wool. Williamsburg No. 10629 (3'10" x 5'6"). Karastan No. 551. Red, light and dark blue, cream and tobacco. Stock item.
▶ TURKISH CHURCH RUG. Adaptation of a handknotted Transylvanian prayer rug. Balkans, 17th or 18th century. All worsted wool. Williamsburg No. 10777 (3'10" x 5'3"); No. 10801 (5'7" x 8'8"); No. 10272 (8'2" x 11'9"). Karastan No. 553. Red, blue, tan and cream. Stock items (small sizes) and special order (largest size).
▶ USHAK RUG. Adaptation of an antique rug. Document at the Brush-Everard House, Colonial Williams-

burg, Va. All worsted wool. Williamsburg No. 10678 (4'3" x 5'9"); No. 10744 (5'8" x 8'11"); No. 10710 (8'3" x 11'7"). Karastan No. 552. Red orange with gold and patterned blue border. Stock item (small sizes) and special order (largest size).

PEERLESS RUG COMPANY

▶ ASHES OF ROSE ISPAHAN. Wilton. Oriental-style pattern. 1900–20. All wool pile. Handknotted fringed ends. No. 6104 (red). Stock item.

▶ CHINESE PEKING. Chinese-style carpet. Asymmetrical pattern, with carved surface and border. All wool. 2' x 4', 4' x 6', 6' x 9', 8' x 10', 9' x 12' and 10' x 14'. Handknotted with fringed ends. No. 9227 (sand with blue, cream and rose); No. 9773 (ivory and peach with blue); No. 9774 (blue with cream, beiges and green). Stock items.

▶ EMERALD ISPAHAN. Wilton. Oriental-style pattern. 1900–20. All wool. Handknotted fringed ends. No. 6105 (green). Stock item.

▶ RED BOKHARA. Wilton. Oriental-style pattern with overall quartered octagons and borders. 1870–1920. All wool pile. No. 6113 (red with dark blue, black and beige). Stock item.

RED BOKHARA. Wilton carpet, Peerless Rug Company. Red with dark blue, black and beige.

APPENDIX

SUPPLIERS

Listed below are floor covering suppliers, presented both alphabetically with complete information and by specialty category. Manufacturers are indicated by (M); representatives and other suppliers by (R). A complete explanation of the floor covering distribution system is provided in the introduction, page 37. As discussed there, some manufacturers produce as well as sell their products directly; others sell through wholesalers, representatives or retailers. To order any of the items presented in the previous catalog listings, contact the manufacturer or representative indicated or your local interior designer. Complete information about each of the items offered by these suppliers can be found under the specialty category presented in the catalog's five time periods. Because the use of floor covering types varied over the years, not all categories appear in all time periods.

AGED WOODS. 147 West Philadelphia Street, York, Pa. 17403 (800) 233-9307, (717) 843-8104. Antique wide-width chestnut, cypress, fir, oak, pine and poplar flooring. (M)

AMERICAN OLEAN TILE COMPANY. Box 271, Lansdale, Pa. 19446-0271 (215) 855-1111. Hexagonal and square ceramic tile. (M)

ARMSTRONG WORLD INDUSTRIES. P.O. Box 3001, Lancaster, Pa. 17604 (717) 397-0611. Contact local suppliers only. Resilient flooring. (M)

A-2-Z. P.O. Box 351389, 5526 West Pico Boulevard, Los Angeles, Calif. 90019 (213) 671-3115. Linoleum. (M)

BANGOR CORK COMPANY. William and D Streets, Pen

Argyl, Pa. 18072 (215) 863-9041. Battleship linoleum. (M)

BLOOMSBURG CARPET INDUSTRIES. 919 Third Avenue, New York, N.Y. 10022 (212) 688-7447. Brussels, Wilton and Axminster carpets. (M)

BRAID-AID. 466 Washington Street, Pembroke, Mass. 02359 (617) 826-6091. Braided-rug supplies. (M)

BRINTONS CARPETS (USA) LIMITED. E-210 Route 4, Paramus, N.J. 07652 (201) 368-0080. Floorcloth and ingrain adaptations; Brussels, Wilton and Axminster carpets. (M)

J. R. BURROWS AND COMPANY. P.O. Box 418, Cathedral Station, Boston, Mass. 02118 (617) 451-1982. Represents Woodward Grosvenor and Company. Pile floorcloth adaptations; Brussels and Wilton carpets. (R)

CARLISLE RESTORATION LUMBER COMPANY. Route 123, Stoddard, N.H. 03464 (603) 446-3937. Wide-width oak and pine flooring. (M)

CARPETS OF WORTH. Severn Valley Mills, Stourport-on-Severn, Worcestershire DY13 9H, England (Stourport 4122). Axminster carpets. (M)

CASA QUINTAO. 30, Rua Ivens 34, 1200 Lisbon, Portugal (36-58-37). Needlepoint rugs. (M)

CASTLE BURLINGAME. R.D. 1, Box 352, Basking Ridge, N.J. 07920 (201) 647-3885. Antique wide-width white pine flooring. (M)

COLEFAX AND FOWLER. 307 Merton Road, London SW18 5JS, England (01-874-6484). Ingrain adaptation; Brussels and Wilton carpets. (M)

COLONIAL WILLIAMSBURG FOUNDATION. Colonial Williamsburg Craft House, Box CH, Williamsburg, Va. 23187 (800) 446-9240, (804) 220-7463. Corn husk matting; rag, Venetian and Oriental rugs. (R)

CONGOLEUM CORPORATION. 195 Belgrove Drive, Kearny, N.J. 07032 (201) 991-1000. Resilient flooring; asphalt tiles. (M)

COUNTRY BRAID HOUSE. Clark Road, R.F.D. 2, Box 29, Tilton, N.H. 03276 (603) 286-4511. Braided rugs. (M)

COURISTAN. 919 Third Avenue, New York, N.Y. 10022 (212) 371-4200. Hooked and Oriental rugs. (R)

THE CRAFTSMAN STUDIO. W. Cushing and Company, Kennebunkport, Maine 04046-0351 (207) 967-3711. Hooked-rug patterns and supplies. (M)

CRAIGIE STOCKWELL CARPETS. 67a Great Titchfield Street, London, W1P 7FL, England (01-580-5935). Associated with Stockwell Riley Hooley. Handtufted, needlepoint and custom carpets. (M)

VICTOR CUSHWA AND SONS. P.O. Box 160, Williamsport, Md. 21795 (301) 223-7700. Colonial brick. (M)

LOUIS DE POORTERE. Millers Road, Warwick CV34 5AS, England (0926-495136). Axminster carpets. (M)

DESIGNS IN TILE. P.O. Box 4983, Foster City, Calif. 94404 (415) 571-7122. Hexagonal and square ceramic tile; encaustic, geometric and Victorian transfer tile. (M)

DLW FLOORING SYSTEMS. Represented by Anderson, Dewald and Associates, 2750 Northaven, Suite 120, Dallas, Tex. 75229 (214) 247-4955. Linoleum. (M)

THE DORR MILL STORE. Box 88, Guild, N.H. 03754 (603) 863-1197. Baize floorcloths. (M)

FAMILY HEIR-LOOM WEAVERS. R.F.D. 3, Box 59E, Red Lion, Pa. 17356 (717) 246-2431. Ingrain carpets. (M)

THE GAZEBO OF NEW YORK. 660 Madison Avenue, New York, N.Y. 10021 (212) 832-7077. Rag, braided and hooked rugs. (M)

GOOD AND COMPANY. Salzburg Square, Route 101, Amherst, N.H. 03031 (603) 672-0490. Traditional floorcloths. (M)

GRIGSBY/HALLMAN STUDIO. 1322 West Broad Street, Richmond, Va. 23220 (804) 353-3738. Traditional floorcloths; stencilling and marbleizing. (M)

HAND PAINTED STENCILS. 6 Polstead Road, Oxford OX2 6TN, England (0865-56072). Custom stenciling. (M)

HANDWOVEN. 6818 54th Avenue, N.E., Seattle, Wash. 98115 (206) 524-9058. Rag rugs. (M)

HARRIS-TARKETT. Wood Flooring Division, 383 East Maple Street, Johnson City, Tenn. 37601-0300 (615) 928-3122. Hardwood and parquet flooring. (M)

HEIRLOOM RUGS. 28 Harlem Street, Rumford, R.I. 02916 (401) 438-5672. Hooked-rug supplies. (M)

HERITAGE RUGS. R.D. 1, Box 404, Lahaska, Pa. 18931

(215) 794-7229. Rag rugs. (M)

IMPORT SPECIALISTS. 82 Wall Street, New York, N.Y. 10005 (212) 709-9633. Matting; rag (flatwoven plaid) rugs. (R)

H AND R JOHNSON TILES. Highgate Tile Works, Tunstall, Stoke-on-Trent ST6 4JX, England (0782-85611). Encaustic and geometric tile. (M)

THE JOINERY COMPANY. P.O. Box 518, Tarboro, N.C. 27886 (919) 823-3306. Antique and remilled wide-width yellow pine flooring. (M)

KARASTAN BIGELOW. P.O. Box 3089, Greenville, S.C. 29602 (803) 299-2000. Oriental rugs, including Colonial Williamsburg Reproductions. (M)

KENTILE FLOORS. 58 Second Avenue, Brooklyn, N.Y. 11215 (718) 768-9500. Resilient flooring. (M)

KENTUCKY WOOD FLOORS. P.O. Box 33276, Louisville, Ky. 40232 (502) 451-6024. Hardwood parquet flooring and borders. (M)

KEYSTONE FABRICATING. Molasses Hill Road, R.D. 1, Lebanon, N.J. 08833 (201) 735-9150. Distributes "L. V. Railroad Rug." (R)

K. V. T. See PENNSYLVANIA WOVEN CARPET MILLS.

LACEY-CHAMPION CARPETS. Box 216, Fairmount, Ga. 30139 (404) 337-5355. Custom handtufted carpets. (M)

LANGHORNE CARPET COMPANY. Box 175, Penndel, Pa. 19047-0824 (215) 757-5155. Pile ingrain adaptation; Brussels and Wilton carpets. (M)

L'ESPERANCE TILEWORKS. 240 Sheridan Avenue, Albany, N.Y. 12210 (518) 465-5586. Encaustic, geometric and embossed glazed tile. (M)

HUGH MACKAY CARPET FACTORY. P.O. Box 1, Dragon Lane, Durham City DH1 2RX, England (0385-6444). Brussels and Wilton carpets. (M)

MANNINGTON MILLS. P.O. Box 30, Salem, N.J. 08079 (609) 935-3000. Linoleum. (M)

MILLIKEN CONTRACT CARPETING. P.O. Box 2956, La Grange, Ga. 30241 (404) 883-5511. Floorcloth adaptation; tufted carpets. (M)

EDWARD MOLINA DESIGNS. 196 Selleck Street, Stamford, Conn. 06902 (203) 967-9445. Brussels, Wilton and Axminster carpets. (R)

MORAVIAN POTTERY AND TILE WORKS. Swamp Road, Doylestown, Pa. 18901 (215) 345-6722. Geometric, mosaic and embossed tile. (M)

MOUNTAIN LUMBER COMPANY. Route 2, Box 43-1, Ruckersville, Va. 22968 (804) 985-3646. Antique wide-width pine flooring; hardwood flooring and parquet borders. (M)

ISABEL O'NEIL STUDIO AND FOUNDATION. 177 East 87th Street, New York, N.Y. 10028 (212) 348-4464. Traditional floorcloths and stencilling. (M)

PATTERSON, FLYNN AND MARTIN. 950 Third Avenue, New York, N.Y. 10022 (212) 751-6414. Pile floorcloth and ingrain adaptations; needlepoint, Brussels, Wilton and custom tufted carpets. (R)

PED PRODUCTS COMPANY. P.O. Box 321, Springfield, Pa. 19064 (215) 328-4950. Forbo linoleum. (R)

PEERLESS IMPORTED RUGS. 3028 North Lincoln Avenue, Chicago, Ill. 60657 (800) 621-6573. Rag, hooked, Oriental and Chinese rugs. (R)

PEMAQUID FLOORCLOTHS BY KATHLEEN MACK. Round Pond, Maine 04564 (207) 529-5633. Traditional floorcloths. (M)

PENNSYLVANIA WOVEN CARPET MILLS. 401 East Allegheny Avenue, Philadelphia, Pa. 19134 (215) 425-5833. Brussels and Wilton carpets. (M)

PERSNICKETY. Box 458, 776 East Walker Road, Great Falls, Va. 22066 (703) 450-7150. Rag and hooked rugs. (M)

RASTETTER WOOLEN MILL. 5802 State Route 39, Millersburg, Ohio 44654 (216) 674-2103. Rag and braided rugs. (M)

ROBBINS BROTHERS. 919 Third Avenue, New York, N.Y. 10022 (212) 421-1050. Represents Axminster Carpets Limited. Axminster carpets. (R)

ROSECORE CARPETS. 979 Third Avenue, New York, N.Y. 10022 (212) 421-7272. Rag rugs; needlepoint, Brussels and Wilton carpets. (R)

THE RUGGING ROOM. 10 Sawmill Drive, Westford, Mass. 01886 (508) 692-8600. Custom hooked rugs, patterns and supplies. (M)

SAXONY CARPET COMPANY. 979 Third Avenue, New York, N.Y. 10022 (212) 755-7100. Needlepoint, Brussels, Wilton and Axminster carpets. (R)

SCALAMANDRE. 950 Third Avenue, New York, N.Y. 10022 (212) 980-3888. Ingrain, needlepoint, Brussels, Wilton and custom handtufted carpets. (M, R)

F. SCHUMACHER AND COMPANY. 939 Third Avenue, New York, N.Y. 10022 (212) 415-3900. Braided rugs; needlepoint, handtufted and custom carpets. (R)

SPECIAL EFFECTS BY SUE. 8113 Oakbrook Lane, S.W., Tacoma, Wash. 98498 (206) 582-7821. Traditional floorcloths. (M)

JANOS P. SPITZER FLOORING COMPANY. 44 West 22nd Street, New York, N.Y. 10010 (212) 627-1818. Hardwood parquet borders. (M)

STARK CARPET CORPORATION. 979 Third Avenue, New York, N.Y. 10022 (212) 752-9000. Matting; rag rugs; needlepoint, Brussels, Wilton and custom tufted carpets. (R)

CHARLES R. STOCK/V'SOSKE. 2400 Market Street, Philadelphia, Pa. 19103 (215) 568-3448. Axminster and handtufted carpets. (R)

STURBRIDGE YANKEE WORKSHOP. Blueberry Road, Westbrook, Maine 04092 (800) 343-1144. Rag and braided rugs. (R)

SUNFLOWER STUDIO. Constance La Lena, 2851 Road B½, Grand Junction, Colo. 81501 (303) 242-3883. Baize floorcloths; ingrain, Jerga and Venetian rugs. (M)

SUSAN'S INTERIORS. 108 North Park, Marshall, Mich. 49068 (616) 781-7777. Distributes "Honolulu House Carpet." (R)

TARKETT. Resilient Flooring Division, Harris-Tarkett, P.O. Box 264, Parsippany, N.J. 07504 (201) 428-9000. Resilient flooring. (M)

TERRA DESIGNS. 241 East Blackwell Street, Dover, N.J. 07801 (201) 539-2999. Solid-colored pictorial mosaic tile. (M)

TOMKINSONS CARPETS. P.O. Box 11, Kidderminster, Worcestershire DY10 2JR, England (0562-745771). Axminster carpets. (M)

ERNEST TREGANOWAN. 306 East 61st Street, New York, N.Y. 10021 (212) 755-1050. Matting. (R)

U.S. AXMINSTER. P.O. Box 877, East Union Extended, Greenville, Miss. 38702-0877 (601) 332-1581. Pile needlepoint adaptations; Axminster carpets. (M)

VINTAGE LUMBER AND CONSTRUCTION COMPANY. 9507 Woodsboro Road, Frederick, Md. 21701 (301) 898-7859. Antique standard and random-width chestnut, fir, oak and pine flooring; new cherry, maple, oak, pine, poplar and walnut flooring.

V'SOSKE. 155 East 56th Street, New York, N.Y. 10022 (212) 688-1150. Custom handtufted carpets. (M)

W. A. G. (WAVENY APPLE GROWERS). Common Road, Aldeby, Beccles, Suffolk NR34 0BL, England (Aldeby 050-277). Matting. (M)

WEAVERS UNLIMITED. P.O. Box 485, Burlington, Wash. 98233-0485 (206) 988-2906. Rag rugs. (M)

EVELYN WOOD. 7738 10th Avenue, N.W., Seattle, Wash. 98117 (206) 784-6902. Hooked rugs. (M)

THOS. K. WOODARD AMERICAN ANTIQUES AND QUILTS. 835 Madison Avenue, New York, N.Y. 10021 (212) 988-2906. Rag, Venetian and checked rugs. (M)

SUPPLIERS BY CATEGORY

For complete information including addresses, telephone numbers and specialties, see previous "Suppliers" listing.

▶ WOOD FLOORING

AGED WOODS
CARLISLE RESTORATION LUMBER COMPANY
CASTLE BURLINGAME
HARRIS-TARKETT
THE JOINERY COMPANY
KENTUCKY WOOD FLOORS
MOUNTAIN LUMBER COMPANY
JANOS P. SPITZER FLOORING COMPANY
VINTAGE LUMBER AND CONSTRUCTION COMPANY

▶ BRICK FLOORING

VICTOR CUSHWA AND SONS

▶ TILE FLOORING

AMERICAN OLEAN TILE COMPANY
DESIGNS IN TILE
H AND R JOHNSON TILES
L'ESPERANCE TILEWORKS

MORAVIAN POTTERY AND TILE WORKS
TERRA DESIGNS

▶ RESILIENT FLOORING

ARMSTRONG WORLD INDUSTRIES
A-2-Z
BANGOR CORK COMPANY
CONGOLEUM CORPORATION
DLW FLOORING SYSTEMS
KENTILE FLOORS
MANNINGTON MILLS
PED PRODUCTS COMPANY
TARKETT

▶ MATTING

COLONIAL WILLIAMSBURG FOUNDATION
IMPORT SPECIALISTS
STARK CARPET CORPORATION
ERNEST TREGANOWAN
W. A. G. (WAVENY APPLE GROWERS)

▶ FLOORCLOTHS AND STENCILLING

BRINTONS LIMITED
J. R. BURROWS AND COMPANY
GOOD AND COMPANY
GRIGSBY/HALLMAN STUDIO
HAND PAINTED STENCILS
ISABEL O'NEIL STUDIO AND FOUNDATION
PEMAQUID FLOORCLOTHS
SPECIAL EFFECTS BY SUE

▶ FLOORCLOTHS: BAIZE

THE DORR MILL STORE
SCALAMANDRE
SUNFLOWER STUDIO

▶ RAG, BRAIDED AND HOOKED RUGS

BRAID-AID
COLONIAL WILLIAMSBURG FOUNDATION
COUNTRY BRAID HOUSE
COURISTAN
CRAFTSMAN STUDIO

THE GAZEBO OF NEW YORK
HANDWOVEN
HEIRLOOM RUGS
HERITAGE RUGS
PEERLESS IMPORTED RUGS
PERSNICKETY
RASTETTER WOOLEN MILL
ROSECORE CARPETS
THE RUGGING ROOM
F. SCHUMACHER AND COMPANY
STARK CARPET CORPORATION
STURBRIDGE YANKEE WORKSHOP
WEAVERS UNLIMITED
EVELYN WOOD
THOS. K. WOODARD

▶ FLATWOVEN CARPETS: INGRAIN, JERGA AND VENETIAN

BLOOMSBURG CARPET INDUSTRIES
COLEFAX AND FOWLER
COLONIAL WILLIAMSBURG FOUNDATION
FAMILY HEIR-LOOM WEAVERS
K. V. T. See PENNSYLVANIA WOVEN CARPET MILLS
LANGHORNE CARPET COMPANY
MILLIKEN CONTRACT CARPETING
PATTERSON, FLYNN AND MARTIN
PENNSYLVANIA WOVEN CARPET MILLS
SAXONY CARPET COMPANY
SCALAMANDRE
SUNFLOWER STUDIO
THOS. K. WOODARD

▶ NEEDLEPOINT AND EMBROIDERED RUGS

CASA QUINTAO
CRAIGIE STOCKWELL CARPETS
PATTERSON, FLYNN AND MARTIN
ROSECORE CARPETS
SAXONY CARPET COMPANY
SCALAMANDRE
F. SCHUMACHER AND COMPANY
STARK CARPET CORPORATION
U.S. AXMINSTER

▶ PILE CARPETS

BLOOMSBURG CARPET INDUSTRIES
BRINTONS CARPETS (USA) LIMITED
J. R. BURROWS AND COMPANY
CARPETS OF WORTH
COLEFAX AND FOWLER
CRAIGIE STOCKWELL CARPETS
LOUIS DE POORTERE
KEYSTONE FABRICATING
K. V. T. See PENNSYLVANIA WOVEN CARPET MILLS
LACEY-CHAMPION CARPETS
LANGHORNE CARPET COMPANY
HUGH MACKAY
MILLIKEN CONTRACT CARPETING
EDWARD MOLINA DESIGNS
PATTERSON, FLYNN AND MARTIN
PENNSYLVANIA WOVEN CARPET MILLS
ROBBINS BROTHERS
ROSECORE CARPETS
SAXONY CARPET COMPANY
SCALAMANDRE
F. SCHUMACHER AND COMPANY
STARK CARPET CORPORATION
CHARLES R. STOCK/V'SOSKE
SUSAN'S INTERIORS
TOMKINSONS CARPETS
U.S. AXMINSTER
V'SOSKE

▶ ORIENTAL RUGS

COLONIAL WILLIAMSBURG FOUNDATION
COURISTAN
KARASTAN BIGELOW
PEERLESS IMPORTED RUGS

ART SQUARE. An inexpensive, seamless, bordered ingrain rug with fringed ends fashionable at the end of the 19th century as a carpet or crumbcloth under a dining table.

ART TILE. Ceramic tile used primarily for architectural decoration around fireplaces or as wainscoting in vestibules during the last quarter of the 19th century. Some tiles were decorated with portraits, scenes, abstracted floral patterns or geometric designs in relief accentuated by clear glaze. Others were decorated by transfer printing using designs printed by copper-plate or lithographic processes. The Art Tile Works, begun by John Gardner Low in Chelsea, Mass., in 1878, was a leading American manufacturer of art tiles; other major potteries were located in New Jersey and Ohio.

AUBUSSON CARPET. A flatwoven, tapestry-type carpet manufactured at Aubusson, a town near Limoges, France, and characterized by soft colors, central medallions and rococo, floral and scroll motifs.

AXMINSTER CARPET. A luxurious cut-pile carpet first produced by handknotting during the mid-18th century in England. Patterns tended to imitate Oriental carpets and were woven in large, seamless pieces. In addition to the handknotted carpets, several looms were invented during the 19th century to weave Axminsters; two of these, the spool and the gripper, are still used today.

BACKING. Woven or nonwoven fabrics used to provide dimensional stability for linoleum, tufted carpets and some woven carpets.

BACKING CLOTH. Fabric of jute, flax or cotton of various weights used as the foundation for linoleum.

BATTLESHIP LINOLEUM. High-quality linoleum made in a solid color and first defined by the U.S. Bureau of Standards in 1915. It is available today from European manufacturers in a limited variety of colors.

BEAT UP. A weaving process in which a new weft is inserted into the fabric. Also, the term for the number of tufts per inch of carpet in Axminster and chenille carpeting; and the "wire" in Wilton and Brussels carpets.

BINDING YARN. Cotton or rayon yarns that run the

length of a woven carpet and hold the tufts of pile firmly in place. Also known as crimp warp or binder warp.

BODY BRUSSELS CARPET. A level-loop pile carpet woven on a multiframe loom. Generally, the patterns are limited to about five colors because all the wool yarns, when not appearing on the surface as pile, are carried within the structure (body) of the carpet. However, with careful planting, up to seven colors can be added to the pattern. See also Brussels Carpet.

BORDER. A separate strip of carpeting that is mitred and stitched to the edges of rugs and wall-to-wall carpeting woven on looms. Bordered carpets were known in the 19th century but appear to have been more popular in England than in America until the last quarter of the 19th century.

BRAIDED RUG. A rug made from strips of new or used cloth that are folded in at the edges and then braided. The braided strips may be worked into the preceding row or sewn together with carpet thread.

BROADLOOM. During the 18th and 19th centuries, any pile-weaving loom more than 27 inches wide; by 1929, any such loom more than 72 inches wide; by 1955, pile carpets wider than 9 feet.

BRUSSELS CARPET. A durable, looped-pile, wool carpet with a linen warp developed in Brussels about 1710 and woven in England by about 1740. Because all the colors that appear in a single lengthwise row of carpet are carried along within the structure of the carpet, the patterns were limited to about five colors plus others added by planting. Color placement was first controlled by the weaver and an assistant operating a draw loom and, after 1825, by a Jacquard attachment. A power loom for weaving Brussels carpeting was invented by Erastus Bigelow in 1849. Production of Brussels carpets ceased about 1930, and today Wilton looms are used to weave level-loop Wilton carpets as a substitute for Brussels. See also Body Brussels.

BUCKLING. An irregular surface of bumps and ridges (puckers) caused by improper installation, uneven weaving or lack of dimensional stability in carpeting.

BURLAP. A coarse, plain-woven fabric made of hemp or

jute and used as a backing for carpeting and linoleum and as a base for most hooked rugs during the 19th century.

CARPET. Any soft floor covering extending nearly across a floor or installed wall to wall and fastened in place. See also Rug.

CARPET BALL. Narrow strips of rags stitched together and wound into a ball in preparation for making rag rugs.

CARPET BEETLE. A small, reddish brown insect (*Anthrenus scrophulariae*) whose larvae devour protein fibers in wool carpets and upholstery.

CARPET BINDING. Cotton, linen or wool twill tape used to bind the raw edges of carpeting to prevent unraveling. Linen or leather tape was used to protect the edges of grass matting.

CARPET PADDING. A layer of material placed under a carpet or rug to provide additional resiliency and insulation, deaden sound, prolong wear and prevent slipping. Until products were developed specifically for this purpose during the last quarter of the 19th century, worn carpets, paper and straw were often used as padding. Today, urethane foams and hair padding are the most common forms of padding.

CARPET TACK. A large-headed tack about ½ inch in length traditionally used to hold wall-to-wall carpeting in place. (Matting was laid with white metal tacks instead of ordinary iron ones to prevent discoloration from rust.) Modern installations use metal or wood tack strips along the edges of the floor.

CARPET WOOL. A low-grade wool used for carpet pile and imported from South America, New Zealand, Australia and parts of Asia. See also Woolens; Worsteds.

CHAIN. An alternate term for warp, the lengthwise structural yarns that together with the weft threads hold carpet pile in place.

CHENILLE, CHENILLE AXMINSTER CARPET. A two-step weaving process patented in 1839 by James Templeton of Glasgow, Scotland, to compete with the more expensive, handknotted Axminster carpets. The first step was to weave the chenille "fur" and the second was to weave the fur into the fabric backing. Templeton's "patent chenille Axminsters" could be woven up to 33 feet wide, making them the first woven broadloom carpets.

COLORWAY. The color or colors in which a specific pattern is manufactured.

CRUMBCLOTH. A cloth of serge, drugget or heavy damask laid over a better floor covering, particularly in a dining room, to protect it from spills. Also known as crumcloth.

CUT PILE. Woven or tufted carpet in which the pile has been cut to produce a velvetlike surface.

DELFT TILE. Glazed ceramic tile manufactured during the 17th century, first in Holland and later in England. Motifs included animals, scenes and figures. Although various colors were used, blue on white was the most common.

DIMENSIONAL STABILITY. The degree to which a fabric or carpet will retain its original shape after use or cleaning.

DOUBLE CLOTH. See Ingrain Carpet.

DOWELED FLOOR. One of several 18th- and 19th-century methods of laying wood floors and also the most expensive. Holes were drilled laterally into the edge of a floorboard and pegs inserted. Each successive board was drilled, pegged and pushed in place.

DRAW LOOM. A hand-operated loom used to weave complex-pattern fabrics, including carpeting, before the invention of the Jacquard attachment in 1801.

DROP MATCH. A pattern that is based on diagonally repeating designs and requires more yardage than a set match when matching seams.

DRUGGET. A durable wool or linen and wool fabric used under dining tables to protect better floor covering. The term came to mean any material used in that manner. See also Crumbcloth.

ELL. A now mainly archaic unit of measure that survives in the textile industry. The Flemish ell was equal to 27 inches, a double ell was 54 inches, and an English ell was 45 inches.

EMBROIDERED RUG. See Needlepoint Rug.

ENCAUSTIC TILE. A thick, durable ceramic tile made

during the 19th century in England and America and modeled on medieval examples. In England the term refers specifically to tiles with patterns made by impressing a design into the soft clay and filling it with a slip (liquid clay) of a different color before firing. See also Geometric Tile.

ENGLISH CARPET. See Ingrain Carpet.

FACE WEIGHT. A qualitative measure referring to the number of ounces of surface yarn in a square yard of carpet exclusive of other construction elements such as the warp, weft and stuffer threads.

FLOORCLOTH. A cotton, linen or jute canvas painted with oil-based paints and commonly used in entry halls and dining rooms beginning in the 18th century. It was sometimes used as a drugget to protect better carpeting. After the first half of the 19th century, the term was superceded by "oilcloth."

4/4, FOUR/QUARTER. A carpet woven 36 inches wide. See also Quarter.

GAUGE. See Pitch.

GEOMETRIC TILE. Floor tile without a pattern produced in a limited number of colors and shapes during the 19th century and used to create floor designs. In England geometrics were distinguished from encaustic tiles, but in America both were marketed as encaustics.

GRANITE. A linoleum pattern resembling terrazzo that became popular during the 1920s and is still produced in England and Europe.

HEARTH RUG. A small rug placed in front of a hearth to protect better carpeting from wear, soil and sparks. During the 19th century many carpet manufacturers wove hearth rugs in patterns that coordinated with their carpet designs.

INGRAIN CARPET. An American term for a flatwoven, reversible, wool carpet resembling a coverlet in which the colors of the design on one side reverse on the other. Also known as English, Kidderminster, Scotch, double cloth and three-ply and two-ply carpeting.

JACQUARD ATTACHMENT. A device invented by Joseph Marie Jacquard about 1801 that is attached to looms and simplifies the weaving of complex patterns.

The attachment uses needles to "read" punched cards, thus automatically controlling the harnesses on a loom. Designed originally to weave fabrics, it was adapted for carpet looms in 1825.

JASPÉ. Linoleum with random striations generally in tones of one color; first produced in the 1920s and still manufactured in England.

JERGA. A flatwoven carpet produced in the American Southwest during the 19th century. Jergas were made of wool and usually contained two colors woven in a twill or herringbone pattern.

JUTE. A strong fiber obtained from two East Indian plants of the linden family that is used to weave burlap and as stuffers, filling and backing for carpets.

KAMPTULICON. A forerunner of linoleum made of India rubber and granulated cork. Invented in England by Elijah Galloway in 1844, kamptulicon was an expensive but durable and resilient floor covering particularly prized because it could be laid below grade or on damp floors. Production ceased about 1920.

KIDDERMINSTER CARPET. See Ingrain Carpet.

LEVEL-LOOP PILE CARPET. A 20th-century term for a looped-pile carpet in which the pile is the same height.

LINOLEUM. A durable floor covering invented in England by Frederick Walton in 1863 and made primarily of linseed oil and flax. The American Linoleum Manufacturing Company of New York City began to market domestically produced goods in 1875. Patterns were either printed or inlaid; surface printing offered more pattern variation but was not as durable as inlaid designs. Linoleum in solid colors, jaspé and granite patterns is still produced in Europe but no longer manufactured in America.

LIST CARPET. A carpet woven using strips of cloth or the selvages of fabric or ingrain carpeting as weft threads. Also known as rag rugs during the 19th century.

MAT. A small rug placed at doorways, bedsides and the base of stairs during the 18th and 19th centuries. Mats were made of rags, vegetable fibers or animal skins.

MATTING. A popular 18th- and 19th-century floor covering woven from various grasses, sometimes with a cotton warp, in the Far East and imported into Europe and America. Also called Canton, Indian or grass matting.

MILLED DRUGGET. A woven fabric printed in colors and sometimes used as a substitute for carpeting during the 19th century.

MOQUETTE. A French term used in America in the last decades of the 19th century to designate a type of very fine machine-woven Axminster carpet.

NAVAJO RUG. A flatwoven wool rug adapted by the Navajo from their traditional handwoven blankets. These became popular at the beginning of the 20th century, particularly for Craftsman-style interiors. Patterns were mainly traditional geometrics colored with either natural or aniline (artificial) dyes.

NEEDLEPOINT RUG. A rug worked in wool on canvas during the 18th and 19th centuries generally using either a tent stitch or cross-stitch. Needlepoint carpets are still made for the American market in Portugal and Brazil.

OILCLOTH. A term for a floorcloth used during the second half of the 19th century to designate a fabric printed in oil-based paints.

ORIENTAL CARPET. Any carpet woven by hand in the Near East or Far East. Generally, these carpets are knotted and have a fairly short pile, but flatwoven carpets, known as kilims, are also made.

PAPER CARPET. Painted paper, sometimes even wallpaper, used to imitate carpeting in the 19th century. These materials were usually finished in several coats of varnish for durability.

PARQUET. A patterned floor made of wood. Originally, the term denoted inlaid and ornately patterned, raised wood floors around the state bed in 17th-century palaces. The English critic Charles Locke Eastlake praised parquet floors in *Hints on Household Taste* (1868), and they became popular during the last quarter of the 19th century. The best parquet is made of hardwood nearly an inch thick and blind-nailed to the subfloor. Often several different types of wood are used to create the designs.

PILE. The looped or cut tufts that make up the surface of

a carpet such as an Axminster, Brussels, Wilton or Oriental.

PITCH. A standard measurement for the quality of a carpet based on the number of warp yarns across the face of a 27-inch woven carpet. The higher the pitch, the more precise the pattern definition. Quality woven carpets have a pitch of 256. Also known as gauge.

PLANTING. A procedure used in some woven carpets (e.g., Axminster, Brussels and Wilton) for inserting extra colors into the pattern.

PLY. The number of layers of fabric interwoven to form an ingrain carpet.

PRIMARY BACKING. The fabric into which tufting, hooking or embroidery is worked to form a carpet.

PRIMARY COLORS. The three hues—red, yellow and blue—from which all other colors are derived.

QUARRY TILE. A thick, solid-colored ceramic tile with a matte finish used for flooring.

QUARTER. A unit of measure based on one-fourth of a yard (9 inches) and used as the standard designation for carpet widths in America. For example, during the 19th century ³/₄ carpet—that is, carpet 27 inches wide—was the standard for woven carpets although other widths were made.

RAG RUG. See List Carpet.

RANDOM WIDTH. A wood floor made of planks in various widths. In the 18th and 19th centuries, random-width floors were the poorest quality. However, during the Colonial Revival era, beginning at the end of the 19th century, such floors were associated with early American interiors and became popular.

RAVEL RUG. A handmade rug produced in America during the 19th century from colored yarns stitched to a backing.

REPEAT. The length required for one complete repetition of a pattern. See also Drop Match and Set Match.

RESILIENT FLOORING. A 20th-century term for any vinyl-type floor covering with a printed surface and spongy underlayer. American manufacturers make only resilient flooring today and produce no linoleum.

ROVING. Thick, loosely spun yarns sometimes used as the weft in Venetian carpets.

RPI (ROWS PER INCH). An indication of carpet quality. The more rows of face pile per inch, the higher the grade of carpet.

RUG. Any soft, generally small, floor covering that is made without seams and is not tacked to the floor. See also Carpet.

RUNNER. A long, narrow floor covering, generally of carpeting but also of matting or floorcloth, that is used in narrow passages such as halls and stairs.

SCATTER RUG. A term coined during the 1920s for small rugs placed on top of wall-to-wall carpeting, linoleum or wood floors. Also called a throw rug.

SCOTCH CARPET. See Ingrain Carpet.

SECONDARY COLOR. A color formed by mixing two primary colors. For example, orange, a secondary color, is created by combining red and yellow.

SERGE. A stout worsted or wool and worsted fabric in a twill weave used during the 19th century as a drugget.

SET MATCH. A pattern that matches straight across the goods. Set matches require less yardage than drop matches when aligning the patterns for seaming. Also known as a straight, block or self-match.

SHIPLAP. A common technique for laying less expensive wood floors during the 18th and early 19th centuries, consisting of cutting a recess on the edge of a board and fitting it to correspond with the recesses on neighboring boards.

SHOT. Weft yarn used to hold in place the pile of carpets such as Wilton.

SMYRNA RUG. A reversible chenille Axminster rug developed in America during the last quarter of the 19th century. The pile is patterned chenille, the warp is cotton and the weft is jute.

STAIR ROD. A plain or decorative rod that, with brackets, was used at the back of stair treads to hold the carpet in place. Stair rods were typically flat until the second quarter of the 19th century, when cylindrical ones became popular. While holding the carpet in place, they also allowed it to be removed for cleaning or shifted to equalize wear. Also known as a carpet rod.

STUFFER. A supplementary warp of jute added to pile carpets for stiffness and bulk.

TAPESTRY BRUSSELS CARPET. A looped-pile wool carpet patented by Richard Whytock of Edinburgh, Scotland, in 1832. Whytock's invention used preprinted warp yarns wound on large drums to form the face of looped-pile carpets, thus reducing the amount of face pile needed for the carpets and allowing a virtually limitless number of colors in the design. See also Body Brussels Carpet.

TERTIARY COLOR. A color formed by mixing two secondary colors. Tertiary color schemes were particularly popular during the last quarter of the 19th century.

3/4, THREE/QUARTER. A carpet woven 27 inches wide. See also Quarter.

TONGUE AND GROOVE. A method for joining floor boards in which one edge has a groove cut into it and the other has a projection that fits the groove on the adjoining board. This process provides an interlocking structure and a smooth, secure surface and was common from the mid-19th century on.

TURKEY CARPET. A carpet woven in Turkey and the Near East during the 17th and 18th centuries as well as handknotted carpets made in England to imitate such carpets.

VELVET CARPET. Originally, a patterned cut-pile carpet woven from drum-printed wool yarns in England during the 1830s, similar to tapestry Brussels. Today, the term refers to a solid-colored carpet with a low-cut pile woven on a wide Wilton loom without a Jacquard attachment or a tufted carpet with a dense, level cut pile.

VENETIAN CARPET. A flatwoven carpet widely used in the 19th century that apparently has no connection with Venice. It is a reversible, multicolored, warp-striped carpet traditionally 36 inches wide with wool warps that cover cotton or jute wefts. A popular 19th-century practice was to use Venetian carpeting in halls, stairways and servants' rooms.

VENETIAN DAMASK. Venetian carpeting in which the stripes are broken into small checked or twill patterns.

WARP. Lengthwise yarns woven in a carpet that, when interlaced with the weft threads, form the pattern or underlayer of the carpet.

WEFT. The crosswise structural yarns used to hold the pattern warp in place.

WILTON CARPET. A cut-pile carpet first woven in England about the mid-18th century. The weaving process is similar to that of Brussels carpeting, with the face yarns carried in the body of the carpet when they do not appear on the surface as pile. Originally woven in 27-inch widths, Wilton is now also made on broadlooms developed in the early 20th century that are up to 18 feet wide.

WIRE. A rod in the form of a flat wire used to create the pile height of a Brussels or Wilton carpet. The rod for Wilton carpets has a knife blade at one end that cuts the loops as the wire is withdrawn. Also, a measure of carpet quality indicated by the number of rows of pile per lengthwise (warp) inch.

WOOD CARPETING. An inexpensive substitute for parquet employing thin pieces of hardwood glued to a fabric or paper backing and face-nailed to the floor. It was a popular solution for covering pine floors during the last quarter of the 19th century.

WOOLENS. Short-staple wool fibers that are carded and spun before use. Previously used for lesser-quality carpets, this is now the dominant wool yarn used in the carpet industry.

WORSTEDS. Long-staple wool fibers that are carded, combed and spun before use. Yarns made of worsted are resilient and durable and are used in the manufacture of the finest carpets.

Adler, Hazel H. *The New Interior: Modern Decorations for the Modern Home.* New York: Century Company, 1916.

Anderson, Susan H. *The Most Splendid Carpet.* Philadelphia: National Park Service, 1978.

Bacon, Richard M. "The Painted Floor Pattern—A Colonial Original," *Yankee,* October 1975, pp. 82–89.

Barnard, Julian. *Victorian Ceramic Tiles.* London: Castell Ltd., 1979.

Beecher, Catharine, and Harriet Beecher Stowe. *The American Woman's Home.* 1869. Reprint. Hartford, Conn.: Stowe-Day Foundation, 1975.

Beitter, Ethyl Jane. *Hooked and Knotted Rugs.* New York: Sterling Publishing, 1973.

Blackman, Leo, and Deborah Dietsch. "A New Look at Linoleum: Preservation's Rejected Floor Covering," *The Old-House Journal,* January 1982, pp. 9–12.

————. "Linoleum: How to Repair It, Install It, and Clean It," *The Old-House Journal,* February 1982, pp. 36–38.

Bradbury, Fred. *Carpet Manufacture.* Belfast, Ireland, 1904. London: R. S. Brinton Carpets, 1919.

Cassidy, Anne R. "Elegance Underfoot: Floor Coverings for American Homes 1700–1860," *The New York-Pennsylvania Collector,* May 1982. Reprinted. Albany: New York State Bureau of Historic Sites, 1984.

Chapman, Pat. "American Inventive Genius: Hooked Rugs to Broadloom," *Modern Floor Coverings,* July 1976, pp. 19–39.

Church, Ella Rodman. *How to Furnish a Home.* New York, 1882.

Comstock, Helen. "Eighteenth-century Floor Cloths," *Antiques,* January 1955, p. 48.

Cook, Alexander N., ed. *A Century of Carpet and Rug Making in America, 1825–1925.* New York: Bigelow-Hartford Carpet Company, 1925.

Cook, Clarence. *The House Beautiful.* New York, 1881.

Crane, Ross. *Interior Decoration: A Comprehensive Study Course for Furniture Men.* Chicago, 1928.

Dedera, Don. *Navajo Rugs: How to Find, Evaluate, Buy and Care for Them.* Flagstaff, Ariz.: Northland Press, 1975.

Dillaway, Theodore M. *Decoration of the School and*

Home. Springfield, Mass.: Milton Bradley, 1914.

Dornsife, Samuel J. "Timetable of Carpet Technology," *Nineteenth Century,* Autumn 1981, pp. 38–41.

Downing, Andrew Jackson. *The Architecture of Country Houses.* 1850. Reprint. New York: Dover Publications, 1969.

Dwyer, Charles P. *The Economic Cottage Builder.* Buffalo, 1856.

Eastlake, Charles Locke. *Hints on Household Taste in Furniture, Upholstery & Other Details.* 4th ed. 1878. Reprint. New York: Dover Publications, 1969.

Eberlein, Harold Donaldson. *Book of Decoration: Upstairs.* The American Home Library Series. New York: Doubleday, Doran, 1931.

Ewing, John S., and Nancy P. Norton. *Broadlooms and Businessmen: A History of the Bigelow-Sanford Carpet Company.* Cambridge, Mass.: Harvard University Press, 1955.

Fraser, Esther Stevens. "Some Colonial and Early American Decorative Floors," *Antiques,* April 1931, pp. 296–301.

Gilbert, Christopher, James Lomax and Anthony Wells-Cole. *Country House Floors: 1660–1850.* Leeds, England: Temple Newsome, 1987.

Hall, Philip A. *The Rug and Carpet Industry of Philadelphia.* Philadelphia, 1917.

Harwood, Buie. *Decorative Painting in Texas 1840–1940: A Survey of the European Influence.* College Station: Texas A&M Press, forthcoming.

Hawley, Walter A. *Oriental Rugs, Antique and Modern.* 1913. Reprint. New York: Dover Publications, 1970.

Hemming, Charles. *Paint Finishes.* London: Quill Publishing, 1985.

Hubel, Reinhard G. *The Book of Carpets.* New York: Praeger Publishers, 1970.

I.C.S. Reference Library. *Carpet, Wallpaper, Linoleum and Architectural Design.* London, 1905.

Innes, Jocasta. *Paint Magic: The Complete Guide to Decorative Finishes.* New York: Van Nostrand Reinhold, 1981.

Jacobs, Bertram. *Axminster Carpets, 1755–1957.* Leigh-on-Sea, England: F. Lewis, 1966.

Jacobsen, Charles W. *Oriental Rugs: A Complete Guide.* Rutland, Vt.: Charles E. Tuttle, 1962.

Jaray, Madeleine. *The Carpets of the Manufacture de la Savonnerie.* Leigh-on-Sea, England: F. Lewis, 1966.

Kent, William Winthrop. *The Hooked Rug.* New York: Mead, 1930.

Kopp, Joel and Kate Kopp. *American Hooked and Sewn Rugs.* New York: E. P. Dutton, 1975.

[A Lady]. *The Workwoman's Guide.* London, 1838.

Landreau, Anthony N. *America Underfoot: A History of Floor Coverings from Colonial Times to the Present.* Washington, D.C.: Smithsonian Institution Press, 1976.

Leslie, Miss [Eliza]. *The Lady's House Book.* 19th ed. Philadelphia, 1854.

Little, Nina Fletcher. *Floor Coverings in New England Before 1850.* Sturbridge, Mass.: Old Sturbridge Village, 1972.

Loudon, John Claudius. *An Encyclopedia of Cottage, Farm, and Villa Architecture and Furniture.* London, 1833.

McMullan, Joseph V. "The Turkey Carpet in Early America," *Antiques,* March 1954, pp. 220–23.

O'Brien, Mildred Jackson. *The Rug and Carpet Book.* New York: Barrows and Company, 1946.

O'Donnell, Bill. "Reconditioning Floors," *The Old-House Journal,* December 1985, p. 201 et seq.

O'Neil, Isabel. *The Art of the Painted Finish for Furniture and Decoration.* New York: William Morrow, 1971.

Pilgrim, Dianne H. "The American Renaissance: Decorative Arts and Interior Design from 1876 to 1917," *Art and Antiques,* January–February 1980, p. 50.

Poore, Patricia. "Restoring a Parquet Floor," *The Old-House Journal,* January–February 1984, pp. 28–29.

Quinn, Richard L. *Carpets and Rugs.* North Canton, Ohio: Hoover Home Institute, 1976.

Roth, Rodris. *Floor Coverings in 18th-Century America.* Washington, D.C.: Smithsonian Institution Press, 1967.

Schoelwer, Susan Prendergast. "Form, Function, and Meaning in the Use of Fabric Furnishings: A Philadelphia Case Study, 1700–1775," *Winterthur Portfolio,* Spring 1979, pp. 25–40.

Scobey, Joan. *Rugs and Wall Hangings.* New York: Dial Press, 1974.

Shoppell, Robert W. *Modern Houses, Beautiful Homes.* New York, 1887.

Skinner, D. S., and Hans van Lemmen. *Minton Tiles, 1835–1935.* Stoke-on-Trent, England: City Museum and Art Gallery, 1984.

Tattersall, C. E. C. *A History of British Carpets.* Revised by Stanley Reed. Leigh-on-Sea, England: F. Lewis, 1966.

Vollmer, William A., ed. *A Book of Distinctive Interiors.* New York: McBride, Nast, 1912.

Von Rosenstiel, Helene. *American Rugs and Carpets from the Seventeenth Century to Modern Times.* New York: William Morrow, 1978.

Webster, Thomas, and Mrs. W. Parkes. *An Encyclopedia of Domestic Economy.* London, 1844.

Weeks, Jeanne G., and Donald Treganowan. *Rugs and Carpets of Europe and the Western World.* New York: Weathervane Books, 1969.

Wheeler, Candance. *How to Make Rugs.* New York: Doubleday, Page, 1902.

Wheeler, Gervase. *Rural Homes; or Sketches of Houses Suited to American Country Life.* New York, 1851.

Winkler, Gail Caskey, and Roger W. Moss. *Victorian Interior Decoration: American Interiors 1830–1900.* New York: Henry Holt, 1987.

AMERICAN SOCIETY OF INTERIOR DESIGNERS. 1430 Broadway, New York, N.Y. 10018

CALIFORNIA HISTORICAL SOCIETY. 2090 Jackson Street, San Francisco, Calif. 94109

CARPET AND RUG INSTITUTE. P.O. Box 2048, Dalton, Ga. 30722-2048

COLONIAL WILLIAMSBURG FOUNDATION. P.O. Box C, Williamsburg, Va. 23187

HELEN ALLEN TEXTILE COLLECTION. University of Wisconsin, 1300 Linden Drive, Madison, Wis. 53706

HENRY FORD MUSEUM AND GREENFIELD VILLAGE. 915 Brady Street, Dearborn, Mich. 48124

LOUISIANA STATE MUSEUM. P.O. Box 2458, New Orleans, La. 70176

METROPOLITAN MUSEUM OF ART. Fifth Avenue at 82nd Street, New York, N.Y. 10028

MUSEUM OF AMERICAN TEXTILE HISTORY. 800 Massachusetts Avenue, North Andover, Mass. 01845

MUSEUM OF EARLY SOUTHERN DECORATIVE ARTS. P.O. Box 10310, Winston-Salem, N.C. 27108

NATIONAL MUSEUM OF AMERICAN HISTORY. Smithsonian Institution, 14th Street and Constitution Avenue, N.W., Washington, D.C. 20560

OAKLAND MUSEUM. History Department, 1000 Oak Street, Oakland, Calif. 94607-4892

OLD STURBRIDGE VILLAGE. Route 20, Sturbridge, Mass. 01566

PENNSYLVANIA FARM MUSEUM OF LANDIS VALLEY. 2451 Kissel Hill Road, Lancaster, Pa. 17601

PHILADELPHIA MUSEUM OF ART. 26th Street and Benjamin Franklin Parkway, Philadelphia, Pa. 19130

SOCIETY FOR THE PRESERVATION OF NEW ENGLAND ANTIQUITIES. 141 Cambridge Street, Boston, Mass. 02114

STRONG MUSEUM. One Manhattan Square, Rochester, N.Y. 14607

TEXTILE MUSEUM. 2320 S Street, N.W., Washington, D.C. 20008

VICTORIA AND ALBERT MUSEUM. Exhibition and Cromwell Roads, London SW 1, England

WINTERTHUR MUSEUM. Route 52, Kennett Pike, Winterthur, Del. 19735

ACKNOWLEDG-
MENTS

This book was written in honor of and is dedicated to Marion A. Von Rosenstiel.

The authors wish to thank the following individuals for their assistance: Penelope Hartshorne Batcheler, Independence National Historical Park, Philadelphia; Gina Bianco, Brooklyn, N.Y.; Peggy B. Jonas, Atlanta, and Lorraine Joynt Bruton and Patricia Eells, New York City, The Wool Bureau; John Dickey, FAIA, Media, Pa.; Samuel J. Dornsife, ASID, Williamsport, Pa.; Anne-Marie McIntyre, New York City; Robert Neiley, AIA, Boston; Nicholas A. Pappas, FAIA, Colonial Williamsburg Foundation, Williamsburg, Va.; and Rodris Roth, Smithsonian Institution, Washington, D.C. Most of the research for the historical essays was conducted at The Athenaeum of Philadelphia, and we particularly want to thank Keith A. Kamm, bibliographer, and Bruce Laverty, archivist, for their assistance. Unless otherwise credited, photographs in the introduction were taken by Louis Meehan, Philadelphia.

We are especially grateful for the generous encouragement and assistance of the floor covering manufacturers, showrooms and representatives who responded so promptly to our requests for information and illustrations. Without their help this book would not have been possible.

The Preservation Press is grateful for the support and asssistance of Robert Herring, Jody Imperato and Ann Martin, Schumacher; and Peggy B. Jonas, The Wool Bureau.

Floor Coverings for Historic Buildings was developed and edited by Diane Maddex, director, The Preservation Press, with editorial assistance from Gretchen Smith and Michelle LaLumia and production assistance from Janet Walker, managing editor, The Preservation Press.

The book was designed by Meadows & Wiser, Washington, D.C., under the direction of Marc Meadows, Robert Wiser and Terri Brand. It was composed in Cloister Old Style by BG Composition, Inc., Baltimore, Md., and printed by Collins Lithographing, Inc., Baltimore, Md.

HELENE VON ROSENSTIEL is the owner of Helene Von Rosenstiel, Inc., Brooklyn, N.Y., a major conservator of textiles and costumes for the past 17 years. She is the author of *American Rugs and Carpets from the Seventeenth Century to Modern Times* (1978, William Morrow). Von Rosenstiel also teaches and lectures extensively on historic floor coverings.

GAIL CASKEY WINKLER, ASID, is the senior partner of LCA Associates, Philadelphia, which provides design and restoration services to museums, corporations, organizations and individuals. With her husband, Roger W. Moss, she is coauthor of *Victorian Exterior Decoration* and *Victorian Interior Decoration* (1986, 1987, Henry Holt), among other writings. She lectures widely and teaches at the University of Pennsylvania.

Helene Von Rosenstiel compiled the catalog entries and Gail Caskey Winkler wrote the historical essays for this book. Both authors provided information for the book's supplemental sections and collaborated on its contents.

Other books in this series include:

FABRICS FOR HISTORIC BUILDINGS. Jane C. Nylander. A primer with a catalog listing 550 fabric reproductions for curtains, upholstery, bed hangings, table covers and other uses. 160 pages, 95 illus., gloss., biblio., append. $13.95 paperbound.

LIGHTING FOR HISTORIC BUILDINGS. Roger W. Moss. A handbook on the history of American lighting with hundreds of fixtures suitable for the colonial era through the 1920s. 192 pages, 175 illus., gloss., biblio., append. $13.95 paperbound.

WALLPAPERS FOR HISTORIC BUILDINGS. Richard C. Nylander. A guide to 350 wallpaper reproductions with advice on choosing the correct pattern. 128 pages, 110 illus., gloss., biblio., append. $13.95 paperbound.

AUTHORS

HISTORIC INTERIORS SERIES